Communications in Computer and Information Science 1497

More information about this series at http://www.springer.com/series/7899

Pantelimon Stănică · Sihem Mesnager ·
Sumit Kumar Debnath (Eds.)

Security and Privacy

Second International Conference, ICSP 2021
Jamshedpur, India, November 16–17, 2021
Proceedings

 Springer

Editors
Pantelimon Stănică [ID]
Naval Postgraduate School
Monterey, CA, USA

Sihem Mesnager [ID]
University of Paris VIII
Paris, France

Sumit Kumar Debnath [ID]
National Institute of Technology Jamshedpur
Jamshedpur, India

ISSN 1865-0929 ISSN 1865-0937 (electronic)
Communications in Computer and Information Science
ISBN 978-3-030-90552-1 ISBN 978-3-030-90553-8 (eBook)
https://doi.org/10.1007/978-3-030-90553-8

This Springer imprint is published by the registered company Springer Nature Switzerland AG
The registered company address is: Gewerbestrasse 11, 6330 Cham, Switzerland

Preface

This volume contains the refereed proceedings papers of the 2nd International Conference on Security and Privacy (ICSP 2021), organized by the National Institute of Technology, Jamshedpur, India, during November 16–17, 2021. The call for papers for ICSP 2021 included the following topics:

- Cryptography
- Secure cryptographic protocols
- Post-quantum cryptography
- Quantum cryptography
- Blockchain and cryptocurrency
- IoT security and privacy
- Cloud security
- Privacy-preserving technologies
- Biometric security
- Security and privacy of big data
- Cloud and edge computing security
- Access control
- Steganography and steganalysis
- Leakage-resilient cryptography
- Cyber-physical security
- Database security
- Embedded systems security
- Lightweight security
- Authentication and authorization
- Social networks security, privacy, and trust
- Wireless security
- Distributed systems security
- Cyber-physical systems security
- Verification of security protocols
- Machine learning in cybersecurity

The proceedings of the conference contain 10 contributed papers, accepted out of the 44 submitted papers. All papers have been thoroughly reviewed by at least three referees. Most of the refereeing was done by members of the Program Committee. We thank all of them for their help. In addition to the contributed papers, we had seven invited lectures given by Elette Boyle (Director of the FACT Research Center and Head of the RRIS International Program, Efi Arazi School of Computer Science, IDC Herzliya, Israel), Craig Costello (Microsoft Research, USA), Ronald Cramer (Head of the Cryptology Group, CWI, and Professor at the Mathematical Institute, Leiden University, The Netherlands), Carmit Hazay (Deputy Director and Head of the Scientific Committee of the Center for Research in Applied Cryptography and Cyber Security,

Bar-Ilan University, Israel), Delaram Kahrobaei (University Dean for Research, City University of New York, USA), Mridul Nandi (Indian Statistical Institute, Kolkata, India), Pantelimon Stănică (Professor and Manager of the Secure Communication Program, Naval Postgraduate School, USA). Many thanks to all for sharing their expertise.

November 2021

Pantelimon Stănică
Sihem Mesnager
Sumit Kumar Debnath

Organization

Program Committee

General Chair

Pantelimon Stănică   Naval Postgraduate School, USA

Program Chairs

Sumit Kumar Debnath   NIT Jamshedpur, India
Sihem Mesnager   University of Paris VIII, France

Technical Program Committee

Kamalesh Acharya	IIT Kharagpur, India
Avishek Adhikari	Presidency University, India
Ravi Anand	University of Hyogo, Japan
Satya Bagchi	NIT Durgapur, India
Daniele Bartoli	University of Perugia, Italy
Chinmoy Biswas	IIT Kharagpur, India
Christina Boura	University of Versailles, France
Andrea Bracciali	University of Stirling, UK
Matteo Campanelli	Aarhus University, Denmark
Claude Carlet	Universities of Paris VIII, France, and University of Bergen, Norway
Tanmay Choudhury	NIT Jamshedpur, India
Dipanwita Roy Chowdhury	IIT Kharagpur, India
Jean-Luc Danger	Telecom Paris, France
Pratish Datta	NTT Research, USA
Sumit Kumar Debnath	NIT Jamshedpur, India
Kunal Dey	NIT Jamshedpur, India
Jintai Ding	University of Cincinnati, USA
Sabyasachi Dutta	University of Calgary, Canada
Subrata Dutta	NIT Jamshedpur, India
Luca De Feo	IBM Research Zürich, Switzerland
Sugata Gangopadhyay	IIT Roorkee, India
Sylvain Guilley	Telecom Paris, France
Sourav Sen Gupta	NTU, Singapore
Shoichi Hirose	University of Fukui, Japan
Tan Chik How	NUS, Singapore
Meenakshi Kansal	IIT Madras, India
Nibedita Kundu	The LNMIIT Jaipur, India

Organizing Committee

Chief Patron

Karunesh Kumar Shukla   NIT Jamshedpur, India

Patron

Sunil Kumar   NIT Jamshedpur, India

Chairman

Sourav Das   NIT Jamshedpur, India

Convener and Organizing Secretary

Sumit Kumar Debnath   NIT Jamshedpur, India

Members

Mahendra Kumar Gupta
Sripati Jha
Snehasis Kundu
Tarni Mandal
Ratnesh Kumar Mishra
Raj Nandkeolyar
Hari Shankar Prasad
Ramayan Singh
Rajat Tripathi

Contents

Cryptanalysis and Other Attacks

Higher Order c-Differentials

Aaron Geary[1], Marco Calderini[2], Constanza Riera[3],
and Pantelimon Stănică[1(✉)]

[1] Applied Mathematics Department, Naval Postgraduate School,
Monterey, CA 93943, USA
{aaron.geary,pstanica}@nps.edu
http://faculty.nps.edu/pstanica/
[2] Department of Informatics, University of Bergen, Postboks 7803,
5020 Bergen, Norway
Marco.Calderini@uib.no
[3] Department of Computer Science, Electrical Engineering and Mathematical
Sciences, Western Norway University of Applied Sciences, 5020 Bergen, Norway
csr@hvl.no

Abstract. In [9], the notion of c-differentials was introduced as a potential expansion of differential cryptanalysis against block ciphers utilizing substitution boxes. Drawing inspiration from the technique of higher order differential cryptanalysis, in this paper we propose the notion of higher order c-derivatives and differentials and investigate their properties. Additionally, we consider how several classes of functions, namely the multiplicative inverse function and the Gold function, perform under higher order c-differential uniformity.

Keywords: Boolean and p-ary function · Higher order differential · Differential uniformity · Differential cryptanalysis

1 Introduction and Background

The newly proposed c-differentials [9] modify the traditional differential cryptanalysis technique by applying a multiple "c" to one of the outputs of an S-box primitive F. If an input pair $(x, x + a)$ with difference "a" results in an output pair $(F(x), F(x+a))$ with difference $b = F(x+a) - F(x)$, then the couple (a, b) is the traditional *differential* traced throughout a cipher. A differential that appears with a high probability is used as the basis of a classical differential attack [3]. The new c-differential uses a modified output pair of $(cF(x), F(x + a))$, and the new output difference is then $b = F(x + a) - cF(x)$. Similar to other extensions and modifications of differential cryptanalysis, c-differentials have been shown to result in higher probabilities than traditional differentials for some functions [9,15], thus potentially resulting in attacks against ciphers that are resistant against other forms of differential cryptanalysis.

P. Stănică et al. (Eds.): ICSP 2021, CCIS 1497, pp. 3–15, 2021.
https://doi.org/10.1007/978-3-030-90553-8_1

The introduction of c-differentials and the corresponding c-differential uniformity (cDU) has been met with substantial interest. Researchers have since submitted multiple papers (see [1,15,16,19,20], just to cite only a few of these works) further exploring the topic. These include investigations of the cDU of various classes of functions, finding functions with low cDU, construction and existence results on the so-called perfect c-nonlinear and almost perfect c-nonlinear functions, and generalizations of cryptographic properties to include the new c-differential.

In this paper, we continue this investigation by considering the extension of c-differentials into higher order. This is motivated by the extension of the original differential cryptanalysis technique into higher order differential cryptanalysis [12,13]. In contrast with the traditional higher order derivatives of Boolean or p-ary functions, the c-derivative and higher order c-derivative do not always reduce the degree of a function. However, in the same spirit as traditional higher order differentials, higher order c-differentials have the potential to allow for a better trace of multiple differences through an encryption scheme, and any resistance against such higher order differentials with large probabilities furthers the case of a cipher's security.

The rest of the paper is organized as follows. In Sect. 2 we provide the necessary notation and definitions to introduce the higher order c-derivative and investigate its properties in Sect. 3. In Sects. 4 and 5 we consider specific higher order c-differential cases of the inverse function and Gold function over finite fields. Section 6 summarizes our findings.

2   Preliminaries

We introduce here some basic notations and definitions on Boolean and p-ary functions (where p is an odd prime); the reader can consult [5,6,8,14,18] for more on these objects. For a positive integer n and p a prime number, we denote by $\mathbb{F}_p^n$ the n-dimensional vector space over $\mathbb{F}_p$, and by $\mathbb{F}_{p^n}$ the finite field with p^n elements, while $\mathbb{F}_{p^n}^* = \mathbb{F}_{p^n} \setminus \{0\}$ will denote the multiplicative group. We call a function from $\mathbb{F}_{p^n}$ (or $\mathbb{F}_p^n$) to $\mathbb{F}_p$ a p-ary function on n variables. For positive integers n and m, any map $F : \mathbb{F}_{p^n} \to \mathbb{F}_{p^m}$ (or, $\mathbb{F}_p^n \to \mathbb{F}_p^m$) is called a vectorial p-ary function, or (n, m, p)-function. If $p = 2$ the function is called a vectorial Boolean function. In any characteristic, when $m = n$ the function F can be uniquely represented as a univariate polynomial over $\mathbb{F}_{p^n}$ (using some identification, via a basis, of the finite field with the vector space) of the form $F(x) = \sum_{i=0}^{p^n-1} a_i x^i$, $a_i \in \mathbb{F}_{p^n}$, whose algebraic degree, denoted by $\deg(F)$, is then the largest weight in the p-ary expansion of i (that is, the sum of the digits of the exponents i with $a_i \neq 0$). To (somewhat) distinguish between the vectorial and single-component output, we shall use upper/lower case to denote the functions.

Given a (n, m, p)-function F, the derivative of F with respect to $a \in \mathbb{F}_{p^n}$ is the (n, m, p)-function

$$D_a F(x) = F(x + a) - F(x), \text{ for all } x \in \mathbb{F}_{p^n}.$$

The distribution of the derivatives of an (n, m, p)-function used in an S-box is important. If we let $\Delta_F(a, b) = \#\{x \in \mathbb{F}_{p^n} : F(x + a) - F(x) = b\}$, then we call the quantity $\delta_F = \max\{\Delta_F(a, b) : a, b \in \mathbb{F}_{p^n}, a \neq 0\}$ the *differential uniformity* of F.

The i-th derivative of F at $(a_1, a_2, \ldots, a_i)$ is defined recursively as

$$D^{(i)}_{a_1, \ldots, a_i} F(x) = D_{a_i}(D^{(i-1)}_{a_1, \ldots, a_{i-1}} F(x)).$$

The new c-differential, which applies a multiplier to one of the outputs, immediately leads to a modified derivative. For an (n, m, p)-function F, and $a \in \mathbb{F}_{p^n}, b \in \mathbb{F}_{p^m}$, and $c \in \mathbb{F}_{p^m}$, the (*multiplicative*) *c-derivative* of F with respect to $a \in \mathbb{F}_{p^n}$ is the function

$$_cD_aF(x) = F(x + a) - cF(x), \text{ for all } x \in \mathbb{F}_{p^n}.$$

Equipped with this new c-derivative, a new c-autocorrelation function was defined in [16], and several cryptographic properties of (n, m, p)-functions were generalized. That work continues in this paper as we extend the c-derivative into higher order, investigate its properties, and then analyze the higher order c-differential uniformity of several functions.

3   Higher Order c-differentials

Inspired by the concept of higher order derivatives of functions between Abelian groups and their applications to cryptography in [13], we propose the following definition.

Definition 31. *Let $F : \mathbb{F}_{p^n} \to \mathbb{F}_{p^m}$ be an (n, m, p)-function. The i-th c-derivative of F at $(a_1, a_2, \ldots, a_i)$ is*

$$_cD^{(i)}_{a_1, \ldots, a_i} F(x) = {}_cD_{a_i}({}_cD^{(i-1)}_{a_1, \ldots, a_{i-1}} F(x)),$$

where $_cD^{(i-1)}_{a_1, \ldots, a_{i-1}} F(x)$ is the $(i-1)$-th derivative of F at $(a_1, a_2, \ldots, a_{i-1})$.

This implies the 0-th c-derivative is the function F itself and the 1st c-derivative is the c-derivative defined in Sect. 2. Notice that, when $c = 1$, we recover the traditional (n, m, p)-function higher order derivative.

Before we explore these new higher order derivatives we need to ensure several basic properties carry over from the traditional (i.e. $c = 1$) case. First, we see that the sum rule holds. That is, that the c-derivative of a sum is the sum of the c-derivatives.

$$\begin{aligned} _cD_a(F + G)(x) &= F(x + a) + G(x + a) - c(F(x) + G(x)) \\ &= F(x + a) - cF(x) + G(x + a) - cG(x) \\ &= {}_cD_aF(x) + {}_cD_aG(x). \end{aligned}$$

A product rule exists for the traditional derivative, $D_a(FG)(x) = F(x + a)D_aG(x) + D_aF(x)G(x)$. We find something similar with the c-derivative,

$$\begin{aligned}
{}_cD_a(FG)(x) &= F(x + a)G(x + a) - cF(x)G(x) \\
&= F(x + a)\left(G(x + a) - cG(x)\right) + \left((F(x + a) - F(x))\, cG(x)\right) \\
&= F(x + a)\, {}_cD_aG(x) + {}_cD_aF(x)\, c\, G(x).
\end{aligned}$$

Now we consider the higher order c-derivatives. When $i = 2$ we have

$$\begin{aligned}
{}_cD^{(2)}_{a_1,a_2} F(x) &= {}_cD_{a_2}({}_cD_{a_1}F(x)) \\
&= {}_cD_{a_2}(F(x + a_1) - cF(x)) \\
&= F(x + a_1 + a_2) - cF(x + a_2) - c(F(x + a_1) - cF(x)) \\
&= F(x + a_1 + a_2) - cF(x + a_2) - cF(x + a_1) + c^2 F(x).
\end{aligned}$$

Taking another iteration, we have

$$\begin{aligned}
{}_cD^{(3)}_{a_1,a_2,a_3} F(x) &= F(x + a_1 + a_2 + a_3) \\
&\quad - c\left[F(x + a_1 + a_2) + F(x + a_1 + a_3) + F(x + a_2 + a_3)\right] \\
&\quad + c^2\left[F(x + a_1) + F(x + a_2) + F(x + a_3)\right] - c^3 F(x).
\end{aligned}$$

We see a similar pattern to Proposition 1 in [13], albeit with the additional complication of powers of c, and we find the following identity:

$$\begin{aligned}
F(x + a_1 + a_2 + a_3) &= {}_cD^{(3)}_{a_1,a_2,a_3} F(x) \\
&\quad + c\left[{}_cD^{(2)}_{a_1,a_2} F(x) + {}_cD^{(2)}_{a_1,a_3} F(x) + {}_cD^{(2)}_{a_2,a_3} F(x)\right] \\
&\quad + c^2\left[{}_cD_{a_1}(F(x)) + {}_cD_{a_2}(F(x)) + {}_cD_{a_3}(F(x))\right] \\
&\quad + c^3 F(x).
\end{aligned}$$

The pattern holds in general, as we now show.

Theorem 32. *Let F be an (n, m, p)-function with ${}_cD^{(i)}_{a_1,\ldots,a_i} F(x)$ the i-th c-derivative of F at $(a_1, a_2, \ldots, a_i)$. Then*

$$F\left(x + \sum_{i=1}^{n} a_i\right) = \sum_{i=0}^{n} \sum_{1 \leq j_1 < \ldots < j_i \leq n} c^{n-i}\, {}_cD^{(i)}_{a_{j_1},\ldots,a_{j_i}} F(x). \tag{1}$$

Proof. Equation (1) can also be written as

$$F\left(x + \sum_{i=1}^{n} a_i\right) = {}_cD^{(n)}_{a_1,\ldots,a_n} F(x) + \sum_{i=0}^{n-1} \sum_{1 \leq j_1 < \ldots < j_i \leq n-1} c^{n-1-i}\, {}_cD^{(i)}_{a_{j_1},\ldots,a_{j_i}} F(x),$$

which implies

$${}_cD^{(n)}_{a_1,\ldots,a_n} F(x) = F\left(x + \sum_{i=1}^{n} a_i\right) - \sum_{i=0}^{n-1} \sum_{1 \leq j_1 < \ldots < j_i \leq n-1} c^{n-1-i}\, {}_cD^{(i)}_{a_{j_1},\ldots,a_{j_i}} F(x).$$

We proceed by induction. For $n = 1$ we see (1) follows directly from the definition and $n = 2, 3$ can be seen in the discussion before the theorem. Assuming Eq. (1) holds for $n - 1$, we have

$$_cD^{(n)}_{a_1,\ldots,a_n} F(x) = {_cD_{a_n}} \left({_cD^{(n-1)}_{a_1,\ldots,a_{n-1}}} F(x) \right)$$

$$= {_cD_{a_n}} \left(F\left(x + \sum_{i=1}^{n-1} a_i \right) - \sum_{i=0}^{n-2} \sum_{1 \leq j_1 < \ldots < j_i \leq n-2} c^{n-2-i} {_cD^{(i)}_{a_{j_1},\ldots,a_{j_i}}} F(x) \right)$$

$$= F\left(x + \sum_{i=1}^{n} a_i \right) - cF\left(x + \sum_{i=1}^{n-1} a_i \right)$$

$$- {_cD_{a_n}} \left(\sum_{i=0}^{n-2} \sum_{1 \leq j_1 < \ldots < j_i \leq n-2} c^{n-2-i} {_cD^{(i)}_{a_{j_1},\ldots,a_{j_i}}} F(x) \right).$$

We apply the induction hypothesis to $cF(x + a_1 + \cdots + a_{n-1})$, and noticing the last double sum is composed of all the c-derivatives that include a_n, we have

$$F\left(x + \sum_{i=1}^{n} a_i \right) - cF\left(x + \sum_{i=1}^{n-1} a_i \right)$$

$$- {_cD_{a_n}} \left(\sum_{i=0}^{n-2} \sum_{1 \leq j_1 < \ldots < j_i \leq n-2} c^{n-2-i} {_cD^{(i)}_{a_{j_1},\ldots,a_{j_i}}} F(x) \right)$$

$$= F\left(x + \sum_{i=1}^{n} a_i \right) - c\left(\sum_{i=0}^{n-2} \sum_{1 \leq j_1 < \ldots < j_i \leq n-2} c^{n-2-i} {_cD^{(i)}_{a_{j_1},\ldots,a_{j_i}}} F(x) \right)$$

$$- \left(\sum_{i=0}^{n-1} \sum_{1 \leq j_1 < \ldots < j_i \leq n-1} c^{n-1-i} {_cD^{(i)}_{a_{j_1},\ldots,a_{j_i},a_n}} F(x) \right)$$

$$= F\left(x + \sum_{i=1}^{n} a_i \right) - \left(\sum_{i=0}^{n-2} \sum_{1 \leq j_1 < \ldots < j_i \leq n-2} c^{n-1-i} {_cD^{(i)}_{a_{j_1},\ldots,a_{j_i}}} F(x) \right)$$

$$+ \left(\sum_{i=0}^{n-1} \sum_{1 \leq j_1 < \ldots < j_i \leq n-1} c^{n-1-i} {_cD^{(i)}_{a_{j_1},\ldots,a_{j_i},a_n}} F(x) \right)$$

$$= F\left(x + \sum_{i=1}^{n} a_i \right) - \left(\sum_{i=0}^{n-1} \sum_{1 \leq j_1 < \ldots < j_i \leq n-1} c^{n-1-i} {_cD^{(i)}_{a_{j_1},\ldots,a_{j_i}}} F(x) \right).$$

The claim is shown.

While we have shown several properties of the c-derivative closely align with the traditional derivative, one key property does not follow. A fundamental property of traditional derivatives is that the degree of a polynomial function is reduced by at least one for every derivative taken. That is, $\deg(D_a F) \leq \deg(F) - 1$. This is not always true in the case of c-derivatives when $c \neq 1$. For example, consider the linearized monomial $F(x) = x^{p^k}$ over $\mathbb{F}_{p^n}$ with k an integer between 0 and n. This function has degree 1 (recall that the p-ary weight of p^k is 1) and the c-derivative of F at a is $(x+a)^{p^k} - cx^{p^k} = (1-c)x^{p^k} + a^{p^k}$, which is also of degree 1 for all $c \neq 1$. Thus, the reduction of degree is not a general property of the c-derivative.

We will now show that higher order c-derivatives are invariant under permutation of the a_i's.

Proposition 33. *Let $F : \mathbb{F}_{p^n} \to \mathbb{F}_{p^n}$, denote $[t] := \{1, \ldots, t\}$, and let $|I|$ be the cardinality of the subsets $I \subseteq [t]$. Then,*

$$_c D^{(t)}_{a_1,\ldots,a_t} F(x) = \sum_{I \subseteq [t]} (-c)^{t-|I|} F\left(x + \sum_{i \in I} a_i\right).$$

In particular, for any permutation π of $\{1, \ldots, t\}$ we have $_c D^{(t)}_{a_1,\ldots,a_t} F(x) = {}_c D^{(t)}_{a_{\pi(1)},\ldots,a_{\pi(t)}} F(x)$.

Proof. It is easy to see that $_c D^{(2)}_{a_1,a_2} F(x) = \sum_{I \subseteq [2]} (-c)^{2-|I|} F(x + \sum_{i \in I} a_i)$, and by induction we get

$$_c D^{(t)}_{a_1,\ldots,a_t} F(x) = {}_c D^{(t-1)}_{a_1,\ldots,a_{t-1}} F(x + a_t) - c \cdot {}_c D^{(t-1)}_{a_1,\ldots,a_{t-1}} F(x)$$

$$= \sum_{I \subseteq [t-1]} (-c)^{(t-1)-|I|} F\left(x + a_t + \sum_{i \in I} a_i\right) - c \sum_{I \subseteq [t-1]} (-c)^{(t-1)-|I|} F\left(x + \sum_{i \in I} a_i\right)$$

$$= \sum_{\substack{I' \subseteq [t] \\ a_t \in I'}} (-c)^{(t-1)-(|I'|-1)} F\left(x + \sum_{i \in I'} a_i\right) + \sum_{\substack{I' \subseteq [t] \\ a_n \notin I'}} (-c)^{t-|I'|} F\left(x + \sum_{i \in I'} a_i\right)$$

$$= \sum_{I \subseteq [t]} (-c)^{t-|I|} F\left(x + \sum_{i \in I} a_i\right).$$

From this we can see that permuting the elements a_i does not change the value of the higher order c-derivative.

One of the key findings of higher order derivatives of binary functions is that if the i inputs are not linearly independent, then the ith derivative is exactly 0. That is, if $a_1, a_2, \ldots, a_i$ are linearly dependent, then $D^{(i)}_{a_1,\ldots,a_i} F(x) = 0$. This limits the number of pairs that can be attempted in a higher order differential attack to the dimension of the vector space and reduces the combinations of differences that can be traced simultaneously. However, this property, and therefore the limits, do not apply for higher order c-derivatives when $c \neq 1$, which can be seen by considering the definition of the c-derivative. If we let $a = 0$, then

$$_c D_0 F(x) = F(x + 0) - cF(x) = (1-c)F(x).$$

Thus, even in the extreme case of zero difference between the input pairs, the c-derivative results in a nonzero function. In higher order c-derivatives this property remains true. For example the 2nd c-derivative has the form

$$_cD^{(2)}_{a_1,a_2}F(x) = F(x + a_1 + a_2) - cF(x + a_2) - cF(x + a_1) + c^2F(x).$$

Even if $a_1 = a_2$ (and thus linearly dependent), the 2nd c-derivative is not identically zero due to the introduction of the c multiplier. This fact increases the input (or output) differences that can be traced through an encryption scheme and potentially increases the vulnerability of a cipher if a c-differential attack is realized in the future.

As for the 1st order derivative, for an (n, m, p)-function we can introduce the *t-order c-differential uniformity* of F at c to be

$$_c\delta^{(t)}_F = \max_{a_1,\ldots,a_t \in \mathbb{F}_{p^n}} \#\{x : {}_cD^{(t)}_{a_1,\ldots,a_t}F(x) = b\}$$

(if $c = 1$, not all a_i's are allowed to be zero). If $t = 1$, we recover the c-differential uniformity $_c\delta^{(1)}_F = {}_c\delta_F$, as defined in [9].

Proposition 34. *For any (n, m)-function F, any order $t \in \mathbb{Z}_+$ (positive integers), and any $c \neq 1$, the t-order c-differential uniformity of F is greater than or equal to its $(t - 1)$-order c-differential uniformity, $\delta^{(t)}_{F,c} \geq \delta^{(t-1)}_{F,c}$.*

Proof. For any (n, m)-function F and any $c \neq 1$, and taking $a_t = 0$, we obtain that $_cD^{(t)}_{a_1,a_2,\ldots,a_{t-1},0}F(x) = (1 - c)\,_cD^{(t-1)}_{a_1,a_2,\ldots,a_{t-1}}F(x)$, which implies our claim.

Another easy fact to check is that for power functions the t-order c-differential uniformity can be computed by considering $a_1 = 1$.

Proposition 35. *Let $F(x) = x^d$ on $\mathbb{F}_{p^n}$ and denote by $_c\Delta(a_1,\ldots,a_t;b) = \#\{x : {}_cD^{(t)}_{a_1,\ldots,a_t}F(x) = b\}$. Then, assuming that not all a_i's are zero (and without loss of generality we can assume that $a_1 \neq 0$), $_c\Delta(a_1,\ldots,a_t;b) = {}_c\Delta\left(1, a_2/a_1 \ldots, a_t/a_1; b/(a_1)^d\right)$.*

4   The Inverse Function

Next we consider an example of a higher order c-derivative and compare it to the traditional higher order derivative (i.e. when $c = 1$). The function we investigate is the multiplicative inverse function over finite fields of characteristic 2, a popular function used in S-boxes that can be represented by a monomial $F : \mathbb{F}_{2^n} \to \mathbb{F}_{2^n}$, $F(x) = x^{2^n-2}$. In [9] the authors investigate the first c-derivative of this function, focusing on the newly defined c-differential uniformity property. Specifically, they count the maximum number of solutions of $_cD_aF(x) = b$ for some $a, b, c \in \mathbb{F}_{2^n}$. In this section we count solutions to the second order c-differential equation $_cD^{(2)}_{a_1,a_2}F(x) = b$ with $c, a_1, a_2, b \in \mathbb{F}_{2^n}$.

The traditional ($c = 1$) second order differential spectrum of the inverse function over $\mathbb{F}_{2^n}$ was recently investigated in [17]. It was shown that for $n \geq 3$ the number of solutions to $D_{a_1,a_2} x^{2^n-2} = b$ is in the set $\{0, 4, 8\}$ and that there are multiple a_1, a_2, b that provide 8 solutions for $n \geq 6$.

With this understanding of the behavior of the second traditional derivative of the inverse function, we now consider the second c-derivative of the inverse function and compare the two. Starting with $_cD_{a_1,a_2}^{(2)} F(x) = b$, we have

$$(x + a_1 + a_2)^{2^n-2} + c(x + a_2)^{2^n-2} + c(x + a_1)^{2^n-2} + c^2 x^{2^n-2} = b. \quad (2)$$

It was shown in [9] that the inverse function has a bijective first c-derivative when $c = 0$. Later in [16] we showed that any permutation will have a bijective (i.e. balanced) first c-derivative when $c = 0$. For the second c-derivative of the inverse function, when $c = 0$, we get $(x + a_1 + a_2)^{2^n-2} = b$. If $b = 0$, $x = a_1 + a_2$ is the only solution. If $b \neq 0$, then $x \neq a_1 + a_2$ and $\frac{1}{x+a_1+a_2} = b$. Thus, $x = \frac{1}{b} + a_1 + a_2$ is the only solution and we see when $c = 0$ the second c-derivative of the inverse function is a bijection, as is in the case of the first c-derivative when $c = 0$.

In fact, from Theorem 32, we see that the nth 0-derivative of a function F is $F(x + a_1 + a_2 + \cdots + a_n)$, which is bijective if and only if F is bijective. Thus permutations have bijective n-th c-derivatives for all n when $c = 0$.

For $c \neq 0$, we consider multiple cases.

Case (i). Let $a_1 = a_2$. Recall this leads to a trivial result in traditional derivatives. Equation (2) becomes $x^{2^n-2} + c^2 x^{2^n-2} = b$, that is, $(1 + c^2)x^{2^n-2} = b$. When $b = 0$, $x = 0$ is the only solution. If $b \neq 0$, then $x \neq 0$ and $\frac{1+c^2}{x} = b$ gives us one solution $x = \frac{1+c^2}{b}$.

Case (ii). $a_1 \neq a_2$, and $x = a_1, a_2, a_1 + a_2,$ or 0. Equation (2) becomes, respectively,

$$a_2^{2^n-2} + c(a_1 + a_2)^{2^n-2} + c^2 a_1^{2^n-2} = b, \text{ or,}$$
$$a_1^{2^n-2} + c(a_1 + a_2)^{2^n-2} + c^2 a_2^{2^n-2} = b, \text{ or,}$$
$$ca_2^{2^n-2} + ca_1^{2^n-2} + c^2(a_1 + a_2)^{2^n-2} = b, \text{ or,}$$
$$(a_1 + a_2)^{2^n-2} + ca_2^{2^n-2} + ca_1^{2^n-2} = b.$$

When $c = 1$ all four of these solutions are the same and can be true simultaneously. However, when $c \neq 1$ we cannot combine all four of these solutions. In fact, the most that can be combined are two. Consider the solutions for a_1 and a_2 (the first two above). If we could combine these, then we would have,

$$a_2^{2^n-2} + c(a_1 + a_2)^{2^n-2} + c^2 a_1^{2^n-2} = a_1^{2^n-2} + c(a_1 + a_2)^{2^n-2} + c^2 a_2^{2^n-2},$$

which simplifies to

$$a_2^{2^n-2} + c^2 a_1^{2^n-2} = a_1^{2^n-2} + c^2 a_2^{2^n-2}, \text{ or,} (1 + c^2)a_1^{2^n-2} = (1 + c^2)a_2^{2^n-2}.$$

For $c \neq 1$ (which is an assumption throughout), a_1 must equal a_2 which is not true in this case. Therefore, the solutions cannot be combined and we have that no more than three solutions can be true simultaneously.

Now we consider the possibility of combining $x = 0$ with $x = a_1 + a_2$. This gives us

$$ca_2^{2^n-2} + ca_1^{2^n-2} + c^2(a_1 + a_2)^{2^n-2} = (a_1 + a_2)^{2^n-2} + ca_2^{2^n-2} + ca_1^{2^n-2},$$

which simplifies to $c^2(a_1+a_2)^{2^n-2} = (a_1+a_2)^{2^n-2}$. This is only true when $c = 1$ or $a_1 = a_2$, neither of which are allowed in this case. From this we immediately see that we can combine at most two of the solutions in Case (ii). There are only at most four values of c which allow the combination of two of these solutions. As we have seen, there are only four possible combinations (which in some cases might be equal): $x = 0$ and $x = a_1$, $x = 0$ and $x = a_2$, $x = a_1 + a_2$ and $x = a_1$, and $x = a_1 + a_2$ and $x = a_2$.

Let $x = 0$ and $x = a_1$ be both solutions of the equation above. Then,

$$(a_1 + a_2)^{2^n-2} + ca_2^{2^n-2} + ca_1^{2^n-2} = a_2^{2^n-2} + c(a_1 + a_2)^{2^n-2} + c^2 a_1^{2^n-2}.$$

Rearranging terms, we arrive at

$$(1 + c)(a_1 + a_2)^{2^n-2} + (1 + c)a_2^{2^n-2} + c(1 + c)a_1^{2^n-2} = 0,$$

which, since $c \neq 1$, simplifies to $(a_1 + a_2)^{2^n-2} + a_2^{2^n-2} + ca_1^{2^n-2} = 0$.

If $a_1 = 0$, then $x = 0$ and $x = a_1$ are the same solution, so we can assume that $a_1 \neq 0$. If $a_2 = 0$, we arrive at the equation $(1 + c)a_1^{2^n-2} = 0$, which only has the forbidden solutions $c = 1$ or $a_1 = 0$. We can then assume that $a_1 a_2 \neq 0$. The equation becomes then $c(a_1 + a_2)a_2 + a_1^2 = 0$, which has a single solution $c_0 = \frac{a_1^2}{(a_1+a_2)a_2}$. It is easy to see that $c_0 = 0$ if and only if $a_1 = 0$. However, it is possible to obtain that $c_0 = 1$ if $a_1^2 + a_2^2 + a_1 a_2 = 0$, which is achievable only if n is even and $a_1 = a_2\omega$ or $a_1 = a_2\omega^2$, where $\mathbb{F}_4 = \{0, 1, \omega, \omega^2\}$. As long as $n \geq 5$, we can always chose valid a_1, a_2 to ensure that $c_0 \neq 1$. By symmetry, $x = 0$ and $x = a_2$ give $c_1 = \frac{a_2^2}{(a_1+a_2)a_1}$, with the same conditions as $x = 0$ and $x = a_1$.

Now, if $x = a_1 + a_2$ and $x = a_1$, then

$$ca_2^{2^n-2} + ca_1^{2^n-2} + c^2(a_1 + a_2)^{2^n-2} = a_2^{2^n-2} + c(a_1 + a_2)^{2^n-2} + c^2 a_1^{2^n-2},$$

which, by rearranging, becomes $(1 + c)a_2^{2^n-2} + c(1 + c)a_1^{2^n-2} + c(1 + c)(a_1 + a_2)^{2^n-2} = 0$, and, since $c \neq 1$, this can be simplified to $a_2^{2^n-2} + ca_1^{2^n-2} + c(a_1 + a_2)^{2^n-2} = 0$. If $a_1 = 0$, then we have the case $x = 0, x = a_2$. If $a_2 = 0$, we do not have two different solutions. We can then assume $a_1 a_2 \neq 0$. Then, the equation is equivalent to $(a_1 + a_2)a_1 + ca_2^2 = 0$, which has the solution $c_2 = \frac{a_1(a_1+a_2)}{a_2^2}$. It is easy to see that $c_2 \neq 0$, and that $c \neq 1$ under the same conditions as for $x = 0$ and $x = a_1$. By symmetry, $x = a_1 + a_2$ and $x = a_1$ gives $c_3 = \frac{a_2(a_1+a_2)}{a_1^2}$.

Case (iii). $a_1 \neq a_2$, $x \neq a_1, a_2, a_1 + a_2$, or 0. Equation (2) becomes

$$\frac{1}{x + a_1 + a_2} + \frac{c}{x + a_1} + \frac{c}{x + a_2} + \frac{c^2}{x} = b.$$

Multiplying through by $(x+a_1+a_2)(x+a_1)(x+a_2)x$, collecting and rearranging terms, we arrive at

$$bx^4 + \left(1 + c^2\right)x^3 + \left(a_2 + ca_2 + ba_2^2 + a_1 + ca_1 + ba_1^2 + ba_1a_2\right)x^2$$
$$+ \left(a_1a_2 + ca_2^2 + c^2a_2^2 + ca_1^2 + c^2a_1^2 + c^2a_1a_2 + ba_1a_2^2 + ba_1^2a_2\right)x \qquad (3)$$
$$+ c^2a_1a_2(a_1 + a_2) = 0.$$

This quartic polynomial has at most four solutions when $b \neq 0$ and at most three when $b = 0$. Without the four guaranteed solutions from Case (ii), we cannot reach the 8 solutions possible when $c = 1$. This means that, as in the case of the first c-derivative of the inverse function, when $c \neq 1$ the differential counts *decreases* from the traditional case. In fact, when combining Cases (ii) and (iii), a maximum of 6 solutions is possible, if $c \neq 1$.

Theorem 1. *Let $n \geq 4$, and $F(x) = x^{2^n-2}$ over $\mathbb{F}_{2^n}$. Then, for any $c \in \mathbb{F}_{2^n} \setminus \{1\}$, ${}_c\delta_F^{(2)} \leq 6$.*

Some computations to demonstrate our findings are captured in Table 1. From here, we see that the maximum is attainable for $n = 8, 9$. We conjecture that it is attainable for all $n \geq 8$.

Table 1. Maximum number of solutions to ${}_cD_{a_1,a_2}^{(2)}x^{2^n-2} = b$

n	$c = 1$	$c \neq 1$	$c = 0$
4	4	5	1
5	4	5	1
6	8	5	1
7	8	5	1
8	8	6	1
9	8	6	1

5   The Gold Function

The c-differential uniformity for quadratic functions was characterized in [1], where the authors focus on the PcN and APcN case though their proof applies for the general case. In particular from Theorem 3.1 in [1] we can obtain the following result.

Theorem 51. *Let $q = p^h$, $F : \mathbb{F}_{p^n} \to \mathbb{F}_{p^n}$ be a quadratic function given by*

$$\sum_{i,j} c_{i,j}x^{q^i+q^j} + \sum_l c_l x^{p^l}.$$

Let $\delta = \max_{b \in \mathbb{F}_{p^n}} |F^{-1}(b)|$. Then, for $c \in \mathbb{F}_{p^{\gcd(n,h)}} \setminus \{1\}$, ${}_c\delta_F^{(t)} = \delta$.

Proof. From the proof of Theorem 3.1 in [1], we have that for $c \in \mathbb{F}_{p^{\gcd(n,h)}} \setminus \{1\}$ the c-derivative $_cD_aF(x)$ equals

$$(1-c)F\left(x + \frac{a}{1-c}\right) + F(a) - (1-c)F\left(\frac{a}{1-c}\right) = (1-c)F\left(x + \frac{a}{1-c}\right) + \beta,$$

with $\beta = F(a) - (1-c)F\left(\frac{a}{1-c}\right)$. From this we can easily see that for any $a_1, \ldots, a_t$ the higher-order c-derivative of F is

$$_cD_{a_1,\ldots,a_t}F(x) = (1-c)^t F\left(x + \frac{a_1 + \cdots + a_t}{1-c}\right) + \beta',$$

for some constant β' depending on the a_i's, and the claim follows.

Theorem 52. *Let $F(x) = x^{p^k+1}$ on $\mathbb{F}_{p^n}$, and $1 \neq c \in \mathbb{F}_{p^n}$. Then, the maximum number of solutions of $_cD^{(2)}_{a_1,a_2}F(x) = b$ is $p^{\gcd(k,n)} + 1$, and there exist some b, a_1, a_2 such that this bound is obtained.*

Proof. The equation $_cD^{(2)}_{a_1,a_2}F(x) = b$ is

$$(x + a_1 + a_2)^{p^k+1} - c(x+a_1)^{p^k+1} - c(x+a_2)^{p^k+1} + c^2 x^{p^k+1} = b,$$

which renders $(1 - 2c + c^2)x^{p^k+1} + (a_1 + a_2)(1-c)x^{p^k} + (a_1+a_2)^{p^k}(1-c)x + (a_1+a_2)^{p^k+1} - c(a_1^{p^k+1} + a_2^{p^k+1}) = b$. Since $c \neq 1$, this yields

$$x^{p^k+1} + \frac{a_1 + a_2}{1-c}x^{p^k} + \frac{(a_1+a_2)^{p^k}}{1-c}x + \frac{(a_1+a_2)^{p^k+1} - c(a_1^{p^k+1} + a_2^{p^k+1})}{(1-c)^2} = \frac{b}{(1-c)^2}.$$

Taking $a_2 = -a_1$, this equation becomes $x^{p^k+1} = \frac{b}{(1-c)^2}$, which has at most $\gcd(p^k+1, p^n-1)$ solutions, and exactly $\gcd(p^k+1, p^n-1)$ solutions for some b. This implies that the maximum number of solutions to $_cD^{(2)}_{a_1,a_2}F(x) = b$ is lower bounded by $\gcd(p^k+1, p^n-1)$ (also derived from Proposition 34).

Taking $a_1 \neq a_2$, and $x = y - \frac{a_1+a_2}{1-c}$, we can write this equation as

$$y^{p^k+1} + (a_1+a_2)^{p^k}\frac{(1-c)^{p^k-1}-1}{(1-c)^{p^k}}y + \frac{a_1^{p^k}a_2 + a_1 a_2^{p^k} - b}{(1-c)^2} = 0.$$

If $(1-c)^{p^k-1} = 1$, then we obtain the equation $y^{p^k+1} + \frac{a_1^{p^k}a_2 + a_1 a_2^{p^k} - b}{(1-c)^2} = 0$, which has at most $\gcd(p^k+1, p^n-1)$ solutions, and exactly $\gcd(p^k+1, p^n-1)$ solutions for some b.

If $(1-c)^{p^k-1} \neq 1$, and $b = a_1^{p^k}a_2 + a_1 a_2^{p^k}$, this equation can be written as

$$y\left(y^{p^k} + (a_1+a_2)^{p^k}\frac{(1-c)^{p^k-1}-1}{(1-c)^{p^k}}\right) = 0,$$ which has at most $\gcd(p^k, p^n-1)+1 = 2$ solutions, and exactly 2 solutions for some a_1, a_2.

Otherwise, taking $z = \alpha y$, where $\alpha^{p^k} = (a_1+a_2)^{p^k}\frac{(1-c)^{p^k-1}-1}{(1-c)^{p^k}}$ (note that the p^k-root exists since, for any p, $\gcd(p^k, p^n-1) = 1$ and x^{p^k} is therefore a permutation on $\mathbb{F}_{p^n}$), we get the equation $z^{p^k+1} + z + \beta = 0$, where $\beta = \alpha^{-(p^k+1)} \frac{a_1^{p^k} a_2 + a_1 a_2^{p^k} - b}{(1-c)^2}$.

It is easy to see that the equation fulfills the conditions imposed in [4], where it is shown that there are either $0,1,2$ or $p^d + 1$ solutions to this equation, where $d = \gcd(k, n)$. Taking $p > 2$, and if $m = \frac{n}{d}$ is even, we have (using [9]) that $\gcd(p^k + 1, p^n - 1) = p^d + 1$. From the results above, this bound is obtained, and we have exactly $p^d + 1$ solutions for the general equation for some a_1, a_2.

If m is odd, for $p \geq 2$, then $m > 2$ since otherwise $n = k$. Then, by [4], the amount of values of β such that there are $p^d + 1$ solutions to the equation is nonzero. Since β is linear on b, the maximum number of solutions taken over all b is $p^d + 1$.

One still has to study the case where $p = 2$ and $m = 2$. In this case, by [9], we have that $\gcd(2^k + 1, 2^n - 1) = \frac{2^{\gcd(2k,n)}-1}{2^{\gcd(k,n)}-1} = \frac{2^{2d}-1}{2^d-1} = 2^d + 1$. So, in that case as well, by the previous results we obtain the bound $p^d + 1$.

The following corollary implies that, for any odd characteristic, we can always obtain functions whose higher differential uniformity is 2, regardless of the order of differentiation.

Corollary 53. *Let $F(x) = x^{p^k+1}$, and let $1 \neq c \in \mathbb{F}_{p^{\gcd(k,n)}}$. Then, the maximum number of solutions to $_cD_{a_1,a_2,\ldots,a_t}^{(t)}F(x) = b$ is $\gcd(p^k + 1, p^n - 1)$.*

Remark 54. *It is not difficult to modify the argument to obtain the same outcome as above for the t-order derivative taken with respect to different c's.*

6   Summary and Further Comments

In this paper we investigate higher order c-differentials, noting that traditional derivatives are a special case of our extension (i.e. when $c = 1$). We also look at the specific case of the inverse function over fields of even characteristic and the Gold function over any characteristic. While many properties of higher order c-differentials are preserved from the traditional higher order derivative, a key difference arises in that the higher order c-derivatives do not require linearly independent input differences. Thus, the higher order c-derivatives we have introduced could potentially allow the use of more input pairs (for encryption or decryption), which in turn could lead to differentials with higher probabilities than traditional higher order differential attacks or the new c-differential attack using one derivative.

References

1. Bartoli, D., Calderini, M.: On construction and (non)existence of c-(almost) perfect nonlinear functions, Finite Fields Appl. **72**, 101835 (2021)
2. Berlekamp, E.R., Rumsey, H., Solomon, G.: On the solutions of algebraic equations over finite fields. Inf. Control **10**, 553–564 (1967)

3. Biham, E., Shamir, A.: Differential cryptanalysis of DES-like cryptosystems. J. Cryptol. **4**(1), 3–72 (1991). https://doi.org/10.1007/BF00630563
4. Bluher, A.W.: On $x^{q+1} + ax + b$. Finite Fields Appl. **10**(3), 285–305 (2004)
5. Budaghyan, L.: Construction and Analysis of Cryptographic Functions. Springer, Cham (2014). https://doi.org/10.1007/978-3-319-12991-4_6
6. Carlet, C.: Boolean Functions for Cryptography and Coding Theory. Cambridge University Press, Cambridge, Cambridge (2021)
7. Coulter, R.S., Henderson, M.: A note on the roots of trinomials over a finite field. Bull. Austral. Math. Soc. **69**, 429–432 (2004)
8. Cusick, T.W., Stănică, P.: Cryptographic Boolean Functions and Applications, 2nd edn, Academic Press, San Diego (2017)
9. Ellingsen, P., Felke, P., Riera, C., Stănică, P., Tkachenko, A.: C-differentials, multiplicative uniformity and (almost) perfect c-nonlinearity. IEEE Trans. Inf. Theory **66**(9), 5781–5789 (2020)
10. Helleseth, T., Kholosha, A.: On the equation $x^{2^{\ell}+1} + x + a = 0$ over $GF(2^k)$. Finite Fields Appl. **14**, 159–176 (2008)
11. Kim, K.H., Choe, J., Mesnager, S.: Solving $x^{q+1} + x + a = 0$ over Finite Fields. Finite Fields Appl. **70**(6), 101797 (2021)
12. Knudsen, L.R.: Truncated and higher order differentials. In: Preneel, B. (ed.) FSE 1994. LNCS, vol. 1008, pp. 196–211. Springer, Heidelberg (1995). https://doi.org/10.1007/3-540-60590-8_16
13. Lai, X.: Higher order derivatives and differential cryptanalysis, In: Blahut, R.E., Costello, D.J., Maurer, U., Mittelholzer, T. (eds.) Communications and Cryptography. The Springer International Series in Engineering and Computer Science (Communications and Information Theory), vol. 276. Springer, Boston, MA (1994). https://doi.org/10.1007/978-1-4615-2694-0_23
14. Mesnager, S.: Bent Functions: Fundamentals and Results, Springer Verlag (2016)
15. Mesnager, S., Riera, C., Stănică, P., Yan, H., Zhou, Z.: Investigations on c-(almost) perfect nonlinear functions IEEE Trans. Inf. Theory **67**(10), 6916–6925 (2021)
16. Stănică, P., Gangopadhyay, S., Geary, A., Riera, C., Tkachenko, A.: C-Differential Bent Functions and Perfect Nonlinearity, to Appear in Discrete Applied Mathematics.
17. Tang, D., Mandal, B., Maitra, S.: Further cryptographic properties of the multiplicative inverse function. https://eprint.iacr.org/2020/920
18. Mesnager, S.: Subclasses of bent functions: hyper-bent functions. In: Bent Functions, pp. 171–205. Springer, Cham (2016). https://doi.org/10.1007/978-3-319-32595-8_9
19. Wu, Y., Li, N., Zeng, X.: New PcN and APcN functions over finite fields. Des., Codes Cryptogr. **89**, 2637–2651 (2021)
20. Zha, Z., Hu, L.: Some classes of power functions with low c-differential uniformity over finite fields. Des. Codes Cryptogr. **89**, 1193–1210 (2021)

First-Order Side-Channel Leakage Analysis of Masked but Asynchronous AES

Antoine Bouvet[1], Sylvain Guilley[1,2], and Lukas Vlasak[1]

[1] Secure-IC S.A.S., Think Ahead Business Line, 35510 Cesson-Sévigné, France
{antoine.bouvet,sylvain.guilley,lukas.vlasak}@secure-ic.com
[2] Télécom ParisTech, 91120 Palaiseau, France
sylvain.guilley@telecom-paristech.fr

Abstract. Masking schemes are classical countermeasures against Side-Channel Attacks on cryptographic implementations. This paper investigates the effectiveness of masking when the code does not run in constant time. We prove that in this case, a first-order Correlation Power Analysis can break an otherwise perfect masking scheme. Furthermore, with an in-depth leakage analysis on traces generated at a pre-silicon stage, we pinpoint the leaking instructions and recover a complex leakage model.

Keywords: Side-Channel Analysis · Masking scheme · Leakage model · Desynchronisation · AES · White-Box · Pre-silicon evaluation

1 Introduction

Cryptographic algorithms are known to be sensitive to physical attacks. While theoretically proven to resist algebraic cryptanalysis, the actual implementations of such an algorithm may leak information about a parameter through its observable physical behavior when running on an end-user device. The parameters which must be kept secret are called Critical Security Parameters (CSPs). The computation of an intermediate value, which depends on these CSPs, leads to a statistically biased activity on the device (*e.g.* its power consumption [22], its electro-magnetic (EM) emanations [17], the execution time [21] or the emitted acoustic waves [18]), which can be measured, recorded and analysed. This is called a Side-Channel Analysis (SCA). Such an analysis can be performed on subkeys, small parts of a CSP, in order to reduce the strength of a cryptosystem (a *Divide-and-Conquer* strategy). Even if not all subkeys have been broken, it may be weakened enough to accomplish a brute-force attack. Fortunately, many countermeasures exist, such as noise addition [12], [20, §2.1], constant time operations [1], shuffling [28] or masking schemes [5, 26]. Each one aims at protecting against specific attacks – for instance, constant time operations resist against Timing Attacks, while masking schemes are effective against vertical SCAs. That is why developers and designers do not use only one countermeasure when designing their software, but a combination of them. The goal is always to secure a device against as many attacks as possible.

P. Stănică et al. (Eds.): ICSP 2021, CCIS 1497, pp. 16–29, 2021.
https://doi.org/10.1007/978-3-030-90553-8_2

Contributions. We present how a first-order SCA such as Differential Power Analysis (DPA) [22] or Correlation Power Analysis (CPA) [8] can break a (possibly higher-order) masking scheme. Normally the usage of an nth-order masking scheme countermeasure protects a device against an nth-order SCA (no subkey can be broken). Nevertheless, we show that instead of increasing the cryptosystem's security, the combination of masking and desynchronisations significantly improves the attack efficiency, allowing to break the whole secret key. More precisely, we prove that, if a Boolean masking scheme is used in combination with asynchronous operations that depend on a CSP, then the masking is completely ineffective. Moreover, our pre-silicon security White-Box evaluation approach, based on traces generated on CPU, allows an in-depth analysis of the leakage source, including the derivation of the optimal leakage model.

Outline. Boolean masking schemes against vertical SCAs and possible reasons for non-constant time cryptographic code are explained in Sect. 2. Our contributions start in Sect. 3; we outline theoretical examples of first-order SCAs against masking schemes. Side-Channel Analyses on pre-silicon traces are carried out in Sect. 4: the leakage is characterised and its source identified. Section 5 discusses general aspects about our results. Eventually, conclusions are given in Sect. 6.

2 Boolean Masking Schemes Against Vertical SCAs

Masking techniques aim to protect implementations against vertical SCAs by avoiding statistical dependencies between CSPs and the processed values, which influence the observable side-channel activity. **Boolean masking** [11,19,23] uses an *exclusive or* (XOR, $\oplus$). For a secret parameter $x \in \mathbb{F}_2^N$, and $d \in \mathbb{N}$ randomly chosen masks $x_1, ..., x_d \in \mathbb{F}_2^N$, every possible masked value $x_0 = x \oplus x_1 \oplus ... \oplus x_d$ has the same probability ($\frac{1}{2^N}$). This widely used masking scheme avoids first-order SCAs and increases the resistance against SCAs of arbitrary order, when $d > 1$.

One could argue that masked implementations ought be designed "constant time" in the first place. This is a good practice we do recommend. We want to underline that there are reasons for some developers – who are generally not security experts – to implement non-constant masked code:

- Blinding for RSA [21] works even if the implementation is non-constant time, but this countermeasure does not intend to protect against vertical SCA.
- One might think randomization would protect the data sufficiently also against Timing Attacks. This is untrue, as shown in [13]. In the next Sect. 3, we will show that even vertical SCAs can be applied on masked code which does not run in constant time.
- A programmer may not be aware that he is implementing non-constant time code. For instance, an AES with tabulated substitution boxes is not constant time, as the lookup time can depend on the address (see [4]). Examples of potentially vulnerable codes are [10,15,16,30], which use tables addressed by sensitive variables. Furthermore, [15,16] resort to conditional control flow in $\mathbb{F}_{256}$ multiplication.

3   First-Order Vertical SCAs Against Masking Schemes

Usually, vertical SCAs require that the activity traces are synchronised – the target nodes are temporally aligned according to a *clock period of interest*. In the case of the AES, common target nodes are the first round S-Box output $S(x_i \oplus k_i)$, where S is the S-Box, x_i and k_i are the ith plaintext and key bytes respectively, or the last round S-Box input $S^{-1}(c_i \oplus k_i)$, where S^{-1} is the inverse S-Box, and c_i is the ith ciphertext byte. In a protected algorithm with first-order Boolean masking, the first round's target node becomes $S(x_i \oplus k_i) \oplus M$, where a random byte value M is used as mask, hence even under the correct key hypothesis the value is unpredictable by an attacker. The current situation can be summarised in the following assertions:

– vertical SCAs are very effective against unprotected algorithms;
– desynchronisations (intentional or not) increase the difficulty of vertical SCA;
– when a cryptographic algorithm is implemented with a first-order (or higher-order) masking scheme, first-order CPAs do fail.

However, we highlight hereafter that *asynchronous* (*i.e.*, non-constant time) activity traces may lead to a side-channel leakage in a masked implementation.

Our study deals with an asynchronous, masked AES (defined in Algorithm 1).

Input   : *plaintext, key,* $(mi, mo) \in \mathbb{F}_{2^8}^2$, $Nr \in \{10, 12, 14\}$
Output : *ciphertext*

1 *KeySchedule* = KeyExpansion(*key*, *Nr*)   // Precomputation of the *Nr* round keys
2 for *byte* = 0 *to* 255 do
3   ⌊ $MS[byte] = S[byte \oplus mi] \oplus mo$ // Precomputation of the masked S-Box
4 $mr = mi \oplus mo$ // Precomputation of the mask refresh
5 for *i* = 0 *to* 15 do
6   ⌊ $state[i] = plaintext[i] \oplus mi$ // Masking the state
7 AddRoundKey(*state*, *KeySchedule*, 0)
8 for *round* = 1 *to* $Nr - 1$ do
9   ShiftRows(*state*)
10   SubBytes(*state*, MS)
11   MixColumns(*state*)
12   RefreshMask(*state*, *mr*)   // $\forall i \in \{0, \ldots, 15\}$, $state[i] \oplus= mr$
13   AddRoundKey(*state*, *KeySchedule*, *round*)
14 ShiftRows(*state*)
15 SubBytes(*state*)
16 AddRoundKey(*state*, *KeySchedule*, *Nr*)
17 for *i* = 0 *to* 15 do
18   ⌊ $ciphertext[i] = state[i] \oplus mo$ // Unmasking the state
19 **return** *ciphertext*

Algorithm 1: Main ciphering function of the masked AES.

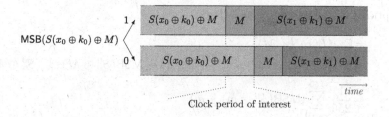

Misaligned traces and the corresponding leakage model.

The desynchronisation occurs in the *xtime* sub-function which is used in *MixColumns*, to multiply a polynomial $b \in \mathbb{F}_2\,[x]\,/\langle x^8 + x^4 + x^3 + x + 1\rangle$ with the monomial x. A pseudo-code of its naive implementation is given in Algorithm 2. As there is a conditional branch which depends on the Most Significant Bit (MSB) of the S-Box output, one gets a parameter-dependent misalignment between the traces. This can be exploited with a high-order Timing Analysis [13] and, as we show, it also opens the door to a first-order vertical SCA.

Input   : $b \in \mathbb{F}_2\,[x]\,/\langle x^8 + x^4 + x^3 + x + 1\rangle$
Output : $res = b \times x$

1   $res \leftarrow b \ll 1$ // Multiplication by x
2   if $b \wedge$ *0x80* then
3   $\lfloor$ $res \leftarrow res \oplus$ 0x11b   // Conditional reduction
4   return res

Algorithm 2: Naive *xtime* (insecure – with conditional branching).

The Fig. 1 illustrates the two paths of execution, depending on line 3 of Algorithm 2 is executed or not. During the *clock period of interest*, if the MSB of the masked S-Box output is 1, the S-Box evaluation is over and the mask is manipulated, whereas if it is 0, at the same time the S-Box evaluation is still ongoing.

Let $i \in \{0, \ldots, 15\}$ and $j \in \{0, \ldots, 7\}$. For the rest of the paper, the notation S^i refers to the S-Box output $S(x_i \oplus k_i)$, and S_j^i to its jth bit. Then the leakage model can be expressed as follows:

$$L(x_0, k_0, M) = \begin{cases} M & \text{if } \mathsf{MSB}(S^0 \oplus M) = 1, \\ S^0 \oplus M & \text{otherwise.} \end{cases}$$

$$= \mathsf{MSB}(S^0 \oplus M) \times M$$
$$+ (1 - \mathsf{MSB}(S^0 \oplus M)) \times (S^0 \oplus M). \tag{1}$$

The *optimal model* can be derived by averaging $L(x_0, k_0, M)$ over M [27]. If this model depends on the sensitive variable $x_0 \oplus k_0$, then a key extraction is possible.

The optimal model computes as follows:

$$\ell(x_0, k_0) = \mathbb{E}_M(L(x_0, k_0, M))$$
$$= \mathbb{E}_M(\mathsf{MSB}(S^0 \oplus M) \times M) + \mathbb{E}_M((1 - \mathsf{MSB}(S^0 \oplus M)) \times (S^0 \oplus M))$$
$$= \frac{1}{256} \sum_{m=0}^{255} (\mathsf{MSB}(S^0 \oplus m) \times m)$$
$$+ \frac{1}{256} \sum_{m=0}^{255} ((1 - \mathsf{MSB}(S^0 \oplus m)) \times (S^0 \oplus m))$$
$$= \frac{1}{256} \sum_{m=0}^{255} \mathsf{MSB}(S^0 \oplus m) \times m \tag{2}$$
$$+ \frac{1}{256} \sum_{m'=0}^{255} (1 - \mathsf{MSB}(m')) \times (m'). \tag{3}$$

using variable change $m' = m \oplus S(x_0 \oplus k_0)$. Notice that (2) does depend on the key, and the term (3) is a constant, thus it can be dropped.

Now, let m_i be the ith bit of $m \in \mathbb{F}_2^8$:

$$\sum_{m=0}^{255} \mathsf{MSB}(S^0 \oplus m) \times m = \sum_{m \in \{0,1\}^8} (S_7^0 \oplus m_7) \times (m_7, \ldots, m_0).$$

For any $i \in \{6, \ldots, 0\}$:

$$\frac{1}{256} \sum_{m \in \{0,1\}^8} (S_7^0 \oplus m_7) \times m_i = \frac{64}{256} \sum_{(m_7, m_i) \in \{0,1\}^2} (S_7^0 \oplus m_7) \times m_i$$
$$= \frac{64}{256} \sum_{m_7 \in \{0,1\}} (S_7^0 \oplus m_7)$$
$$= \frac{64}{256}(S_7^0 + (1 - S_7^0)) = \frac{1}{4},$$

and for the particular case $i = 7$:

$$\frac{1}{256} \sum_{m \in \{0,1\}^8} (S_7^0 \oplus m_7) \times m_i = \frac{128}{256} \sum_{m_7 \in \{0,1\}} (S_7^0 \oplus m_7) \times m_7 = \frac{128}{256}(1 - S_7^0),$$

hence we can conclude:

$$\ell(x_0, k_0)_7 = \frac{1}{2}(1 - \mathsf{MSB}(S(x_0 \oplus k_0))). \tag{4}$$

It turns out that the optimal model for a SCA on Fig. 1 is simply the selection signal of the unmasked target node. Correlation coefficients between measures and optimal model (4) are shown in Fig. 2, the correct key can easily be recovered.

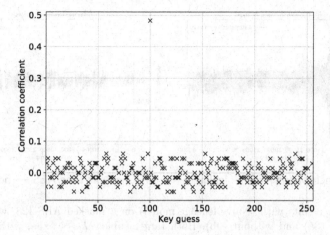

Fig. 2. CPA coefficients obtained for leakage (1) and leakage model (4) (correct key is $k_0 = 100$) – Ideal setup of Fig. 1.

However, if the traces are realigned, the leakage model does not depend on the MSB. Therefore we confirm that the code is first-order perfectly masked. Interestingly, this leakage would not have been detected by a static analysis method, such as the one of Barthe *et al.* [2], because this approach is unaware of timing issues between executions with different data.

4   Experiments on a Real-World AES Code

In Sect. 3, a theoretical example of leakages due to the combination of masking and desynchronisation, has been studied. In the present section, we consider a real use-case.

4.1   Target Agnostic Analysis on CPU

Traces Generation. In order to pinpoint such leakages, we analyse at a pre-silicon stage, a masked AES-128 which uses the *xtime* structure presented in Algorithm 2, through a target agnostic approach as introduced in [6]. The implementation is protected with first-order Boolean masking, which theoretically resists first-order SCAs. Static leakage detection tools, such as [2], cannot detect the vulnerabilities we encounter (since they do not have a notion of time). Dynamic tools, such as SLEAK [29], can be used in this respect.

Our traces are generated at a binary level – on a CPU, using a debugger (gdb) as measurement tool which records the values of multiple registers –, while running on a 64-bit x86 architecture. That is why in the following sections, bit indices of a byte can exceed 7 and extend up to 63. We need to record only the RAX[1] register values. In such a White-Box context, we can map each RAX

---

[1] RAX is the name of the accumulator register in x86 assembly.

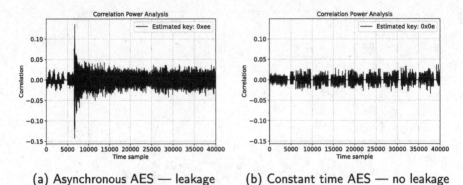

(a) Asynchronous AES — leakage   (b) Constant time AES — no leakage

Fig. 3. CPA results with (Naive leakage model) on a masked AES-128, with desynchronisation (3a) and without (3b). Both target subkey $k_0 = $ Oxee, with the same number of traces. The subkey is broken only in case of desynchronisation.

Input   : $b \in \mathbb{F}_2\,[x] \,/\langle x^8 + x^4 + x^3 + x + 1\rangle$
Output : $res = b \times x$
1 **return** $(b \ll 1) \oplus (((b \gg 7) \land 1) \times \mathtt{0x11b})$

Algorithm 3: Constant time *xtime*.

sample with its address, and are therefore able to find the corresponding line of the C source code [7] (leveraging DWARF format).

Naive Analysis. We use the Pearson's correlation as distinguisher and target the AES first round using the Hamming Weight leakage model:

$$\ell_N(x_0, k_0) = \mathtt{HW}(S(x_0 \oplus k_0)) \qquad \text{(Naive leakage model)}$$

where HW refers to the *Hamming Weight* function. Obviously, such analysis is not optimal, since the AES traces are not synchronised on the targeted operation sample. Nevertheless, one can easily break the secret key as if no mask was used, as shown in Fig. 3a. One may think that the implemented masking scheme is not really effective (*e.g.* in reality some sensitive intermediate value is not masked), however the countermeasure itself is well implemented. The linearity of the *xtime* function in $\mathbb{F}_2^8$ guarantees that the sensitive values stay perfectly masked. Besides, when repeating the same analysis on a constant time version described by Algorithm 3, there is no first-order leakage (Fig. 3b). The AES is perfectly masked end-to-end, according to the requirement of Blömer *et al.* [5]. This observation is consistent with the situation in Sect. 3, that a protected AES leaks in first-order, when the traces are misaligned. Furthermore, it should be noted that the constant time *xtime* (Algorithm 3) increases the computation time by 46%, compared to Algorithm 2. This again explains a possible motivation for non-constant solutions in practice.

Table 1. Classes of each of the 2^5 possible combinations for $\mathcal{C}$.

$\mathcal{L}_1$	$\mathcal{L}_2$	$\mathcal{L}_3$	$\mathcal{L}_4$	$\mathcal{L}_5$	$\mathcal{L}_6$
$\{0;0;1;1;1\}$	$\{1;1;1;1;-\}$	$\{0;1;1;0;-\}$	$\{0;0;1;1;0\}$	$\{0;1;0;-;-\}$	$\{1;1;0;-;-\}$
		$\{1;0;0;1;-\}$	$\{0;0;1;0;-\}$	$\{0;1;1;1;-\}$	$\{1;1;1;0;-\}$
			$\{0;0;0;-;-\}$	$\{1;0;1;1;-\}$	
				$\{1;0;-;0;-\}$	

Real Leakage Model. In White-Box evaluations on CPU, we can map each time sample with its source code. We can narrow this analysis down to the Points of Interest (PoIs) – the samples with the highest Pearson's correlation. We pinpoint all the used addresses, which can differ from one trace to another. If the situation matches with the theoretical one (Sect. 3), we should get two addresses (as Fig. 1 shows two execution paths at the clock period of interest). But actually, more than two addresses correspond to the analysed sample, therefore the leakage model is far more complicated than expected. After mapping the assembly instructions to the corresponding algorithmic values, we want to understand the conditions leading to these values. In fact, in our case, each call to the *xtime* function creates a misalignment of up to 2 samples, depending only on the MSB of *xtime* input. This leads to a global misalignment of up to 38 samples when targeting k_0, depending on the following MSB:

$$\mathcal{C} = \{\mathrm{MSB}(M); \mathrm{MSB}(\mathrm{xtime}(M)); \mathrm{MSB}(a); \mathrm{MSB}(\mathrm{xtime}(a)); \mathrm{MSB}(d)\}$$

where $a = S(x_0 \oplus k_0) \oplus M$, and $d = S(x_{15} \oplus k_{15}) \oplus M$. By classifying the traces according to this condition $\mathcal{C}$, we observe six different classes $\mathcal{L}_1, \ldots, \mathcal{L}_6$, at the leaking sample (defined in Table 1).

As a consequence, the real leakage model $\hat{L} = L(x_0, k_0, x_{15}, k_{15}, M)$, outlined in Fig. 4, can be expressed as follows:

$$\hat{L} = \begin{cases} 1 & \text{if } \mathcal{C} \in \mathcal{L}_1, \\ 0 & \text{if } \mathcal{C} \in \mathcal{L}_2, \\ d \ll 1 & \text{if } \mathcal{C} \in \mathcal{L}_3, \\ \mathrm{xtime}(d) & \text{if } \mathcal{C} \in \mathcal{L}_4, \\ d & \text{if } \mathcal{C} \in (\mathcal{L}_5 \cup \mathcal{L}_6). \end{cases} \tag{5}$$

Figure 4 also highlights that there are six execution paths. They happen not to be of the same duration. However, if they were, Timing Analyses [4] would not be possible, but the first-order SCA could still be carried out in the same way. Interestingly, we can check the consistency of this leakage model by comparing the theoretical and the experimental leaking values distributions.

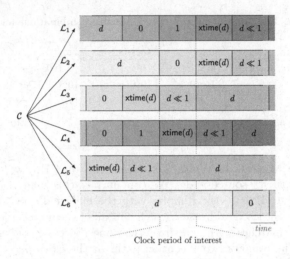

Fig. 4. Symbolic values in the registers, depending on the condition $\mathcal{C}$.

Indeed, over $2^5 = 32$ possible combinations (Table 1):

- $\mathcal{L}_1$ (symbolic value: 1) contains only 1 combination;
- $\mathcal{L}_2$ (symbolic value: 0) clusters 2 combinations;
- $\mathcal{L}_3$ (symbolic value: $d \ll 1$) clusters 4 combinations;
- $\mathcal{L}_4$ (symbolic value: xtime(d)) clusters 7 combinations;
- $\mathcal{L}_5$ and $\mathcal{L}_6$ (symbolic value: d) cluster respectively $12 + 6 = 18$ combinations.

As shown in Fig. 5, the experimental distribution is close to the theoretical one, which validates this leakage model as realistic.

4.2 Optimal Leakage Model

Note that the former CPA breaks subkey k_0 (Fig. 3a) by algorithmic values which never depend on x_0 or k_0 (Fig. 4). Therefore, below we compute the optimal leakage model $\ell(x_0, k_0)$ by deriving the real leakage model $\hat{L}$, which is deduced from symbolic values stored in the registers.

Lemma 1 (Expression of the optimal leakage model). *Let* $i \in \mathbb{N}_{<64}$. *The optimal leakage model* $\ell_{O,i} = \ell_O(x_0, k_0)_i$ *for the* i^{th} *bit of* $\hat{L}$ *expresses as follows:*

$$\ell_{O,0} = \frac{1}{2^4}\begin{pmatrix} 2\,S_7^0 S_6^0 & + \\ 2^2(\neg S_7^0) & + \\ 2^2 S_7^0(\neg S_6^0) & + \\ 2\,S_7^0 & + \\ 2(\neg S_6^0) & + \\ 2^2(\neg S_7^0)S_6^0 \end{pmatrix}, \quad \ell_{O,i\in\{1,\ldots,7\}} = \frac{1}{2^4}\begin{pmatrix} (2^2+1)S_7^0 S_6^0 & + \\ 2^2(\neg S_7^0) & + \\ 2^2 S_7^0(\neg S_6^0) & + \\ 2\,S_7^0 & + \\ 2(\neg S_6^0) & + \\ 2^2(\neg S_7^0)S_6^0 \end{pmatrix},$$

$$\ell_{O,8} = \frac{1}{2^4}\begin{pmatrix} 2^2 S_7^0 S_6^0 & + \\ 2(\neg S_7^0) & + \\ 2\,S_7^0(\neg S_6^0) \end{pmatrix}, \quad \ell_{O,i\in\{9,\ldots,63\}} = 0.$$

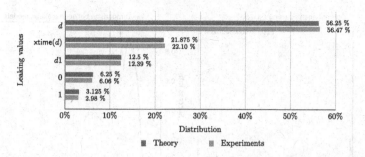

Fig. 5. Leaking values distribution for the leakage model: theory *v.s.* experiments (based on 9,356 execution traces).

Proof. First, we are concerned with x_0, in order to guess k_0 since the leaking values and the different combinations are functions of x_0, k_0, x_{15} and k_{15}. However, we disregard k_{15} which is constant, and x_{15}. Moreover, M is unknown, hence $\ell_O(x_0, k_0) = \mathbb{E}_{M,d}(\hat{L})$. While $\hat{L}$ depends on specific bits' value, which leads to exclusive conditions, we bit-wise construct the optimal leakage model. For instance, assume $\mathcal{C} \in \mathcal{L}_1$, then $\hat{L} = 1$:

$$\mathbb{E}_M(\hat{L}) = \frac{1}{2^8} \sum_{m \in \mathbb{F}_{256}} 1 \wedge \mathcal{C} = \frac{1}{2^8} \sum_{(m_7,\ldots,m_0) \in \mathbb{F}_2^8} \underbrace{(0 \wedge \mathcal{C}, \ldots, 0 \wedge \mathcal{C}, 1 \wedge \mathcal{C})}_{8 \text{ bits}}.$$

Now, $\mathcal{C}$ does not depend on $m_5, \ldots, m_0$. Thus the first bit of $\mathbb{E}_M(\hat{L})$ becomes:

$$\mathbb{E}_M(\hat{L})_0 = \frac{1}{2^2} \sum_{(m_7, m_6) \in \mathbb{F}_2^2} (\neg m_7)(\neg m_6)(S_7^0 \oplus m_7)(S_6^0 \oplus m_6)(S_7^{15} \oplus m_7).$$

$$\mathbb{E}_{M,d}(\hat{L})_0 = \frac{1}{2^8} \sum_{x_{15} \in \mathbb{F}_{256}} \mathbb{E}_M(\hat{L})_0 = \frac{1}{2^8} \sum_{S^{15} \in \mathbb{F}_{256}} \mathbb{E}_M(\hat{L})_0 = \frac{1}{2} \sum_{S_7^{15} \in \mathbb{F}_2} \mathbb{E}_M(\hat{L})_0$$

$$= \frac{1}{2^3} S_7^0 S_6^0.$$

Finally, for every register bit $i \in \{0, \ldots, 63\}$ and all possible values of $\hat{L}$ (5), the optimal leakage model is obtained by summing $\mathbb{E}_{M,d}(\hat{L})_i$ using the Python library SymPy dedicated to symbolic mathematics [24]. □

We perform a new SCA with this optimal leakage model and the maximum likelihood (ML) distinguisher [9], on the same traces as previously:

$$\mathcal{D}_{\mathsf{ML}}(X, \ell_O(x_0, k_0)) = \operatorname*{argmax}_{k \in \mathbb{F}_8} \sum_{i \in \mathbb{F}_{64}} \|\rho(X, \ell_O(x_0, k_0)_i)\|^2, \tag{6}$$

where ρ is the Pearson's correlation, X the simulated side-channel activity, and k the key guess. Results are shown in Fig. 6.

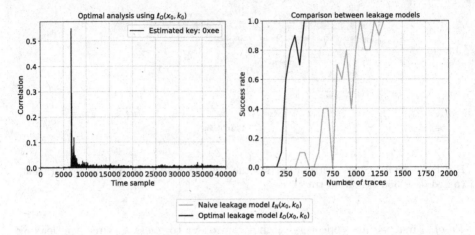

Fig. 6. Maximum likelihood analysis performed on the asynchronous masked AES-128 using the optimal leakage model (left figure). The subkey k_0 is broken with $9,356$ traces. Its success rate is compared to the naive leakage model in the right figure, averaging over 10 analyses, with randomly chosen traces.

Again, a peak is clearly visible at the first AES round (left figure), which corresponds to the correct key, confirming this model is effective. We estimate the number of traces needed for breaking the key, to compare it with the leakage model defined in (Naive leakage model). The success rates, using both the naive and the optimal leakage models, are given in the right figure: around 400 traces are needed with $\ell_O(x_0, k_0)$, whereas $1,300$ traces are necessary through the naive approach. This confirms, once again, that the side-channel leakage due to the combination of the masking scheme with some misalignment is not a coincidence, but an exploitable vulnerability.

5   Discussion

The first-order leakage on the non-constant time masked AES could as well be detected using metrics such as Quantitative Masking Strength (QMS [14]), Normalized Inter-Class Variance (NICV [3, 25]), or Information Leakage Amount (ILA [31]). However, those statistical tools do not help in understanding the root-cause for the leakage – which is crucial for developers to fix their cryptographic implementations.

Our methodology, based on a study of the symbolic values stored in the registers (recall Fig. 4) allows to attribute the bias to the C code of Algorithm 2. Such an approach makes non-regression security testing possible, *i.e.*, evaluating and fixing an implementation before any integration on end-user devices.

6   Conclusions

We studied an end-to-end masked AES algorithm. The masking implementation has been analysed and proven correct. Still, we present a successful first-order analysis. In order to track the leakage back to its responsible code lines, we used an emulated environment and identified that the leakage is produced by a peculiarity of the code: it has some non-constant time structures. As a consequence, the leaking code lines differ from one trace to the other, which complicates the leakage investigation. Evaluation tools which permit to perform Side-Channel Analyses at register level are good solutions for both, understanding leakages in general and improving analyses on end-user devices. Indeed, combining the analysis on symbolic values during the execution and a simulation at register level, allows to attribute the leakages to the corresponding non-constant time operations. The emerging problem is not trivial, as we are not aware of static tools for leakage detection which work turnkey, when masking is in place.

Again, we must point out the importance of a constant execution time: not only can it be exploited by timing- or cache-based attacks, but as we have shown, it can also ruin a masking scheme.

References

1. Almeida, J.B., Barbosa, M., Barthe, G., Dupressoir, F., Emmi, M.: Verifying constant-time implementations. In: 25th USENIX Security Symposium, USENIX Security 2016, Austin, TX, USA, 10–12 August 2016, pp. 53–70 (2016)
2. Barthe, G., Belaïd, S., Dupressoir, F., Fouque, P.-A., Grégoire, B., Strub, P.-Y.: Verified proofs of higher-order masking. In: Oswald, E., Fischlin, M. (eds.) EURO-CRYPT 2015. LNCS, vol. 9056, pp. 457–485. Springer, Heidelberg (2015). https://doi.org/10.1007/978-3-662-46800-5_18
3. Bhasin, S., Danger, J.L., Guilley, S., Najm, Z.: NICV: normalized inter-class variance for detection of side-channel leakage. In: International Symposium on Electromagnetic Compatibility (EMC 2014/Tokyo). IEEE (May 12–16 2014), Session OS09: EM Information Leakage. Hitotsubashi Hall (National Center of Sciences), Chiyoda, Tokyo, Japan (2014)
4. Bhattacharya, S., Maurice, C., Bhasin, S., Mukhopadhyay, D.: Branch prediction attack on blinded scalar multiplication. IEEE Trans. Comput. **69**(5), 633–648 (2020)
5. Blömer, J., Guajardo, J., Krummel, V.: Provably secure masking of AES. In: Selected Areas in Cryptography, pp. 69–83 (2004)
6. Bos, J.W., Hubain, C., Michiels, W., Teuwen, P.: Differential computation analysis: hiding your white-box designs is not enough. In: Gierlichs, B., Poschmann, A.Y. (eds.) CHES 2016. LNCS, vol. 9813, pp. 215–236. Springer, Heidelberg (2016). https://doi.org/10.1007/978-3-662-53140-2_11
7. Bouvet, A., Bruneau, N., Facon, A., Guilley, S., Marion, D.: Give me your binary, I'll tell you if it leaks. In: 13th International Conference on Design & Technology of Integrated Systems In Nanoscale Era, DTIS 2018, Taormina, Italy, 9–12 April 2018, pp. 1–4 (2018)

8. Brier, E., Clavier, C., Olivier, F.: Correlation power analysis with a leakage model. In: Joye, M., Quisquater, J.-J. (eds.) CHES 2004. LNCS, vol. 3156, pp. 16–29. Springer, Heidelberg (2004). https://doi.org/10.1007/978-3-540-28632-5_2
9. Bruneau, N., Guilley, S., Heuser, A., Marion, D., Rioul, O.: Optimal side-channel attacks for multivariate leakages and multiple models. J. Cryptogr. Eng. **7**(4), 331–341 (2017). https://doi.org/10.1007/s13389-017-0170-9
10. Census Labs: Masked AES (2012). http://census-labs.com/
11. Chari, S., Jutla, C.S., Rao, J.R., Rohatgi, P.: Towards sound approaches to counteract power-analysis attacks. In: Wiener, M. (ed.) CRYPTO 1999. LNCS, vol. 1666, pp. 398–412. Springer, Heidelberg (1999). https://doi.org/10.1007/3-540-48405-1_26
12. Coron, J.-S., Kizhvatov, I.: An efficient method for random delay generation in embedded software. In: Clavier, C., Gaj, K. (eds.) CHES 2009. LNCS, vol. 5747, pp. 156–170. Springer, Heidelberg (2009). https://doi.org/10.1007/978-3-642-04138-9_12
13. Danger, J.L., Debande, N., Guilley, S., Souissi, Y.: High-order timing attacks. In: Proceedings of the First Workshop on Cryptography and Security in Computing Systems, CS2 2014, pp. 7–12. ACM, New York (2014)
14. Eldib, H., Wang, C., Taha, M., Schaumont, P.: QMS: evaluating the side-channel resistance of masked software from source code. In: Proceedings of the The 51st Annual Design Automation Conference on Design Automation Conference, DAC 2014, pp. 209:1–209:6. ACM, New York (2014)
15. French ANSSI: Secure AES128 for ATMega8515 (2021). https://github.com/ANSSI-FR/secAES-ATmega8515/tree/master/src/Version2. Accessed 14 May 2021
16. French ANSSI: Secure AES128 for STM32 (2021). https://github.com/ANSSI-FR/SecAESSTM32/blob/master/src/aes/. Accessed 14 May 2021
17. Gandolfi, K., Mourtel, C., Olivier, F.: Electromagnetic analysis: concrete results. In: Koç, Ç.K., Naccache, D., Paar, C. (eds.) CHES 2001. LNCS, vol. 2162, pp. 251–261. Springer, Heidelberg (2001). https://doi.org/10.1007/3-540-44709-1_21
18. Genkin, D., Shamir, A., Tromer, E.: RSA key extraction via low-bandwidth acoustic cryptanalysis. In: Garay, J.A., Gennaro, R. (eds.) CRYPTO 2014, Part I. LNCS, vol. 8616, pp. 444–461. Springer, Heidelberg (2014). https://doi.org/10.1007/978-3-662-44371-2_25
19. Goubin, L., Patarin, J.: DES and differential power analysis the "duplication" method. In: Koç, Ç.K., Paar, C. (eds.) CHES 1999. LNCS, vol. 1717, pp. 158–172. Springer, Heidelberg (1999). https://doi.org/10.1007/3-540-48059-5_15
20. Güneysu, T., Moradi, A.: Generic side-channel countermeasures for reconfigurable devices. In: CHES, pp. 33–48 (2011)
21. Kocher, P.C.: Timing attacks on implementations of Diffie-Hellman, RSA, DSS, and other systems. In: Koblitz, N. (ed.) CRYPTO 1996. LNCS, vol. 1109, pp. 104–113. Springer, Heidelberg (1996). https://doi.org/10.1007/3-540-68697-5_9
22. Kocher, P.C., Jaffe, J., Jun, B.: Differential power analysis. In: Proceedings of the 19th Annual International Cryptology Conference on Advances in Cryptology, CRYPTO 1999, pp. 388–397. Springer, London (1999)
23. Maghrebi, H., Danger, J.L., Flament, F., Guilley, S., Sauvage, L.: Evaluation of countermeasure implementations based on boolean masking to thwart side-channel attacks. In: 2009 3rd International Conference on Signals, Circuits and Systems (SCS), pp. 1–6. IEEE (2009)
24. Meurer, A., et al.: SymPy: symbolic computing in Python. PeerJ Comput. Sci. **3**, e103 (2017)

25. Moradi, A., Guilley, S., Heuser, A.: Detecting hidden leakages. In: Boureanu, I., Owesarski, P., Vaudenay, S. (eds.) ACNS 2014. LNCS, vol. 8479, pp. 324–342. Springer, Cham (2014). https://doi.org/10.1007/978-3-319-07536-5_20
26. Nassar, M., Souissi, Y., Guilley, S., Danger, J.L.: RSM: a small and fast countermeasure for AES, secure against 1st and 2nd-order zero-offset SCAs. In: 2012 Design, Automation & Test in Europe Conference & Exhibition, DATE 2012, Dresden, Germany, 12–16 March 2012, pp. 1173–1178 (2012)
27. Prouff, E., Rivain, M., Bevan, R.: Statistical analysis of second order differential power analysis. IEEE Trans. Computers **58**(6), 799–811 (2009)
28. Veyrat-Charvillon, N., Medwed, M., Kerckhof, S., Standaert, F.-X.: Shuffling against side-channel attacks: a comprehensive study with cautionary note. In: Wang, X., Sako, K. (eds.) ASIACRYPT 2012. LNCS, vol. 7658, pp. 740–757. Springer, Heidelberg (2012). https://doi.org/10.1007/978-3-642-34961-4_44
29. Walters, D.T., Hagen, A., Kedaigle, E.A.: SLEAK: a side-channel leakage evaluator and analysis kit (November 2014), technical paper (Case Number 14–3463). https://www.mitre.org/publications/technical-papers/sleak-a-side-channel-leakage-evaluator-and-analysis-kit. Accessed 24 Sept 2020
30. Yao, Y.: Masked AES implementation, 4 February 2020. https://github.com/Secure-Embedded-Systems/Masked-AES-Implementation/find/master. Accessed 2 June 2021
31. Zhang, L., Ding, A.A., Fei, Y., Luo, P.: A unified metric for quantifying information leakage of cryptographic devices under power analysis attacks. In: Iwata, T., Cheon, J.H. (eds.) ASIACRYPT 2015. LNCS, vol. 9453, pp. 338–360. Springer, Heidelberg (2015). https://doi.org/10.1007/978-3-662-48800-3_14

Side-Channel Analysis
of CRYSTALS-Kyber and A Novel
Low-Cost Countermeasure

Meziane Hamoudi[1]([✉]), Amina Bel Korchi[3], Sylvain Guilley[1,2],
Sofiane Takarabt[1], Khaled Karray[1], and Youssef Souissi[1]

[1] Secure-IC S.A.S, Paris, France
`meziane.hamoudi@secure-ic.com`
[2] LTCI, Télécom Paris, Institut Polytechnique de Paris, Palaiseau, France
[3] Secure-IC S.A.S., Cesson-Sévigné, France

Abstract. In this paper, we propose a vertical side-channel leakage detection on the decryption function of the third round implementation of CPA-secure public-key encryption scheme underlying CRYSTALS-Kyber, a lattice-based key encapsulation mechanism, which is a candidate to the NIST Post-Quantum Cryptography standardization project. Using a leakage assessment metric, we show that the side-channel information can be efficiently used to pinpoint operations leaking the secret variable and how masking countermeasures can be applied. We detect leakages in the polynomial multiplication between the secret key and the ciphertext. We propose and evaluate two different masking countermeasures, based on additive and multiplicative masking. To the best of our knowledge, the multiplicative masking has not been proposed before as a countermeasure to CRYSTALS-Kyber vulnerabilities. We demonstrate their efficiency and discuss their impact in terms of performance. Our work is beneficial to assess and enhance the security of Post-Quantum Cryptography against advanced vertical side-channel analysis.

Keywords: Post-quantum cryptography · Lattice-based cryptography · CRYSTALS-Kyber · Side-channel analysis · Masking countermeasure · Additive masking · Multiplicative masking

1 Introduction

Public-key cryptography made it possible to share a common secret-key between two entities communicating over a non-trusted channel. The most used public-key cryptographic algorithms are Rivest Shamir Adleman (RSA) [36] and Elliptic Curve Cryptography (ECC) [26]. The security of these two cryptosystems relies respectively on the hardness of the integer factorization for RSA and discrete logarithm problem for ECC. These two problems are supposed to be impossible to solve using classical computers.

However, quantum computers have recently been the subject of a substantial amount of research. They are known to have the potential to provide the

---

The original version of this chapter was revised: The author's name has been corrected as "Bel Korchi, Amina". The correction to this chapter is available at https://doi.org/10.1007/978-3-030-90553-8_11

P. Stănică et al. (Eds.): ICSP 2021, CCIS 1497, pp. 30–46, 2021.
https://doi.org/10.1007/978-3-030-90553-8_3

power to brute force current public key encryption standards in a relatively short amount of time. These computers can break standard and complex cryptographic algorithms such as RSA and ECC, as reported in [37,38]. For this purpose, National Institute of Standards and Technology (NIST) called for a proposal to standardize Post-quantum Cryptography (PQC) schemes. The main functions of a typical PQC scheme in the NIST evaluation process are Public Key Encryption (PKE), Key Encapsulation Mechanism (KEM) and digital signature. The NIST submissions rely on different hard problems: error correcting code, Learning With Errors (LWE), hash-based, multivariate and super-singular isogeny. The most important and commonly known families of PQC algorithms are LWE and those based on the hardness of decoding linear codes (also known as code-based algorithms).

PQC schemes based on lattice theory, mainly variant of LWE and Learning With Rounding (LWR) can be efficiently implemented on hardware and software. The best known and competitive algorithms in NIST competition are CRYSTALS-Dilithium for digital signature and CRYSTALS-Kyber for KEM.

In addition to the provided security against quantum computers, submitters must also take into consideration the protection against Side-Channel Attacks (SCA). Several works have been carried out to evaluate the security of PQC against physical attacks based on power acquisition or Electro-Magnetic emanation (EM), and fault injection. Some of them and other works, proposed also a set of countermeasures which can provide security against physical attacks. The NIST desires the PQC schemes to be resistant to side channel attacks at minimal cost.

Contributions. In this paper we evaluate the masking of the linear part of the current (reference implementation of the third round) submission of CRYSTALS-Kyber, especially the CPA-secure decryption function underlying this post-quantum cryptography scheme. After time constancy check using *time-cop* tool [27], we proceed to a practical application of ISO/IEC 17825 [19]; Namely we check if the implementation is properly masked by applying a vertical leakage detection and evaluation leveraging the Normalized Inter-Class Variance (NICV) metric [8] on the secret key. This allows to detect any vulnerabilities related to the long-term key. We evaluate an additive masking countermeasure at machine-code level, discuss the results of the leakage detection, and the impact on the performance. As a second contribution, we propose an alternative countermeasure based on a multiplicative masking which is faster and induces less overhead. The overall execution time of the decryption procedure has an overhead of about 15% for the multiplicative masking versus 32% for the additive one. We discuss the provided security level of this proposition to protect the polynomial multiplication as well as its impact on the performance. A comparison between these two schemes is provided, where we explain in which respect our multiplicative masking scheme happens to be better than the additive one in some other implementations.

Outline. This paper is organized as follows: Sect. 2 covers the related works on the lattice based post-quantum cryptography, side-channel attacks on this topic and the possible countermeasures. We summarize the recent analyses performed on lattice based implementation of the NIST competition previous round. Section 3 explains our analysis methodology, our attack scenario and the used leakage detection metric. Section 4 shows our experimental results on the reference implementation of CRYSTALS-Kyber, on the additive masking countermeasure, and on our proposition based on a multiplicative scheme. Finally, Sect. 5 concludes our paper.

2   Related Works and Background

2.1   Overview

Lattice-based cryptography [25] is a very promising PQC family. It offers a very strong security, and also a great simplicity, flexibility as well as an efficient implementation. Lattices are the most actively studied techniques and are used to construct key exchanges schemes, digital signature schemes, and fully homomorphic encryption schemes.

However, lattice-based cryptosystems have some disadvantages which restricts their usage in practical applications. One of them is the large size of the public key, the secret key, and ciphertexts. Thus, researchers introduce new algorithms based on LWE, which have the same hardness as the worst-case lattice problems.

CRYSTALS-Kyber [4] is a lattice-based KEM. It is one of the official finalist schemes of the NIST third-round competition. The security of this scheme is based on the difficulty of the Ring-LWE (R-LWE) problem. There are three variants of the scheme, namely Kyber512, Kyber768 and Kyber1024, which offer similar levels of security to AES-128, AES-192 and AES-256 respectively.

2.2   Notation

The algebraic structure used in CRYSTALS-Kyber scheme is the polynomial ring $R_q = \mathbb{Z}_q[X]/f(X)$, with $f(X) = X^n + 1$. We note $R = \mathbb{Z}[X]/f(X)$ where $\mathbb{Z}[X]$ is the polynomial ring with coefficients in $\mathbb{Z}$ and $f(X)$ is a cyclotomic polynomial. Elements of R are polynomials of degree less than n and coefficients in $\mathbb{Z}$. Elements of $R_q = \mathbb{Z}_q[X]/f(X)$ are polynomials of degree less than n and coefficients modulo q, where $\mathbb{Z}_q[X]$ is the polynomial ring with coefficients modulo q. Elements of the ring R_q are noted in lowercase ($a \in R_q$), we denote by $[a]_q$ the elements in R obtained by computing all its coefficients modulo q, $a + b$ (resp. $a \cdot b$) is the addition (resp. multiplication) of two polynomials a and b in R_q. In the case where a and b are two vectors in R_q^l with elements a_i and b_i in R_q, the addition of a and b is $a + b$ is a vector of l elements $a_i + b_i$ in R_q and the canonical scalar product is used for the multiplication $a \cdot b$ which is a vector of l elements $a_i b_i$ in R_q. For $x \in \mathbb{R}$ we denote by $\lfloor x \rceil$ rounding to the nearest integer, $\lceil x \rceil$, and $\lfloor x \rfloor$ rounding up and down. In practice, $n = 256$ and $q = 3329$ is a prime number.

2.3   LWE/R-LWE Problems

In 2005, Regev [34] introduced the LWE problem, which consists in finding a secret in the middle of noisy linear equations. Regev has shown that solving the LWE problem in the average case by a quantum algorithm involves solving the SIVP [2] and gapSVP [10] problems in the worst case. R-LWE [23] is the polynomial ring version of LWE problem. CRYSTALS-Kyber is based on the decision version of the RLWE problem, which consists in distinguishing between RLWE samples and uniformly random ones. The problem is described in the mathematical ring formed by degree d polynomials over a finite field such as the integers modulo a prime number q. Let $\phi(x)$ be a cyclotomic polynomial of degree d, and $q \geq 2$ a modulus depending on a security level λ. For a random $s \in R_q$ and a distribution $\chi = \chi(x)$ over R, the problem consists in distinguishing $(a, [a \cdot e + s]_q)$ from a random pair sampled uniformly from $R_q * R_q$, where a is a random element of R_q and e a noise term from χ.

For any cyclotomic ring R of degree n, modulus $q < 2^{poly(n)}$ and error distribution χ of error rate $0 < \alpha < 1$ where $\alpha q \geq 2\sqrt{n}$, solving the $RLWE_{q,\chi,m}$ problem is at least as hard as quantumly solving the SVP_γ problem on arbitrary ideal lattices in R, for some $\gamma = poly(n)/\alpha$.

2.4   Side-Channel Attacks on Lattice-Based Cryptography

SCA on lattice-based Post-quantum cryptography has been performed. Xu et al. propose in [40] an SCA with carefully constructed ciphertext on CRYSTALS-Kyber, and demonstrate that special chosen ciphertexts attack allows an adversary to modulate the leakage of a target device and enable full key extraction through Simple Power Analysis (SPA). Pess et al. in [29] introduced several improvements to the usage of belief propagation, which underlies the single trace attack and changed the target encryption instead of decryption which limited attacks to the recovery of the transmitted symmetric key, but in turn, increased attack performance. Ravi et al. demonstrated in [33] a generic and a practical SCA using a chosen ciphertext attack over multiple LWE/LWE-based PKE and KEM secure in the Chosen Ciphertext Attack (IND-CCA). They showed that the side-channel information can be efficiently used to instantiate a plaintext checking oracle, which provides binary information about the output of decryption, typically concealed within IND-CCA secure PKE/KEM, thereby allowing such attacks. In [31], Ravi et al. reported an important exploitable vulnerability through side-channel attacks for message recovery in five lattice-based PKE and KEM implementations namely NewHope, Kyber, Saber, Round5 and LAC. The reported vulnerabilities exist in the message decoding function which is a fundamental kernel used in lattice-based PKE/KEM. Further analyses of the implementations in the public *pqm4* library revealed that this function is implemented in a similar manner in all the identified schemes, and thus they all share the common side-channel vulnerability that leaks individual bits of the secret message. They demonstrate that the identified vulnerability can be exploited through a number of practical electromagnetic side-channel attacks, fault attacks and combined attacks on implementations from the $pqm4$ library running on ARM Cortex-M4 microcontroller.

Ravi et al. demonstrated in [32] practical fault attacks over a number of lattice-based schemes based on the hardness of the LWE problem. One of the common traits of all the considered LWE schemes is the use of nonce as domain separators to sample the secret components of the LWE instance, and showed that simple faults targeting the usage of nonce can result in a nonce-reuse scenario which allows for key recovery and message recovery attacks.

2.5   Countermeasures

To prevent SCA, some countermeasures can be adopted and applied to a given algorithm. In the following, we give the most important countermeasures, from the basic ones to prevent timing attacks [21], to the most advanced ones to prevent as well vertical and template attacks.

Constant Time. When the execution time of an algorithm is constant whatever the inputs, it becomes impossible to mount any timing attack. It is sufficient to implement constant-time operations only for the sensitive ones. In fact, if the timing variation is independent from sensitive data, or does not involve the key, the attacker cannot learn anything about the secret. Besides, some countermeasures are based on delay insertion, jitter and fake operations to intentionally desynchronize the traces and make vertical attacks more difficult to achieve. Thus, the algorithm is vulnerable only if the timing variation depends on the secret key (or any sensitive data).

Vertical Side Channel Attacks – Masking. The masking countermeasure is used to make the power consumption independent from the processed data. Thus, it makes attacks such as Differential Power Analysis (DPA) and Template attack non-effective. Masking was used in order to construct side-channel resistant implementations for some lattice-based schemes such as CRYSTALS-Dilithium [14], qTESLA [15] and SABER [5]. When the intermediate data are randomized, the attacker cannot build a leakage model that correlates with the physical leakage. Particularly, the power consumption and EM emanations become independent from the secret data. The principle of this countermeasure is to split the sensitive variable into random shares in order to eliminate the computation dependency on the secret data. Usually, the sum of the shares is equal to the secret data. In that case, we talk about additive masking. Besides, another type of masking exists: multiplicative masking, where any value is expressed as a product of shares. Some masking techniques have already been presented in [28,35] for the R-LWE public-key encryption scheme. In parallel to our research, a completely masked implementation of CRYSTALS-Kyber using only additive and Boolean masking for the Chosen Plaintext Attack (IND-CPA) decrypt has been presented in [9]. The main difference of this paper with ours is that we propose a multiplicative masking on this purpose which induces less overhead on the performances.

Countermeasures Against Fault Injection. Deterministic algorithms are more sensitive to fault injection [6,39]. Many algorithmic countermeasures have been proposed based on redundancy. However, in most of the cases, the overhead is very important. Some of them checks only certain variables and thus, limits the complexity [7]. Hardware-based countermeasures like sensors can also be used to detect any abnormal change on the clock, voltage, or temperature. These countermeasures can detect global and even local fault injection like EM or Laser injection. In the case of signature based on public key encryption, all deterministic protocols are vulnerable to fault attacks [30]. Additional randomness to make signature non-deterministic is an effective way to counteract all proposed Differential Fault Attack (DFA). In the case of Crystal-Dilithium, the authors of [12] showed that additional randomness is proved to be the most effective countermeasure.

3   Analysis Methodology

3.1   Our Objective

Official reference and optimized implementation of CRYSTALS-Kyber are unprotected against SCA. In this section, we describe a test to pinpoint side channel leakages. It plays two roles on the sequel:

- It allows to identifying the lines of code which are leaking.
- In case no leakage is detected it allows to prove that implementation is not leaking information.

We first check the time constancy of the CYSTALS-Kyber implementation indeed SCA requires traces to be aligned. For this purpose we use time constancy checking tool *timecop*. Results showed that the NIST third round submission of CRYSTALS-Kyber is constant-time and does not contain timing leakages.

In our analysis scenario the key generation function of CRYSTALS-Kyber is only executed one time in order to generate the long-term key-pair, the attacker can only acquire one trace. Thus operations performed in the key generation function are vulnerable only to one trace based attacks, such as SPA and Template attacks. without being helped by a cryptanalysis attack, those attacks have a small chance of success then we do not cover them. Once the long-term key-pair is generated, the public key is used to encapsulate a (symmetric) secret key. In the other side, the secret key is used to decapsulate the ciphertext. An attacker that has access to the decryption step, can give different inputs and record EM or power activity. In addition to single trace based attacks, the decryption is also vulnerable to vertical attacks such as DPA [20] and Correlation Power Analysis (CPA) [11].

The most critical operation of the decryption step is the polynomial multiplication denoted by o which multiplies elements of the ciphertext and the secret key and accumulates the obtained result(line 4 of Algorithm 1). This function allows to avoid timing leakages by using Montgomery Reduction. However is stills vulnerable to vertical side-channel attacks cited above as presented in [17,18]. In this paper, the goal is not to mount a CPA/DPA attacks, but rather to detect potential leakages that could be exploited by these attacks.

Algorithm 1: KYBER.CPAPKE.Dec(sk, c): Decryption

Input: Secret key sk
Input: Cipherext $c = (u, v) \in R_q$
Output: Message m

1   $u := Decompress_q(Decode_{d_u}(c), d_u)$
2   $v := Decompress_q(Decode_{d_v}(c + d_u.k.n/8), d_v)$
3   $\hat{s} := Decode_{12}(sk)$
4   $m := Encode_1(Compress_q(v - NTT^{-1}(\hat{s} \circ NTT(u)), 1))$
5   **return** m

The *Compress* function, when applied to a vector in R_q^k, takes each coefficient in $x \in \mathbb{Z}_q$ and outputs an integer in $0, \ldots, 2^d - 1$ where $d < log_2(q)$. Formally $Compress(x, d) = \lfloor \frac{2^d}{q} \times x \rceil \bmod 2^d$ and $Decompress(x, d) = \lfloor \frac{q}{2^d} \times x \rceil$. $Decode_l$ function is used to transform an array of $32l$ bytes into a polynomial $f = f_0 + f_1 X + \ldots + f_{255} X^{255}$ where $f_i \in 0, \ldots, 2^{l-1}$. The function $Encode_l$ is the inverse of $Decode_l$. The Number Theoretic Transform (NTT) [22] is an efficient way to perform multiplication of two polynomials in R_q. The complexity of a polynomial multiplication using NTT method is $\mathcal{O}(n \log(n))$ instead of $\mathcal{O}(n^2)$ in the case of naïve multiplication.

3.2 Leakage Detection Test

Leakage Detection Metric. The NICV [8] can be used to detect inherent leakage of a given parameter. The traces are classified with respect to the parameter value to compute the inter-class variance. When normalized by the total variance, only the samples where the parameter is manipulated will yield peaks.

The NICV is defined as follows:

$$NICV(Y, X) = \frac{\mathbb{V}\left[\,\mathbb{E}\left(Y \mid X\right)\,\right]}{\mathbb{V}[Y]} \tag{1}$$

where Y is the traces and X refers to the parameter used to classify Y. The NICV is a bounded quantity: $0 \leq NICV(Y, X) \leq 1$. When the NICV is small (resp. large), the implementation is secure (resp. insecure).

Definition 1. *An implementation is secure if NICV is lower than 0.3 on all samples of a traces.*

Discussion: *Indeed, as one will see on the NICV traces, there is some estimation error, which is empirically evaluated to 0.1 for 500 traces. Thus 0.3 is a conservative value: choosing less than 0.3 would have led to false alarms, whereas choosing a larger threshold would have led to undetected leaks.*

We performed NICV on the polynomial multiplication function, using the secret key $\hat{s}$ where $\hat{s} := Decode(sk)$, and identified the leaking operations (lines of code). The NICV on the ciphertext u, where $u := Decompress_q(Decode_{du}(c), d_u)$ showed common leaking operations. Thus, those operations are critical and sensitive, when an attacker can acquire many traces with random ciphertexts.

We proposed an additive masking scheme, and showed the efficiency of this countermeasure and its impact on the implementation performance. Finally, we implemented our proposed variant based on a multiplicative masking, which has less impacts in terms of performance.

4 Experimental Results

4.1 Flow

In order to generate traces of the polynomial multiplication we simulate the SCA activity of the target implementation based on the CPU register content. Indeed, while performing step by step execution, all CPU registers are observed and their content is extracted after each executed instruction. Finally the Hamming Distance (HD) is computed over the CPU register content acquired from $instruction_i$ and $instruction_{i+1}$. This simulates efficiently the SCA activity of the implementation which is highly correlated with the number of switching bits. As a result, the number of samples of each obtained trace equals the number of instructions.

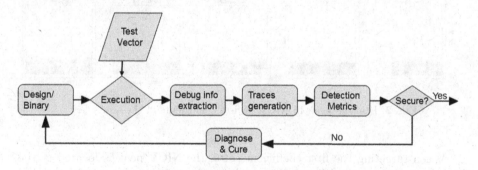

Fig. 1. Workflow of our analysis methodology.

The general workflow of our evaluation methodology from the design implementation to the trace simulation is illustrated in Fig. 1:

– We use the binary as design to evaluate the implementation.
– The test vectors are the inputs to the binary and consist of:

• 500 random ciphertexts to detect leakages depending on the ciphertext.
• 500 random secret keys to detect leakages depending on the secret key.

- Executing the binary, observing and storing registers of the CPU.
- Simulating traces of EM from the register content using the HD model.
- Using NICV to check the security of the implementation. The implementation is secure if NICV is lower than 0.3.
- If the implementation is not secure, performing diagnose and cure phase in order to provide protection.

4.2   Analysis of CRYSTALS-Kyber – Reference Implementation

Using the reference implementation of the official submission of CRYSTALS-Kyber, we have generated 500 traces of the point-wise multiplication with fixed ciphertext and random secret key in order to locate all the leaking operations. Each trace makes 142761 samples corresponding to each instruction of that function. We then capture the NICV coefficients of the secret key $\hat{s}$ (obtained at line 3 of Algorithm 1) which has $256 \times k$ coefficients where $k \in \{2, 3, 4\}$ fixes the lattice dimension, and is the main mechanism in CRYSTALS-Kyber to scale security of different levels.

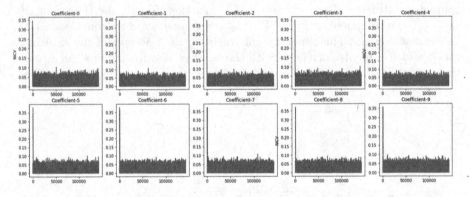

Fig. 2. Leakage peak in NICV of first coefficients of the secret key

When targeting the first coefficients of $\hat{s}$, the NICV peak is located at the beginning of the trace (Fig. 2). The peak is offset with respect to the targeted coordinate index. This represents exactly the way how the decryption function is implemented: the leakage corresponds to the pointwise multiplication "$\hat{s}$ ∘ $NTT(u)$" at line 4 of Algorithm 1. When targeting the last ones (Fig. 3), the NICV peaks are located at the end of the trace. It is easy to see that the peaks are located at equally spaced positions, which is consistent with the $\hat{s}$ coordinates being consumed one after the other. The same results are observed using the ciphertext thus, both parameters are leaking at same samples. The tool used for the analysis allows to map samples to the corresponding lines of code. By applying a threshold of 0.3 on the results of the NICV, we obtain the elementary operations and functions that are leaking. The leaking function are:

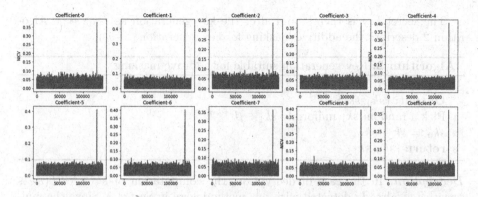

Fig. 3. Leakage peak in NICV of last ten coefficients of the secret key

- *basemul* called by *poly_basemul_montgomery*, multiplication of two polynomials in NTT domain. *basemul* is a multiplication of two polynomials in $\mathbb{Z}q[x]/(x^2 - \zeta)$, where ζ is $256 - th$ root of unity modulo q, used to multiply two elements in R_q.
- *fqmul* (called by *basemul*) which is a multiplication followed by a *Montgomery reduction*.
- *montgomery_reduction* called by *fqmul* bit integer $a \times R^{-1} \bmod q$, where $R = 2^{16}$ (Beware that R stands here for the Montgomery constant, and it not the lattice ring introduced in Sect. 2.2).

Those functions can be found at the reference source code of CRYSTALS-Kyber implementation [1].

The value of the NICV peaks are upper than 0.3 thus the implementation is not secure we therefore go to diagnose and cure step. To eliminate those vulnerabilities, we implement and evaluate the masking countermeasure. This will be detailed in the next sub-sections.

4.3 Analysis of Masked CRYSTALS-Kyber Implementation – Additive Masking

Additive masking consists of randomly splitting secret data into several shares. This solution will be used to protect sensitive data in the algorithms of the key generation and the decryption of CRYSTALS-Kyber

Key Generation. At the key generation step, the secret key $sk = NTT(s)$ should not be stored in clear. A random sk_1 is picked uniformly in $\beta^{24 \cdot k \cdot n/8 + 96}$, where β is the set of 8-bit unsigned integers (we denote by β^k the set of byte arrays of length k). Then, the second member sk_0 is computed as

$$sk_0 = sk - sk_1.$$

The secret key is then stored after the key generation as (sk_0, sk_1). Algorithm 2 describes the additive masking for key generation.

Algorithm 2: Key generation suitable for additive masking

Input: (sk)
Output: (sk_0, sk_1)
1 Pick a random sk_1 uniformly $sk_1 \in \beta^{24 \cdot k \cdot n/8 + 96}$
2 $sk_0 := sk - sk_1$
3 **return** (sk_0, sk_1)

Decryption. In the case of decryption, the computation of $\hat{s}^T \circ NTT(u)$ is sensitive as already detected with our methodology in Sect. 4.2. Since the multiplication is performed in NTT domain, the computation of $\hat{s}^T \circ NTT(u)$ is equivalent to the polynomial product $s^T \cdot u$. Remember that $\hat{s} = NTT(s)$, the secret key $sk = sk_0 + sk_1$ and the first element u of the ciphertext $c = (u, v)$ is in $\beta^{du \cdot k \cdot n/8}$. With the additive masking, the polynomial multiplication is performed as:

$$\hat{s}^T \circ NTT(u) = \hat{s_0}^T \circ NTT(u) + \hat{s_1}^T \circ NTT(u).$$

This property leverages the linearity of the NTT.

The total overhead of the additive masking is k point-wise multiplications in R_q, and k additions in R_q. Algorithm 3 describes the additive masking for decryption step.

Algorithm 3: Decryption – protected by additive masking

Input: $u, (sk_0, sk_1)$
Output: $\hat{s}^T \circ NTT(u)$
1 $\hat{s_0} := Decode(sk_0)$
2 Compute $\hat{s_0}^T \circ NTT(u)$
3 $\hat{s_1} := Decode(sk_1)$
4 Compute $\hat{s_1}^T \circ NTT(u)$
5 $\hat{s}^T \circ NTT(u) := \hat{s_0}^T \circ NTT(u) + \hat{s_1}^T \circ NTT(u)$
6 **return** $\hat{s}^T \circ NTT(u)$

Each trace of the polynomial multiplication using the additive masking algorithm is made up of 285527 samples which is almost two times the size of the unprotected one (142761), indeed this operation is performed twice (line 5 of Algorithm 3). This gives us a first idea about how this protection impacts the implementation overall performance this will be discussed in Sect. 4.5.

The NICV on CRYSTALS-Kyber using additive masking shows the efficiency of this countermeasure. The results show that the secret key is no longer leaking in the polynomial multiplication. Figure 4 shows the NICV on the 10 first coefficients of the secret key and there is no significant peak (all peaks are lower than 0.3). Same results are observed for all the coefficient of the unpacked secret key.

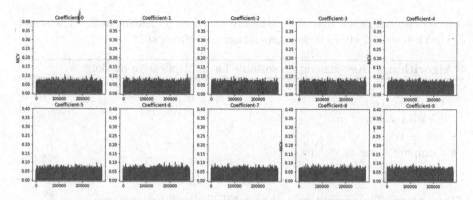

Fig. 4. NICV on the secret key after additive masking countermeasure

This should prevent an attacker from building a vertical SCA, such as DPA, to recover the secret key.

Despite that the additive masking offers resistance against DPA, the overall execution time of the implementation is hampered. In Sect. 4.4, we propose an alternative masking countermeasures, providing the same resistance against vertical SCA with less impact on the overall performance of the decryption.

4.4 Analysis of Masked CRYSTALS-Kyber Implementation – Multiplicative Masking

The idea of the multiplicative masking is to write sk as $r^{-1} \times (r \times sk)$. r can be chosen as a random number in $\mathbb{Z}_q^*$. In our case, we suggest to use a random integer r. As q is a prime number, r is invertible in $\mathbb{Z}_q$.

Notice that multiplicative masking employs a non-uniform random (since it cannot be null), hence is subject to first-order attacks. For instance, the multiplicative masking on AES by Akkar and Giraud [3] has been attacked by Golić and Tymen [16], though some repairs are possible (in hardware [24]). However, multiplicative masking on asymmetric algorithms is still common practice, as operands are largers than 8-bits (case of AES). Hence the first-order leakage decreases. For instance, multiplicative masking is suggested by Kocher on RSA [21] (also known as base blinding), then later on by Coron on ECC [13] (also known as randomized projective coordinates). We leverage this countermeasure for lattice-based cryptography.

Key Generation. At the key generation step, the secret key $sk = NTT(s)$ is not returned in this way. The secret key is *randomized* as described in Algorithm 4. A random r is picked uniformly in $\mathbb{Z}_q^*$. The member $rsk \in \beta^{24 \cdot k \cdot n/8 + 96}$ is computed as:

$$rsk = r \times sk.$$

The member r_inv is computed as $r\_inv = r^{-1} \bmod q$. This inversion can be performed with an algorithm like the extended Euclidean algorithm, or using a pre-computed table, that stores the inverse of each element in $\mathbb{Z}_q$. The secret key is then stored after the key generation as (r_inv, rsk).

Algorithm 4: Key generation suitable for multiplicative masking

Input: sk
Output: (r_inv, rsk)
1 Pick a random r in $\mathbb{Z}_q^*$
2 $rsk := r \times sk$
3 Compute r_inv as $r^{-1} \bmod q$
4 **return** (r_inv, rsk)

Decryption. The computation of $\hat{s}^T \circ NTT(u)$ will be performed as:

$$\hat{s}^T \circ NTT(u) = \hat{rs}^T \circ (r\_inv \times NTT(u))$$

owing to the invariance of the NTT by scaling by 1 (recall $1 = r\_inv \times r$).

In the case of the multiplicative masking, the total overhead is n multiplications in $\mathbb{Z}_q$. Algorithm 5 describes the multiplicative masking for the decryption step. The overhead incurred over unprotected version is negligible compared to the overhead in the additive masked decryption.

Algorithm 5: Decryption – protected by multiplicative masking

Input: $u, (r\_inv, rsk)$
Output: $\hat{s}^T \circ NTT(u)$
1 $\hat{rs} := Decode(rsk)$
2 Compute $r\_inv \times NTT(u)$
3 $\hat{s}^T \circ NTT(u) := \hat{rs}^T \circ (r\_inv \times NTT(u))$
4 **return** $\hat{s}^T \circ NTT(u)$

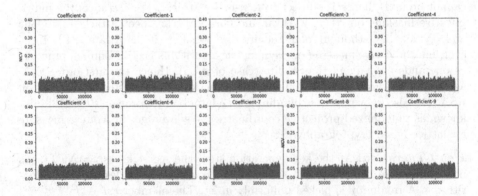

Fig. 5. NICV on the secret key after multiplicative masking countermeasure

The results of NICV on the 10 first coefficients of the secret key are shown in Fig. 5. As for the case of the additive masking scheme, no significant peak is detected. Furthermore, this masking countermeasure does not impact the overall cost of CRYSTALS-Kyber implementation because only one polynomial multiplication is performed.

4.5 Discussion

In this work, we have tested the different analysed implementations on a host machine equipped with an Intel core (i7-6700K CPU 4.00 GHz). We have measured the average and the median execution time to see the impact of each countermeasure in terms of performance.

Table 1. Performance benchmarks for different implementation of CRYSTALS-Kyber-512 decryption – Intel (R) Core (TM) i7-6700K CPU 4.00 GHz.

Implementation	#Cycles		Overhead (%)
	Average	Median	
Unprotected (Ref.)	210694	197150	–
Protected (Additive)	278772	260292	32%
Protected (Multiplicative)	243151	234521	15%

We reported the performance of each implementation in Table 1. The results show that the overall execution time of the decryption procedure has an overhead of about 32% and 15% for the additive and the multiplicative masking respectively. We notice that the key generation outputs the secret key on NTT domain. Thus, in the decryption stage, we do not need to convert the secret key shares. In the additive masking implementation, only the ciphertext (the variable u) is converted on the NTT domain. This explains why the overhead is not doubled, as we know that the most consuming part is the polynomial multiplication. Only a point-wise multiplication is performed in this case, which is not a full polynomial multiplication for instance. If the secret key is not outputted on NTT domain, the overhead will be more significant in the case of additive masking, but not for the multiplicative variant, where no addition point-wise (or polynomial) multiplication is needed. This may be more interesting for other variants of LWE algorithms where the usage of NTT is not possible (for example when the modulus in not a prime).

5 Conclusion

In this paper, we identified vertical side-channel vulnerabilities in the current version of the lattice-based PQC algorithm CRYSTALS-Kyber which is a KEM finalist candidate of the NIST standardization project. We experimentally demonstrated with the leakage detection metric NICV, the presence of leakages depending on the secret key in the NTT domain polynomial multiplication, used in the IND-CPA decryption function. We then study additive masking proposed previously in the literature and propose to the best of our knowledge for the first time, a multiplicative masking solution adapted to CRYSTALS-Kyber. We show the efficiency of each masking scheme against vertical attacks, namely by computing and showing that the NICV does not feature any significant peak that may be interpreted as a leakage based on the same number of traces as in the first experiment. Finally, we compare the overhead of each proposed counter-measure (compared to the vanilla reference code available from NIST submission website) and we show that the multiplicative masking performs better for the same security level.

References

1. Implementation of CRYSTALS-Kyber. https://github.com/pq-crystals/kyber
2. Aggarwal, D., Chung, E.: A note on the concrete hardness of the shortest independent vectors problem in lattices. arXiv preprint arXiv:2005.11654 (2020)
3. Akkar, M.-L., Giraud, C.: An implementation of DES and AES, secure against some attacks. In: Koç, Ç.K., Naccache, D., Paar, C. (eds.) CHES 2001. LNCS, vol. 2162, pp. 309–318. Springer, Heidelberg (2001). https://doi.org/10.1007/3-540-44709-1_26
4. Avanzi, R., et al.: CRYSTALS-Kyber algorithm specifications and supporting documentation. NIST PQC Round 2, 4 (2019)
5. Van Beirendonck, M., D'Anvers, J.-P., Karmakar, A., Balasch, J., Verbauwhede, I.: A side-channel resistant implementation of saber. Cryptology ePrint Archive, Report 2020/733 (2020). https://eprint.iacr.org/2020/733
6. Beringuier-Boher, N., Lacruche, M., El-Baze, D., Dutertre, J.-M., Rigaud, J.-B., Maurine, P.: Body biasing injection attacks in practice. In: Proceedings of the Third Workshop on Cryptography and Security in Computing Systems, CS2@HiPEAC, Prague, Czech Republic, 20 January 2016, pp. 49–54 (2016)
7. Bertoni, G., Breveglieri, L., Koren, I., Maistri, P., Piuri, V.: Error analysis and detection procedures for a hardware implementation of the advanced encryption standard. IEEE Trans. Comput. 52(4), 492–505 (2003)
8. Bhasin, S., Danger, J.-L., Guilley, S., Najm, Z.: NICV: normalized inter-class variance for detection of side-channel leakage. In: 2014 International Symposium on Electromagnetic Compatibility, Tokyo, pp. 310–313. IEEE (2014)
9. Bos, J.W., Gourjon, M., Renes, J., Schneider, T., van Vredendaal, C.: Masking kyber: first-and higher-order implementations. IACR Cryptol. ePrint Arch. 2021:483 (2021)
10. Brakerski, Z.: Fully homomorphic encryption without modulus switching from classical GapSVP. In: Safavi-Naini, R., Canetti, R. (eds.) CRYPTO 2012. LNCS, vol. 7417, pp. 868–886. Springer, Heidelberg (2012). https://doi.org/10.1007/978-3-642-32009-5_50
11. Brier, E., Clavier, C., Olivier, F.: Correlation power analysis with a leakage model. In: Joye, M., Quisquater, J.-J. (eds.) CHES 2004. LNCS, vol. 3156, pp. 16–29. Springer, Heidelberg (2004). https://doi.org/10.1007/978-3-540-28632-5_2
12. Bruinderink, L.G., Pessl, P.: Differential fault attacks on deterministic lattice signatures. IACR Trans. Cryptogr. Hardw. Embed. Syst., 21–43 (2018)

13. Coron, J.-S.: Resistance against differential power analysis for elliptic curve cryptosystems. In: Koç, Ç.K., Paar, C. (eds.) CHES 1999. LNCS, vol. 1717, pp. 292–302. Springer, Heidelberg (1999). https://doi.org/10.1007/3-540-48059-5_25

14. Direction Générale de l'Armement. Masking dilithium: Efficient implementation and side-channel evaluation

15. Gérard, F., Rossi, M.: An efficient and provable masked implementation of qTESLA. In: Belaïd, S., Güneysu, T. (eds.) CARDIS 2019. LNCS, vol. 11833, pp. 74–91. Springer, Cham (2020). https://doi.org/10.1007/978-3-030-42068-0_5

16. Golić, J.D., Tymen, C.: Multiplicative masking and power analysis of AES. In: Kaliski, B.S., Koç, K., Paar, C. (eds.) CHES 2002. LNCS, vol. 2523, pp. 198–212. Springer, Heidelberg (2003). https://doi.org/10.1007/3-540-36400-5_16

17. Huang, W.-L., Chen, J.-P., Yang, B.-Y.: Correlation power analysis on NTRU prime and related countermeasures. IACR Cryptol. ePrint Arch., 100 (2019)

18. Huang, W.-L., Chen, J.-P., Yang, B.-Y.: Power analysis on NTRU prime. IACR Trans. Cryptogr. Hardw. Embed. Syst., 123–151 (2020)

19. ISO/IEC JTC 1/SC 27/WG 3. ISO/IEC 17825:2016: Information technology - Security techniques - Testing methods for the mitigation of non-invasive attack classes against cryptographic modules. https://www.iso.org/standard/60612.html

20. Kocher, P., Jaffe, J., Jun, B.: Differential power analysis. In: Annual international Cryptology Conference, pp. 388–397. Springer (1999)

21. Kocher, P.C.: Timing attacks on implementations of Diffie-Hellman, RSA, DSS, and other systems. In: Koblitz, N. (ed.) CRYPTO 1996. LNCS, vol. 1109, pp. 104–113. Springer, Heidelberg (1996). https://doi.org/10.1007/3-540-68697-5_9

22. Longa, P., Naehrig, M.: Speeding up the number theoretic transform for faster ideal lattice-based cryptography. Cryptology ePrint Archive, Report 2016/504 (2016). https://eprint.iacr.org/2016/504

23. Lyubashevsky, V., Peikert, C., Regev, O.: On ideal lattices and learning with errors over rings. In: Gilbert, H. (ed.) EUROCRYPT 2010. LNCS, vol. 6110, pp. 1–23. Springer, Heidelberg (2010). https://doi.org/10.1007/978-3-642-13190-5_1

24. De Meyer, L., Reparaz, O., Bilgin, B.: Multiplicative masking for AES in hardware. IACR Trans. Cryptogr. Hardw. Embed. Syst. **2018**(3), 431–468 (2018)

25. Micciancio, D.: Lattice-based cryptography. In: van Tilborg, H.C.A., Jajodia, S. (eds) Encyclopedia of Cryptography and Security, pp. 147–191. Springer, Boston (2009). https://doi.org/10.1007/978-1-4419-5906-5_417

26. Miller, V.S.: Use of elliptic curves in cryptography. In: Williams, H.C. (ed.) CRYPTO 1985. LNCS, vol. 218, pp. 417–426. Springer, Heidelberg (1986). https://doi.org/10.1007/3-540-39799-X_31

27. Neikes, M.: Timecop: Automated dynamic analysis for timing side-channels

28. Oder, T., Schneider, T., Pöppelmann, T., Güneysu, T.: Practical CCA2-secure and masked ring-LWE implementation. Cryptology ePrint Archive, Report 2016/1109 (2016). https://eprint.iacr.org/2016/1109

29. Pessl, P., Primas, R.: More practical single-trace attacks on the number theoretic transform. In: Schwabe, P., Thériault, N. (eds.) LATINCRYPT 2019. LNCS, vol. 11774, pp. 130–149. Springer, Cham (2019). https://doi.org/10.1007/978-3-030-30530-7_7

30. Poddebniak, D., Somorovsky, J., Schinzel, S., Lochter, M., Rösler, P.: Attacking deterministic signature schemes using fault attacks. In: 2018 IEEE European Symposium on Security and Privacy (EuroS&P), pp. 338–352. IEEE (2018)

31. Ravi, P., Bhasin, S., Roy, S.S., Chattopadhyay, A.: Drop by Drop you break the rock-Exploiting generic vulnerabilities in Lattice-based PKE/KEMs using EM-based Physical Attacks. IACR Cryptol. ePrint Arch. 2020:549 (2020)

32. Ravi, P., Roy, D.B., Bhasin, S., Chattopadhyay, A., Mukhopadhyay, D.: Number "Not Used" once - practical fault attack on *pqm4* implementations of NIST candidates. In: Polian, I., Stöttinger, M. (eds.) COSADE 2019. LNCS, vol. 11421, pp. 232–250. Springer, Cham (2019). https://doi.org/10.1007/978-3-030-16350-1_13

33. Ravi, P., Roy, S.S., Chattopadhyay, A., Bhasin, S.: Generic Side-channel attacks on CCA-secure lattice-based PKE and KEMs. IACR Trans. Cryptogr. Hardw. Embed. Syst., 307–335 (2020)

34. Regev, O.: The learning with errors problem (invited survey). In: Proceedings of the 25th Annual IEEE Conference on Computational Complexity, CCC 2010, Cambridge, Massachusetts, USA, 9–12 June 2010, pp. 191–204. IEEE Computer Society (2010)

35. Reparaz, O., Roy, S.S., Vercauteren, F., Verbauwhede, I.: A masked ring-LWE implementation. Cryptology ePrint Archive, Report 2015/724 (2015). https://eprint.iacr.org/2015/724

36. Rivest, R.L., Shamir, A., Adleman, L.: A method for obtaining digital signatures and public-key cryptosystems. Commun. ACM **21**(2), 120–126 (1978)

37. Shor, P.W.: Algorithms for quantum computation: discrete logarithms and factoring. In: Proceedings 35th Annual Symposium on Foundations of Computer Science, pp. 124–134. IEEE (1994)

38. Shor, P.W.: Polynomial-time algorithms for prime factorization and discrete logarithms on a quantum computer, vol. 41, pp. 303–332 (1999)

39. Tunstall, M., Mukhopadhyay, D., Ali, S.: Differential fault analysis of the advanced encryption standard using a single fault. In: Ardagna, C.A., Zhou, J. (eds.) WISTP 2011. LNCS, vol. 6633, pp. 224–233. Springer, Heidelberg (2011). https://doi.org/10.1007/978-3-642-21040-2_15

40. Xu, Z., Pemberton, O., Roy, S.S., Oswald, D.F.: Magnifying side-channel leakage of lattice-based cryptosystems with chosen ciphertexts: the case study of kyber. IACR Cryptol. ePrint Arch. 2020:912 (2020)

Symmetric Cryptography and Hash Functions, Mathematical Foundations of Cryptography

A Suitable Proposal of S-Boxes (Inverse-Like) for the AES, Their Analysis and Performances

Said Eddahmani[1,2]([envelope]) and Sihem Mesnager[1,2,3]

[1] Department of Mathematics, University of Paris VIII, 93526 Saint-Denis, France
said.eddahmani@etud.univ-paris8.fr, smesnager@univ-paris8.fr
[2] Laboratory Geometry, Analysis and Applications, LAGA, University Sorbonne Paris Nord, CNRS, UMR 7539, 93430 Villetaneuse, France
[3] Telecom Paris, 91120 Palaiseau, France

Abstract. Vectorial Boolean functions are widely applied to block ciphers' design in cryptography, where they are used to create the so-called substitution boxes, or S-boxes, whose input and output are then both sequences of bits. A prominent example of a block cipher is the AES, or Rijndael, which contains an $(8,8)$-function at its core. This paper presents a simple (but efficient) method for building S-boxes for AES with good cryptographic properties and analyzing their security. Using our approach, we exhibit an S-box example and explore its main algebraic and statistical properties such as Strict Avalanche Criterion (SAC), Distance to SAC, and algebraic complexity. We also analyze its resistance to block ciphers' most popular attacks, namely differential attack, boomerang attack, linear attack, and differential-linear attack. Although the proposed S-box is finally proved to be affinely equivalent to the inverse function, when it is involved in a block cipher, it has enhanced properties at a better level compared to AES (for example, it has better algebraic and statistical criteria such as periodicity, algebraic complexity, strict avalanche, and distance to SAC) by preserving the same security level concerning several main cryptanalyses (for example, it is differentially 4-uniform as well). Consequently, the proposed S-box is more resistant to any attack based on statistical cryptanalysis. We present its strength, including in terms of efficient implementation, and we emphasize that our proposed S-box offers, in addition, more flexibly thanks to the choices of the parameter in its conception, leading to an attractive and suitable alternative for an S-box to be involved in a block cipher.

Keywords: Symmetric cryptography · Block cipher · S-box · AES · Inverse function

Subject Classification: 94A60 · 06E30 · 94C10

© Springer Nature Switzerland AG 2021
P. Stănică et al. (Eds.): ICSP 2021, CCIS 1497, pp. 49–63, 2021.
https://doi.org/10.1007/978-3-030-90553-8_4

1 Introduction

Block ciphers are one of the cornerstones of our cryptographic landscape today and are used to ensure security for a significant fraction of our daily communication. Their design and analysis are well advanced, and with today's knowledge designing a secure block cipher is a problem that is largely considered solved. The Advanced Encryption Standard (AES) block cipher [26] is among the most crucial symmetric cryptosystem. It is widely used in various cryptographic applications. In symmetric cryptography, multi-output Boolean functions are called *S-boxes* (substitution-boxes). They are fundamental parts of block ciphers and essential component of symmetric key algorithms which performs substitution. Being the only source of nonlinearity in these ciphers, S-boxes play a central role in their robustness by providing confusion necessary to withstand known (and hopefully future) attacks. An (n, m)-function, or vectorial Boolean function, is any mapping F from $\mathbb{F}_{2^n}$ to $\mathbb{F}_{2^m}$ (where $\mathbb{F}_{2^n}$ is the finite field of order 2^n). A prominent example is the AES, or Rijndael, block cipher, which contains an $(8, 8)$-function at its core [26]. After more than 20 years of investigations, it still withstands all cryptanalytic attacks. Its S-box mainly guarantees the security of AES against algebraic and statistical attacks. There are various possible attacks on block ciphers such as linear cryptanalysis [24], differential cryptanalysis [4], boomerang cryptanalysis [34], and differential-linear cryptanalysis based on the differential-linear connectivity table (DLCT) [2,18]. To measure the resistance of a block cipher to such attacks, the S-box should satisfy a variety of algebraic and statistical criteria such as bijection, fixed points, Strict Avalanche Criterion (SAC) [36], distance to SAC (see. e.g. [8]), periodicity, algebraic complexity, differential uniformity [30], boomerang uniformity [5,9], nonlinearity [28,29] and differential-linear uniformity [3]. A very recent precious book in this context is the one written by Carlet [8]. The whole algorithm of AES is straightforward to implement and has strong security guarantees. Nevertheless, a large number of researchers have investigated ways to propose new S-boxes with enhanced cryptographic properties. In [11], the proposed S-box is constructed by a function of the form $f(x) = A \cdot (A \cdot x + a)^{-1} + a$ where A is a 8×8 circular matrix of bits and $a \in \mathbb{F}_{2^8}$ is a constant. In various papers, the S-box is obtained by applying a function of the form $f(x) = \frac{ax+b}{cx+d}$ where a, b, c, d are constant elements of $\mathbb{F}_{2^8}$ (see [1,16,17,32]). Very recently, the form $f(x) = \frac{A \cdot x + b}{A \cdot x + d}$ was proposed in [27] with enhanced properties compared to AES where A is a 8×8 matrix of bits, and b, d are constants in $\mathbb{F}_{2^8}$.

In this paper, we present a new approach to build further suitable S-boxes over $\mathbb{F}_{2^n}$ and adapt it to AES. We use the transformation S defined over $\mathbb{F}_{2^n}$ by

$$S(x) = \begin{cases} \dfrac{aA \cdot x + b}{cA \cdot x + d} & \text{if } x \neq A^{-1} \cdot \dfrac{d}{c}, \\[2ex] \dfrac{a}{c} & \text{if } x = A^{-1} \cdot \dfrac{d}{c}, \end{cases}$$

where A is a $n \times n$ invertible matrix with entries in $\mathbb{F}_2$, and $a, b, c, d \in \mathbb{F}_{2^n}$ are fixed constants such that $ad + bc \neq 0$. Here, x is represented by a n-dimensional vector of bits, and $A \cdot x$ is the multiplication of A by x. We adapt the transformation to $\mathbb{F}_{2^8}$, and with extensive experiments and simulations, we find a specific value for the parameters A, a, b, c, d such that the correspondent transformation S has enhanced cryptographic criteria compared to AES. Typically, the algebraic complexity is increased from 9 to 255; the period is increased from the set $\{2, 27, 59, 81, 87\}$ to the optimal value 256, and the distance to SAC is decreased from 432 to 324. Moreover, we study the resistance of the proposed S-box against the main attacks, specifically, against differential attacks [4], boomerang attacks [34], linear attacks [24], and differential-linear connectivity attacks [2,18]. We show that the proposed S-box is affine equivalent to the inverse function, and consequently, it preserves the level of security of the involving cryptosystem as the original AES regarding resistance against linear, differential, and boomerang cryptanalysis. Despite the affine equivalence, our S-box has many advantages; particularly, it has better algebraic and statistical criteria such as periodicity, algebraic complexity, strict avalanche, and distance to SAC. As a consequence, it is more resistant to any attack based on such methods. All the computations related to the criteria and the tables mentioned in this paper were performed by programming the related properties using the Maple algebra system.

The rest of the paper is organized as follows. In Sect. 2, we recall the algebraic structure of the S-box involved in the AES cipher. In Sect. 3, we present a method to find S-boxes over $\mathbb{F}_{2^n}$ whose expression is close to the inverse function. In Sect. 4, we study our proposed S-box's main structural and statistical properties, and in Sect. 5, we examine its resistance to the differential, linear and boomerang attacks. In Sect. 6, we deeply compare the properties of the proposed S-box and former ones. We also emphasize the advantages of using our S-box and present its strength. We conclude the paper in Sect. 7.

2   Description of the AES

The arithmetic of AES [26]. is based on the addition, the multiplication and inversion of bytes. Each byte α is an element of the finite field $\mathbb{F}_{2^8}$ and can be represented by a bit string $\alpha = (\alpha_7, \alpha_6, \alpha_5, \alpha_4, \alpha_3, \alpha_2, \alpha_1, \alpha_0) \in \mathbb{F}_2^8$ or by a polynomial $p(\alpha) = \alpha_7 x^7 + \alpha_6 x^6 + \alpha_5 x^5 + \alpha_4 x^4 + \alpha_3 x^3 + \alpha_2 x^2 + \alpha_1 x + \alpha_0 \in \mathbb{F}_2[x]$. The addition is the XOR operation, while multiplication and inversion are performed modulo the irreducible polynomial $x^8 + x^4 + x^3 + x^2 + x + 1$. The S-box of AES is a 16×16 table of bytes computed by applying a permutation of $\mathbb{F}_{2^8}$ of the form $I(x) = A \cdot x^{-1} + a$ if $x \neq 0$, and $I(0) = a$, where A is a fixed 8×8 matrix of bits, and $a \in \mathbb{F}_{2^8}$ is also fixed.

3   Generating Suitable S-Boxes for Block Ciphers

This section presents a generic function aiming to create further S-boxes whose algebraic expression is close to the inverse function and highlights specific parameters that give rise to an S-box with good cryptographic properties.

3.1   A General Approach

Let $a, c \in \mathbb{F}_{2^n}^*$ and $b, d \in \mathbb{F}_{2^n}$. Let A be an invertible $n \times n$ matrix with entries in $\mathbb{F}_2$. We consider the function $S : \mathbb{F}_{2^n} \to \mathbb{F}_{2^n}$ satisfying

$$S(x) = \begin{cases} \dfrac{aA \cdot x + b}{cA \cdot x + d} & \text{if } x \neq A^{-1} \cdot \dfrac{d}{c}, \\ \dfrac{a}{c} & \text{if } x = A^{-1} \cdot \dfrac{d}{c}. \end{cases} \tag{1}$$

Then, under the condition $ad + bc \neq 0$, the function S is a permutation of $\mathbb{F}_{2^n}$.

3.2   A Proposal S-Box for AES

To find an S-box for AES with good cryptographic properties, we have performed intensive search by generating random parameters A, a, b, c and d where A is an 8×8 bit invertible matrix, and $ad + bc \neq 0$. To this end, a thousand parameters were tested during 60 days on a computer with Intel(R) Core(TM) i5-8250U CPU 1.60 GHz, 8.0 GO. Among all potential candidates, we chose the following parameters.

$$A_0 = \begin{pmatrix} 1&0&0&0&1&1&1&1 \\ 1&0&1&0&0&0&1&1 \\ 1&0&0&1&0&1&1&1 \\ 0&1&0&1&1&0&0&0 \\ 0&0&1&1&0&0&0&0 \\ 0&1&0&0&0&0&1&1 \\ 0&0&1&1&1&1&0&0 \\ 0&1&1&1&0&0&1&0 \end{pmatrix}, A_0^{-1} = \begin{pmatrix} 0&0&1&1&1&1&1&0 \\ 1&0&1&1&0&0&0&0 \\ 1&1&0&0&1&0&1&0 \\ 1&1&0&0&0&0&1&0 \\ 0&1&1&0&0&0&1&0 \\ 0&1&1&0&1&0&0&0 \\ 1&0&1&1&1&0&0&1 \\ 0&0&0&0&1&1&0&1 \end{pmatrix}, \begin{cases} a_0 = 0x14 & b_0 = 0x4a \\ c_0 = 0x0c & d_0 = 0x5c. \end{cases}$$

Then the parameters $(A_0, a_0, b_0, c_0, d_0)$ define a permutation S_0 of $\mathbb{F}_{2^8}$ with

$$S_0(x) = \begin{cases} \dfrac{0x14(A_0 \cdot x) + 0x4a}{0x0c(A_0 \cdot x) + 0x5c} & \text{if } x \neq A_0^{-1} \cdot \dfrac{0x5c}{0x0c} = 0x25, \\ \dfrac{0x14}{0x0c} = 0x03 & \text{if } x = A_0^{-1} \cdot \dfrac{0x5c}{0x0c} = 0x25. \end{cases} \tag{2}$$

Applying S_0 to $\mathbb{F}_2^8$, we get the S-box as presented in Table 1.

4   Algebraic and Statistical Properties of the Proposed S-Box

This section studies some algebraic and statistical properties of our S-box.

Table 1. The proposed S-box

	0	1	2	3	4	5	6	7	8	9	a	b	c	d	e	f
0	9b	9a	3e	70	c0	df	91	b3	7d	54	77	a1	eb	65	17	4b
1	53	60	a2	34	4a	21	45	07	f6	b5	e9	4d	e5	20	62	15
2	72	9d	ab	5b	5a	03	61	69	fc	59	01	ec	89	49	c8	23
3	7a	ea	0e	68	9f	0c	f7	84	d6	0d	a8	13	06	30	a0	19
4	b7	c1	80	85	29	66	4c	41	75	95	16	28	6f	e2	2d	fa
5	e1	0b	6a	73	14	5d	af	58	f9	64	5e	ad	6b	50	a5	f3
6	f4	1c	43	f2	51	6c	db	11	ca	3c	7b	98	d1	dd	1a	02
7	10	b6	c7	c5	2c	ce	c9	90	b2	93	b4	0a	44	bc	de	e7
8	8a	f8	c4	46	5c	09	bd	a6	3a	c3	8c	9c	be	7c	47	48
9	3d	40	aa	00	79	1d	fd	81	3b	18	d0	ef	05	32	d4	c6
a	f5	b8	31	cd	96	12	cf	4e	25	87	36	d2	6d	b1	0f	ba
b	d9	7e	27	dc	26	86	9e	d5	38	5f	42	08	cc	97	3f	67
c	bb	8b	f0	2a	33	a9	bf	83	e6	2f	99	7f	55	8d	63	c2
d	ac	52	37	ff	e0	d8	d3	2e	24	8f	1b	35	1e	82	04	b0
e	f1	78	cb	71	e3	a7	39	ed	6e	e4	8e	74	fe	56	da	76
f	1f	2b	22	ee	b9	a4	ae	88	4f	92	d7	a3	fb	e8	57	94

4.1 Bijectivity of the Proposed S-Box

The following result shows that S is a bijection and gives its inverse.

Proposition 1. *Let S be a vectorial Boolean function defined by the parameters (A, a, b, c, d) with an invertible matrix A and $ad + bc \neq 0$. Then S is a bijection of $\mathbb{F}_2^n$ and its inverse is*

$$S^{-1}(y) = \begin{cases} A^{-1} \cdot \dfrac{dy + b}{cy + a} & \text{if } y \neq \dfrac{a}{c}, \\ A^{-1} \cdot \dfrac{d}{c} & \text{if } y = \dfrac{a}{c}. \end{cases}$$

The inverse of S_0 as defined by the parameters (2) is S_0^{-1} with

$$S_0^{-1}(y) = \begin{cases} A_0^{-1} \cdot \dfrac{0x5c\, y + 0x4a}{0x0c\, y + 0x14} & \text{if } y \neq \dfrac{0x14}{0x0c} = 0x03, \\ A_0^{-1} \cdot \dfrac{0x5c}{0x0c} = 0x25 & \text{if } y = \dfrac{0x14}{0x0c} = 0x03. \end{cases}$$

The inverse S-box related to S_0^{-1} is presented in Table 2.

4.2 Fixed Points and Opposite Points

For an S-box S, defined over $\mathbb{F}_2^n$, a fixed point is a point x satisfying $S(x) + x = 0$. From Table 1, we see that the proposed S-box has no fixed point. Similarly, an

Table 2. The inverse of the new S-box

	0	1	2	3	4	5	6	7	8	9	a	b	c	d	e	f
0	93	2a	6f	25	de	9c	3c	17	bb	85	7b	51	35	39	32	ae
1	70	67	a5	3b	54	1f	4a	0e	99	3f	6e	da	61	95	dc	f0
2	1d	15	f2	2f	d8	a8	b4	b2	4b	44	c3	f1	74	4e	d7	c9
3	3d	a2	9d	c4	13	db	aa	d2	b8	e6	88	98	69	90	02	be
4	91	47	ba	62	7c	16	83	8e	8f	2d	14	0f	46	1b	a7	f8
5	5d	64	d1	10	09	cc	ed	fe	57	29	24	23	84	55	5a	b9
6	11	26	1e	ce	59	0d	45	bf	33	27	52	5c	65	ac	e8	4c
7	03	e3	20	53	eb	48	ef	0a	e1	94	30	6a	8d	08	b1	cb
8	42	97	dd	c7	37	43	b5	a9	f7	2c	80	c1	8a	cd	ea	d9
9	77	06	f9	79	ff	49	a4	bd	6b	ca	01	00	8b	21	b6	34
a	3e	0b	12	fb	f5	5e	87	e5	3a	c5	92	22	d0	5b	f6	56
b	df	ad	78	07	7a	19	71	40	a1	f4	af	c0	7d	86	8c	c6
c	04	41	cf	89	82	73	9f	72	2e	76	68	e2	bc	a3	75	a6
d	9a	6c	ab	d6	9e	b7	38	fa	d5	b0	ee	66	b3	6d	7e	05
e	d4	50	4d	e4	e9	1c	c8	7f	fd	1a	31	0c	2b	e7	f3	9b
f	c2	e0	63	5f	60	a0	18	36	81	58	4f	fc	28	96	ec	d3

opposite point is a point x satisfying $S(x) + x = 0xff$. From Table 1, we also see that our S-box has no opposite point.

4.3   Strict Avalanche Criterion and Distance to SAC

The strict avalanche criterion (SAC) was proposed by Webster and Tavares [36] to study the security of S-boxes. For an (n, m)-vectorial Boolean function F, SAC is fulfilled if each output bit is changed with probability $\frac{1}{2}$ whenever a single bit is changed in the input. It uses the weight $wt(x)$, which is the number of bits equal to 1 in the binary representation of $x \in \mathbb{F}_2^n$.

Definition 1. *Let F be an (n, m)-vectorial Boolean function. Then F satisfies the strict avalanche criterion if and only if, for every $\alpha \in \mathbb{F}_2^n$ with $wt(\alpha) = 1$, we have $\sum_{x \in \mathbb{F}_2^n} (F(x) + F(x + \alpha)) = (2^{n-1}, \dots, 2^{n-1})$.*

For S_0 as defined by (2), Table 3 presents the values of $\sum_{x \in \mathbb{F}_2^8}(S_0(x) + S_0(x+\alpha))$ for all elements $\alpha = (\alpha_7, \alpha_6, \alpha_5, \alpha_4, \alpha_3, \alpha_2, \alpha_1, \alpha_0) \in \mathbb{F}_2^8$ and $wt(\alpha) = 1$.

Definition 2. *Let F be an (n, m)-vectorial Boolean function. The distance to SAC denoted DSAC is defined by*

$$DSAC(F) = \sum_{\substack{\alpha \in \mathbb{F}_2^n \\ wt(\alpha)=1}} \sum_{i=1}^{m} \left| \sum_{x \in \mathbb{F}_2^n} (F_i(x + \alpha) + F_i(x)) - 2^{n-1} \right|.$$

Table 3. SAC of the proposed S-box

α	Bit 7	Bit 6	Bit 5	Bit 4	Bit 3	Bit 2	Bit 2	Bit 1	Mean
00000001	136	128	136	132	136	120	128	120	129.5
00000010	124	128	144	140	132	132	136	128	133.0
00000100	136	128	132	132	132	120	128	120	128.5
00001000	128	136	132	124	132	128	128	132	130.0
00010000	136	128	116	124	120	136	128	128	127.0
00100000	132	136	128	128	144	120	136	140	133.0
01000000	140	132	140	136	124	132	128	128	132.5
10000000	136	120	128	132	132	132	128	132	130.0

According to Definition 1 and Definition 2, the optimal value for DSAC is 0. DSAC is 432 for AES [11] and 324 for our-S-box which is more optimal.

4.4 Periodicity of the Proposed S-Box

In [11,35], the periodicity of some S-boxes is studied.

Definition 3. *Let $F : \mathbb{F}_{2^n} \to \mathbb{F}_{2^n}$ be a vectorial Boolean function. The period of $x \in \mathbb{F}_{2^n}$ relatively to F is the smallest positive integer r such that $F^{(r)}(x) = x$ where $F^{(r)}$ is the composition of r functions F.*

For the AES, the periods are 2, 27, 59, 81, and 87. For the S-box defined by (2), the unique period is 256. This makes any possible attack based on the periods uniformly distributed for our S-box.

4.5 Algebraic Complexity

A vectorial Boolean function F, defined over $\mathbb{F}_2^n$ can be determined by a polynomial $p_S(x) \in \mathbb{F}_2^n[x]$, which can be determined by Lagrange's interpolation theorem [22]

$$p_S(x) = \sum_{i=0}^{2^n-1} a_i x^i = \sum_{i=0}^{2^n-1} S(x_i) \prod_{j=0, j \neq i}^{2^n-1} \frac{x - x_j}{x_i - x_j}.$$

The algebraic structure of a block cipher is important to avoid some algebraic attacks such as XSL [10], Gröbner Basis algorithms, interpolation [19], and SAT-solvers.

For the AES, the S-box can be represented by the polynomial (see [12])

$$P(x) = 05x^{254} + 09x^{253} + f9x^{251} + 25x^{247} + f4x^{239} + 01x^{223}$$
$$+ b5x^{191} + 8fx^{127} + 63,$$

with an algebraic complexity of 9 monomials. For the S-box S_0 defined by (2), the polynomial $p_{S_0}(x)$ is $p_{S_0}(x) = dax^{254} + 1ax^{253} + 78x^{251} + \cdots + 9cx + 9b$. The list of the coefficients is represented in Table 4. It shows that the algebraic complexity of our S-box is 255, which is optimal.

Table 4. Algebraic expression of our proposed S-box

	f	e	d	c	b	a	9	8	7	6	5	4	3	2	1	0
f	00	da	1a	78	f7	37	3d	d5	37	41	77	84	55	1d	b6	fc
e	b9	77	65	d9	45	9b	2c	5a	c9	d1	02	06	32	4a	6a	f9
d	f1	b9	cd	52	1e	14	78	29	07	8d	d5	58	67	b1	f9	03
c	1a	fb	b0	84	17	86	41	fb	a7	38	45	44	12	29	da	71
b	f9	6b	48	d0	6b	c9	6a	46	05	ab	36	19	62	ad	fa	7e
a	cc	dc	f7	85	9a	75	58	04	17	0a	b3	66	5c	6d	7f	3f
9	db	1b	bd	42	f5	51	11	a8	09	79	76	7c	93	b4	60	38
8	3f	b7	35	8c	39	46	ae	79	a8	87	3d	7a	e5	2b	b0	ca
7	a3	c0	bd	03	9c	9e	9d	b6	42	0b	c1	80	15	62	81	22
6	20	8e	58	75	12	0d	db	6c	67	61	78	72	ba	e4	46	4c
5	0f	3f	2b	44	ff	27	2b	3e	d4	79	7c	f7	a4	b4	7d	54
4	e9	a3	c9	b1	0c	70	6b	08	a2	10	ab	b0	fd	7c	52	2a
3	e2	cb	34	aa	f7	14	78	a4	6d	90	09	4f	92	b0	a9	9c
2	48	b5	e3	74	12	8a	41	e2	8c	d8	5f	23	60	90	9d	38
1	47	85	14	ea	93	05	af	93	ab	f9	c3	23	e0	5d	bd	c4
0	47	a4	91	b4	8d	de	eb	83	cc	5c	44	53	aa	27	9c	9b

On the other hand, the inverse S-box of S_0 as defined by (2) has algebraic complexity of 254, while it is 255 for the inverse S-box of AES. Table 5 presents the coefficients of the polynomial $p_{S_0^{-1}}(x)$.

Some algebraic attacks, such as interpolation attacks [19] are based on the simplicity of the algebraic expression of the polynomial $p_S(x)$. Since the algebraic complexity of both the proposed S-box and its inverse is optimal and almost optimal, such attacks are avoidable.

Table 5. Algebraic expression of the inverse of the proposed S-box

	f	e	d	c	b	a	9	8	7	6	5	4	3	2	1	0
f	00	da	f3	91	15	ea	1b	81	b9	fa	e6	b3	15	83	c4	2d
e	59	62	2b	e6	01	c2	d8	9b	fc	7a	83	74	4a	b1	15	f7
d	d2	a8	41	3f	d3	4f	bd	79	d1	6f	47	d2	4d	a0	f4	b7
c	7c	c2	a2	b8	be	93	38	31	8e	0f	24	c4	42	f8	5b	2b
b	55	0c	b0	d9	b9	8a	8f	a3	f1	85	3e	cd	f3	8b	62	01
a	a5	f9	36	63	4a	03	75	1b	65	0d	26	76	14	50	fc	d8
9	4e	24	a0	f8	30	5f	59	d8	97	5d	2a	50	b3	58	41	3b
8	50	c5	83	7f	75	d7	6a	cd	40	64	24	6e	79	81	48	fa
7	11	99	cf	7e	09	ff	d4	3e	eb	00	9a	0b	4c	a4	0e	b9
6	37	68	48	2d	0c	18	41	ff	ca	89	23	b4	35	e7	4f	bf
5	04	c1	b4	13	a2	54	52	cd	b5	13	95	02	54	f4	49	f3
4	93	26	a8	7d	d2	bd	8a	38	35	20	21	fb	05	c1	65	74
3	57	63	65	6b	28	81	ec	1f	6f	41	b6	dc	19	42	a2	2b
2	50	53	8b	9f	51	8e	56	68	85	78	08	69	5d	49	83	be
1	01	a3	51	e5	70	de	c8	2e	16	f8	47	2e	c0	0d	74	89
0	0a	5f	e8	7d	ca	78	11	fa	4d	17	f3	e3	46	be	07	93

5 Cryptanalysis of the Proposed S-Box

In this section, we analyze the cryptographic properties of our S-box for the resistance against the main attacks, namely differential attacks, linear attacks, boomerang attacks, and Differential-Linear Connectivity attacks.

5.1 Equivalences of Our S-Box with the Inverse Function

In this section, as proved below, we show that our S-box is affine equivalent to the S-box of the AES, via the inverse function. Two functions F and F' are affine equivalent if $F' = G \circ F \circ H$ where G and H are two affine permutations of $\mathbb{F}_{2^n}$.

Proposition 2. *Let S be the function defined by the parameters (A, a, b, c, d) with $a, b, c, d \in \mathbb{F}_{2^n}$, with $ac \neq 0$, and $ad + bc \neq 0$. Let G and H be the functions defined by $G(x) = \frac{ad+bc}{c}x + \frac{a}{c}$, and $H(x) = cA \cdot x + d$. Then $S = G \circ I \circ H$ where I is the inverse function defined by $I(x) = x^{-1}$ if $x \neq 0$, and $I(0) = 0$.*

Proof. Let S be the function defined by the parameters (A, a, b, c, d) as in 1. Define the functions G and H by $G(x) = \frac{ad+bc}{c}x + \frac{a}{c}$, and $H(x) = cA \cdot x + d$. First, for $x = A^{-1} \cdot \frac{d}{c}$, we have $cA \cdot x + d = 0$. Then $I \circ H(x) = 0$, and $G \circ I \circ H(x) = \frac{a}{c} = S(x)$. Next, suppose that $x \neq A^{-1} \cdot \frac{d}{c}$. Then $G \circ I \circ H(x) = G\left(\frac{1}{cA \cdot x + d}\right) = \frac{ad+bc}{c}\frac{1}{cA \cdot x + d} + \frac{a}{c} = \frac{aA \cdot x + b}{cA \cdot x + d} = S(x)$. Summarizing, we have $S = G \circ I \circ H$. □

Since the function S is affine equivalent to the inverse function by Proposition 2, both S-boxes have similar cryptographic properties. More specifically, they have the same algebraic degree, the same differential uniformity, the same boomerang uniformity [5], the same linear uniformity, and the same differential-linear uniformity [21].

5.2   Differential Cryptanalysis

An essential parameter for evaluating the resistance of a block cipher against differential attacks is the differential uniformity [6, 30].

Definition 4. *Let F be an (n, m)-vectorial Boolean function. The Differential Distribution Table (DDT) of F is an $2^n \times 2^m$ table where the entry at $(u, v) \in \mathbb{F}_2^n \times \mathbb{F}_2^m$ is $DDT(u, v) = \#\{x \in \mathbb{F}_2^n \mid F(x) + F(x + u) = v\}$. Moreover, the differential uniformity of F is $\delta(F) = \max_{u \in \mathbb{F}_2^n, u \neq 0, v \in \mathbb{F}_2^m} DDT(u, v)$.*

Since the S-box defined by S_0 in (2) is affine equivalent to the inverse function, then $\delta(S_0) = 4$ with $DDT(0x01, 0x59) = 4$.

5.3   Boomerang Cryptanalysis

Introduced in 1999 by Wagner [34], the boomerang attack is an adaptive chosen plaintext attack based on differential cryptanalysis. Various properties and applications of boomerang attack and BCT can be found in [5, 9, 13, 15, 33]. To evaluate the resistance of a function F to the boomerang attack, Cid et al. [9] introduced the *Boomerang Connectivity Table* (see also [7, 21]).

Definition 5. *Let F be a permutation of $\mathbb{F}_2^n$ and F^{-1} its inverse. The boomerang connectivity table (BCT) is a $2^n \times 2^n$ table where the entry at row $\alpha \in \mathbb{F}_2^n$ and column $\alpha_1 \in \mathbb{F}_2^n$ is defined by*

$$BCT_F(\alpha, \alpha_1) = \#\left\{x \in \mathbb{F}_2^n, F^{-1}\left(F(x) + \alpha_1\right) + F^{-1}\left(F(x + \alpha) + \alpha_1\right) = \alpha\right\}.$$

Also, in [5], the boomerang uniformity of F is defined as

$$BU(F) = \max_{\substack{(\alpha, \alpha_1) \in \mathbb{F}_2^n \times \mathbb{F}_2^n \\ \alpha, \alpha_1 \neq 0}} BCT_F(\alpha, \alpha_1).$$

For the S-box defined by S_0 in (2), for all $\alpha, \alpha_1 \in \mathbb{F}_{2^8}$, we have $BCT_S(\alpha, \alpha_1) \in \{0, 2, 4, 6, 256\}$, and the boomerang uniformity is $BU(S_0) = 6$. It is the same as the boomerang uniformity of AES.

5.4   Linear Cryptanalysis

In 1993, Matsui [24] introduced a technique to attack the block cipher DES. The technique, known as linear cryptanalysis, is based on the nonlinearity of the function.

Definition 6. *Let F be an (n, m)-vectorial Boolean function. The nonlinearity of F is defined by*

$$\mathcal{NL}(F) = 2^{n-1} - \frac{1}{2} \max_{u \in \mathbb{F}_2^n, v \in \mathbb{F}_2^m, v \neq 0} \left| \sum_{x \in \mathbb{F}_2^n} (-1)^{u \cdot x + v \cdot F(x)} \right|.$$

For an even number n of variables, an upper bound for the nonlinearity is $2^{n-1} - 2^{\frac{n}{2}-1}$ and is attained by the so-called bent functions (see, e.g. [8,25]). For $n = 8$, the upper bound is then 120. For both AES and our S-box, the nonlinearity is 112 which is close to 120.

5.5 Differential-Linear Connectivity Cryptanalysis

In 2018, Kim et al. [18] and Bar-On et al. [2], introduced independently a new tool, called the *differential-linear connectivity table* (DLCT) to test the differential-linear attacks.

Definition 7. *Let F be an (n, m)-vectorial Boolean function. The Differential-Linear Connectivity Table (DLCT) of F is a $2^n \times 2^m$ table where the entry at $(u, v) \in \mathbb{F}_2^n \times \mathbb{F}_2^m$ is $DLCT_F(u, v) = \#\{x \in \mathbb{F}_2^n \mid v \cdot (F(x) + F(x + u)) = 0\} - 2^{n-1}$. The maximum of all values $|DLCT_F(u, v)|$ with $uv \neq 0$ is called the differential-linear uniformity of F.*

For both AES and our S-box defined by (2), the DLCT is represented by a $2^8 \times 2^8$ table where the entries are in $\{-16, -12, -8, -4, 0, 4, 8, 12, 16, 128\}$. For AES and our S-box, the differential-linear uniformity is 16. This shows that they have equivalent resistance to the differential-linear attacks [14,20,23].

6 Comparison of Cryptographic Properties Between the Proposed S-Box and Former S-Boxes

In this section, we compare the security and the efficiency of the proposed S-Box with existing S-Boxes.

6.1 Security

Many S-Boxes have been proposed for AES with various techniques and cryptographic properties. In Table 6, we present a comparison of the main cryptographic properties of S-Boxes of the proposed S-Box with AES and two former S-Boxes. Note the resistance against boomerang attacks has already been discussed previously.

Moreover, the proposed S-box has the same boomerang uniformity and differential-linear uniformity as AES. On the other hand, our method for finding new S-boxes is based on the parameters (A, a, b, c, d) where A is a 8×8 invertible matrix of $\mathbb{F}_2$, and $a, b, c, d \in \mathbb{F}_{2^n}$. This gives more possibilities to find good

Table 6. Comparison of our proposed S-box with two former S-boxes

Cryptographic parameter	AES S-box	Cui et al. S-Box [11]	Nitaj et al. S-Box [27]	Proposed S-box	Optimal value
Nonlinearity	112	112	112	112	120
Differential uniformity	4	4	4	4	4
Periodicity	≤ 87	256	256	256	256
Algebraic Complexity	9	255	255	255	255
Inverse Algebraic Complexity	255	253	254	254	255
Distance to SAC	432	372	328	324	0

S-boxes for AES. To sum up, the inverse function and AES are well known, well studied, and have good criteria to resist cryptographic attacks, such as the differential, linear, and boomerang cryptanalysis. Meanwhile, some algebraic and statistical criteria of the inverse function and AES are not satisfactory. We propose using the homographic function defined by (1) for several reasons. Firstly, the homographic function is affine equivalent to the inverse function. This makes the homographic function cryptographically as secure as the inverse function and AES. Secondly, with the homographic function, it is possible to generate a large number of S-boxes. Finally, by carefully choosing the parameters A, a, b, c, d, it is possible to improve the quality of the S-box regarding algebraic and statistical criteria, such as periodicity, algebraic complexity, strict avalanche, and distance to SAC.

6.2 Efficiency

For processors with word lengths 32 bits or greater, Daemen and Rijmen [12] have presented a fast implementation method. It combines the SubBytes, ShiftRows, and MixColumns transformations of AES into four look-up tables T_0, T_1, T_2, and T_3. We adopt the same technique for the proposed S-box to build four new look-up tables: T_0^N, T_1^N, T_2^N, and T_3^N where only the output values of SubBytes are different. This technique reduces the j-th column after SubBytes, ShiftRows, and MixColumns transformations in each round transformation to $[b_{0,j}, b_{1,j}, b_{2,j}, b_{3,j}]^T = T_0^N[a_{0,j+C_0}] \oplus T_1^N[a_{1,j+C_1}] \oplus T_2^N[a_{2,j+C_2}] \oplus T_3^N[a_{3,j+C_3}]$, where a is the input, b is the output, $b_{i,j}$ is the byte at i-th row and j-th column, and C_i is a constant corresponding to ShiftRows. This technique has to be completed by AddRoundKey, where each column is XORed with a 4-byte look-up. Moreover, the T_i^N's tables are rotations of each other. As a consequence, the look-up table implementation can be performed with only one table. This enables us to claim that our proposed S-box can be efficiently implemented in a large variety of processors, as is the case for the standard AES.

7 Conclusions

This paper introduced a simple (but efficient) transformation on a finite field with characteristic 2 and adapted it to derive a good alternative S-box for the AES. The new transformation description is detailed, and specific parameters were proposed to build an S-box for the AES. We have analyzed our S-box's algebraic and statistical criteria and its resistance to the main attacks on block ciphers. Our S-box has enhanced properties compared to AES. A typical improvement is a distance to SAC, which is decreased from 432 to 320, the optimal value for the distance to SAC being 0. Another distinct improvement is the proposed S-box's algebraic expression, which increased the optimal value from 9 to 255 terms. Besides, we have analyzed our S-box's security and showed that it preserves AES's security levels. Finally, the advantages of using the proposed S-box as a choice to the one of the AES and its strength, including efficient implementation, were also discussed.

References

1. Altaleb, A., Sarwar Saeed, M., Hussain, I., Aslam, M.: An algorithm for the construction of substitution box for block ciphers based on projective general linear group. AIP Adv. **7**, 035116 (2017)
2. Bar-On, A., Dunkelman, O., Keller, N., Weizman, A.: DLCT: a new tool for differential-linear cryptanalysis. In: Ishai, Y., Rijmen, V. (eds.) EUROCRYPT 2019. LNCS, vol. 11476, pp. 313–342. Springer, Cham (2019). https://doi.org/10.1007/978-3-030-17653-2_11
3. Picek, S., Batina, L., Jakobović, D., Ege, B., Golub, M.: S-box, SET, Match: a toolbox for S-box analysis. In: Naccache, D., Sauveron, D. (eds.) WISTP 2014. LNCS, vol. 8501, pp. 140–149. Springer, Heidelberg (2014). https://doi.org/10.1007/978-3-662-43826-8_10
4. Biham, E., Shamir, A.: Differential cryptanalysis of DES-like cryptosystems. J. Cryptol. **4**(1), 3–72 (1991)
5. Boura, C., Canteaut, A.: On the boomerang uniformity of cryptographic Sboxes. IACR Trans. Symmetric Cryptol. Ruhr Universität Bochum **2018**(3), 290–310 (2018)
6. Canteaut, A.: Lecture notes on cryptographic Boolean functions, 10 March 2016. https://www.rocq.inria.fr/secret/Anne.Canteaut/poly.pdf
7. Canteaut, A., Klösch, L., Li, C., Li, C.K., Li, L., Qu, F.: Wiemer: On the Differential-Linear Connectivity Table of vectorial Boolean functions (2019). https://arxiv.org/abs/1908.07445v1
8. Carlet, C.: Boolean Functions for Cryptography and Coding Theory. Cambridge University Press, Cambridge (2021)
9. Cid, C., Huang, T., Peyrin, T., Sasaki, Y., Song, L.: Boomerang connectivity table: a new cryptanalysis tool. In: Nielsen, J.B., Rijmen, V. (eds.) EUROCRYPT 2018. LNCS, vol. 10821, pp. 683–714. Springer, Cham (2018). https://doi.org/10.1007/978-3-319-78375-8_22
10. Courtois, N.T., Pieprzyk, J.: Cryptanalysis of block ciphers with overdefined systems of equations. In: Zheng, Y. (ed.) ASIACRYPT 2002. LNCS, vol. 2501, pp. 267–287. Springer, Heidelberg (2002). https://doi.org/10.1007/3-540-36178-2_17
11. Cui, J., Huang, L., Zhong, H., Chang, C., Yang, W.: An improved AES S-box and its performance analysis. Int. J. Innov. Comput. Inf. Control **7**(5(A)), 2291–2302 (2011)
12. Daemen, J., Rijmen, V.: The Design of Rijndael: AES - The Advanced Encryption Standard. Springer, Heidelberg (2002). https://doi.org/10.1007/978-3-662-04722-4

13. Dunkelman, O., Keller, N., Ronen, E., Shamir, A.: The Retracing Boomerang Attack, Cryptology ePrint Archive, Report 2019/1154 (2019). https://eprint.iacr.org/2019/1154
14. Dunkelman, O., Indesteege, S., Keller, N.: A differential-linear attack on 12-round serpent. In: Chowdhury, D.R., Rijmen, V., Das, A. (eds.) INDOCRYPT 2008. LNCS, vol. 5365, pp. 308–321. Springer, Heidelberg (2008). https://doi.org/10.1007/978-3-540-89754-5_24
15. Gorski, M., Lucks, S.: New related-key boomerang attacks on AES. In: Chowdhury, D.R., Rijmen, V., Das, A. (eds.) INDOCRYPT 2008. LNCS, vol. 5365, pp. 266–278. Springer, Heidelberg (2008). https://doi.org/10.1007/978-3-540-89754-5_21
16. Hussain, I., Shah, T., Mahmood, H., Gondal, M.A.: A projective general linear group based algorithm for the construction of substitution box for block ciphers. Neural Comput. Appl. **22**(6), 1085–1093 (2012)
17. Hussain, I., Shah, T., Gondal, M.A., Khan, M., Khan, W.A.: Construction of new S-box using a linear fractional transformation. World Appl. Sci. J. **14**(12), 1779–1785 (2011)
18. Hyunwoo, K., Seonggyeom, K., Deukjo, H., Jaechul, S., Seokhie, H.: Improved differential-linear cryptanalysis using DLCT. J. Korea Inst. Inf. Secur. Cryptol. **28**(6), 1379–1392 (2018)
19. Jakobsen, T., Knudsen, L.R.: The interpolation attack on block ciphers. In: Biham, E. (ed.) FSE 1997. LNCS, vol. 1267, pp. 28–40. Springer, Heidelberg (1997). https://doi.org/10.1007/BFb0052332
20. Langford, S.K., Hellman, M.E.: Differential-Linear cryptanalysis. In: Desmedt, Y.G. (ed.) CRYPTO 1994. LNCS, vol. 839, pp. 17–25. Springer, Heidelberg (1994). https://doi.org/10.1007/3-540-48658-5_3
21. Kangquan, L., Qu, L., Sun, B., Li, C.: New results about the boomerang uniformity of permutation polynomials. IEEE Trans. Inf. Theor. **65**(11), 7542–7593 (2019)
22. Lidl, R., Niederreiter, H.: Finite Fields. Cambridge University Press, Cambridge (1983)
23. Lu, J.: A methodology for differential-linear cryptanalysis and its applications. Des. Codes Cryptography **77**(1), 11–48 (2015)
24. Matsui, M.: Linear cryptanalysis method for DES cipher. In: Helleseth, T. (ed.) EUROCRYPT 1993. LNCS, vol. 765, pp. 386–397. Springer, Heidelberg (1994). https://doi.org/10.1007/3-540-48285-7_33
25. Mesnager, S.: Bent Functions: Fundamentals and Results. Springer, Cham (2016). https://doi.org/10.1007/978-3-319-32595-8
26. National Institute of Standards and Technology. Federal Information Processing Standards Publication 197: Announcing the Advanced Encryption Standard (AES). http://csrc.nist.gov/publications/fips/fips197/fips-197.pdf
27. Nitaj, A., Susilo, W., Tonien, J.: A new improved AES S-box with enhanced properties. In: Liu, J.K., Cui, H. (eds.) ACISP 2020. LNCS, vol. 12248, pp. 125–141. Springer, Cham (2020). https://doi.org/10.1007/978-3-030-55304-3_7
28. Nyberg, K.: Perfect nonlinear S-boxes. In: Davies, D.W. (ed.) EUROCRYPT 1991. LNCS, vol. 547, pp. 378–386. Springer, Heidelberg (1991). https://doi.org/10.1007/3-540-46416-6_32
29. Nyberg, K.: On the construction of highly nonlinear permutations. In: Rueppel, R.A. (ed.) EUROCRYPT 1992. LNCS, vol. 658, pp. 92–98. Springer, Heidelberg (1993). https://doi.org/10.1007/3-540-47555-9_8
30. Nyberg, K.: Differentially uniform mappings for cryptography. In: Helleseth, T. (ed.) EUROCRYPT 1993. LNCS, vol. 765, pp. 55–64. Springer, Heidelberg (1994). https://doi.org/10.1007/3-540-48285-7_6

31. Pommerening, K.: Quadratic equations in finite fields of characteristic, 2 February 2012. http://www.staff.uni-mainz.de/pommeren/MathMisc/QuGlChar2.pdf
32. Sarfraz, M., Hussain, I., Ali, F.: Construction of s-box based on Mobius transformation and increasing its confusion creating ability through invertible function. Int. J. Comput. Sci. Inf. Secur. (IJCSIS) **14**(2), 187 (2016)
33. Song, L., Qin, X., Hu, L.: Boomerang Connectivity Table Revisited, Cryptology ePrint Archive, Report 2019/146 (2019). https://eprint.iacr.org/2019/146
34. Wagner, D.: The boomerang attack. In: Knudsen, L. (ed.) FSE 1999. LNCS, vol. 1636, pp. 156–170. Springer, Heidelberg (1999). https://doi.org/10.1007/3-540-48519-8_12
35. Wang, Y.B.: Analysis of structure of AES and its S-box. J. PLA Univ. Sci. Technol. **3**(3), 13–17 (2002)
36. Webster, A.F., Tavares, S.E.: On the design of S-Boxes. In: Williams, H.C. (ed.) CRYPTO 1985. LNCS, vol. 218, pp. 523–534. Springer, Heidelberg (1986). https://doi.org/10.1007/3-540-39799-X_41

A Method of Integer Factorization

Zhizhong Pan[1,2(✉)] and Xiao Li[1,2]

[1] State Key Laboratory of Information Security, Institute of Information Engineering, Chinese Academy of Sciences, Beijing 100093, People's Republic of China
panzhizhong@iie.ac.cn
[2] School of Cyber Security, University of Chinese Academy of Science, Beijing 100093, People's Republic of China

Abstract. Suppose that we want to factor integer where $N = pq$, p, q are two distinct odd primes. Then we can reduce the problem of integer factorization to computing the generators of the Mordell-Weil group of $E_{Nr} : y^2 = x^3 - Nrx$, where r is a suitable integer with $(r, N) = 1$. We consider the family of elliptic curves E_{Nr}. As r varies in $\mathbb{Z}$, we get two results. Firstly, we estimate the probability of $r_{E_{Nr}} \geq 1$. Secondly, we estimate probability that the points on E_{Nr} can factor N. Finally we conduct some experiments to illustrate our method.

Keywords: Elliptic curve · Integer factorization · Analytic rank

1 Introduction

Integer factorization is the most direct attack method for RSA public key cryptosystem, and it has extremely important theoretical value and practical significance for its research.

In dark age of integer factorization, we have Lehman's method, Pllard's ρ method, and Shanks's class group method. The time complexity of these algorithms are all exponential. Then it comes to modern age of integer factorization, the class group method due to Schnorr and Lenstra is the first sub-exponential method which required a negligible amount of space, another prominent method having characteristic is the elliptic curve method. Later, there are another two powerful factoring algorithm are put forward, the quadratic method and the number field sieve. To this day, there are still many algorithms that optimize the original methods or completely new methods have been proposed. In this paper, we try to come up with a method to factoring integer through the rational points on a special family of elliptic curves. We continue our study on elliptic curves and integer factorization problems, and obtain some theoretical and experimental results. But still we have not found an efficient method to find points on the elliptic curve in the application, this will be our next work.

Our original idea comes from Burhanuddin and Huang [3,4]. In 2004 they related the problem of integer factoring to the problem of computing the Mordell-Weil group of an elliptic curve from a special family. Specially, they considered the family of elliptic curves $E = E_D : y^2 = x^3 - Dx$, where $D = pq$ with p and q

© Springer Nature Switzerland AG 2021
P. Stănică et al. (Eds.): ICSP 2021, CCIS 1497, pp. 64–76, 2021.
https://doi.org/10.1007/978-3-030-90553-8_5

distinct prime integers, $p \equiv q \equiv 3 \ mod \ 16$, and $(\frac{p}{q}) = 1$. Furthermore they speculated that the problem of integer factorization and the problem of computing the rational points of the elliptic curve can be polynomial-time equivalent. This method is completely different from the Lenstra's method of factoring integers by computing the order of elliptic curve over finite field, and provides a new idea for integer factorization.

Later, in 2014 Li and Zeng [9] studied a family of elliptic curves $E = E_{2Dr}$: $y^2 = x^3 - 2Drx$, where $D = pq$ is a product of two distinct odd primes and $2Dr$ is square-free. They proved that there are infinitely many $r \geq 1$ such that E_{2Dr} has conjectural rank one and $v_p(x(kP)) \neq v_q(x(kP))$ for any odd integer k, where P is the generator of $E_{2Dr}(\mathbb{Q})/E_{2Dr}(\mathbb{Q})_{tors}$. Furthermore, assuming the Generalized Riemann hypothesis, they showed the minimal value of r is in $O(\log^4(D))$. This will inspire us we can choose a small r such that the points on $E = E_{2Dr} : y^2 = x^3 - 2Drx$ can factor D.

Then, in 2021 Pan and Li [11] considered a larger family of elliptic curves $E = E_{Dr} : y^2 = x^3 - Drx$, where $D = pq$ is the integer we want to factor and r is an arbitrary integer. Employing the method of two-descent, they reduce the problem of factoring integer to computing the Mordell-Weil group of $E_{Nr} : y^2 = x^3 - Nrx$. Furthermore, they give a method to compute the 2-Selmer group.

In this paper, we continue the research on on elliptic curves and Integer Factorization problems. We want to show that while $r \in \mathbb{Z}$, there are enough numbers of r such that points on the elliptic curve E_{Nr} can factor N. So we should guarantee that there are enough curves have rank equal or greater than 1 in the family of curves E_{Nr} firstly. This will ensure that when we choose r randomly, there are still points with infinity order on the curve E_{Nr}. The theorem is as follows.

Theorem 1. *Let $E_{Nr} : y^2 = x^3 - Nrx$ be a family elliptic curves defined over $\mathbb{Q}$, where $N = pq$, $r \in \mathbb{Z}$ and $(r, N) = 1$. As r varies in $\mathbb{Z}$, donating the probability of $r_{E_{Nr}} \geq 1$ as P_1, then $P_1 > \frac{1}{2}$.*

Remark 1. $r_{E_{Nr}}$ donates the rank of Mordell-Weil group of E_{Nr}.

Then we estimate the probability of the point on E_{Nr} can factor N while r varies in $\mathbb{Z}$.

Theorem 2. *Let $E_{Nr} : y^2 = x^3 - Nrx$ be a family elliptic curves defined over $\mathbb{Q}$, where $N = pq$, $r \in \mathbb{Z}$ and $(r, N) = 1$. When we randomly select $r = (-1)^m 2^n \prod_{i=1}^{n_1} p_i \prod_{j=1}^{n_2} q_j^2 \prod_{k=1}^{n_3} r_k^3 \in \mathbb{Z}$, donating the probability that the points on E_{Nr} can factor N as P_2, then $P_2 > \frac{2}{n_1+2}(\frac{c}{6} - \frac{1}{2^{n_1+1}})$.*

Remark 2. This lower bound we estimate is extremely smaller than the practical, this is why P_2 seems to be negative while n_1 is small. In fact, we conduct some experiment when $n_1 = 1, 2, 3, 4, 5$. It shows that P_2 is around 0.3 when $n_2 = 0$, while $n_2 > 0$ it turns to be around 0.1. In spite of the lower bound is smaller than practical, it is enough for us. We can infer that by just picking a small number of r, we can factor N. The experiment result will be shown later.

Remark 3. The constant c in Theorem 2 is the probability of $r_{E_{Nr}} = 1$ and $\text{III}(\phi) = \text{III}'(\phi) = 1$ while r varying in $\mathbb{Z}$. According to Miller [10], if $r_E \leq 1$, there are algorithms to compute both the Mordell-Weil group $E(\mathbb{Q})$ and the Shafarevich-Tate group III. We can regard c as a constant. Furthermore, we check Cremona's database of elliptic curves defined over $\mathbb{Q}$ with conductor less than 130000 [6]. There are 568824 curves in this database, in which 217401 curves have rank one and only 55979 curves have nontrivial Shafarevich-Tate group. So it's believed that c is big enough. In specific family of curves $E_{Nr} : y^2 = x^3 - Nrx$, we roughly find that $c > 0.1$ through experiments.

We conclude our method. When we want to factor an integer N, we can choose an integer r randomly. Theorem 1 guarantees that the curve E_{Nr} have infinite order points while Theorem 2 guarantees that the points on E_{Nr} can factor N. The next step is searching a non-torsion point $P = (x, y)$ on E_{Nr}. If $GCD(x, N) \neq 1, N$, the factorization process successes. Otherwise choose another r, searching again. The Theorem 2 guarantees that this process can be down by selecting a small number of r, and its depended on N. Beside standard methods, there are two other methods of searching for a point of infinite order. One method is the canonical height search algorithm, the other method is the Heegner point algorithm when $r_E^{an} = 1$. But both methods are still quite impractical in general if N is greater than 10^{20}. So this is still far away from factor RSA number. So the next work should be how to find an efficient method to search points on E_{Nr} for an arbitrary integer r.

This paper is organized as follows. In Sect. 2 we do some preprocess to our elliptic curve and introduce the theorem to compute the torsion subgroup. By applying the parity conjecture, we prove Theorem 1. In Sect. 3 we introduced how to reduce the problem of factoring integer to computing the Mordell-Weil group of $E_{Dr} : y^2 = x^3 - Drx$ by Pan and Li [11]. In Sect. 4 we prove Theorem 2 by analytic combination of the structure of 2-Selmer Group and the factors of r. In Sect. 5, we give some experiments result to illustrate our results.

2 Parity Conjecture and the Rank

2.1 Notations

At the beginning, we fix some notations. For the elliptic curve $E_D : y^2 = x^3 - Dx$, if $D = A^4 D'$, that is $y^2 = x^3 - A^4 D'x$. Divide both sides by A^6 to obtain $\frac{y^2}{A^6} = \frac{x^3}{A^6} - D'\frac{x}{A^2}$. Let $x' = \frac{x}{A^2}, y' = \frac{y}{A^3}$, and we get a new curve $E_{D'} : y'^2 = x'^3 - D'x'$. So the relation gives a one-to-one correspondence $(x, y) \leftrightarrow (\frac{x}{A^2}, \frac{y}{A^3})$ of the points between E_D and $E_{D'}$.

According to that, we begin to preprocess the elliptic curve. By removing D's quartic factors, we obtain the new elliptic curve $E_D : y^2 = x^3 - Dx$, where $D = (-1)^m 2^n \prod p_i \prod q_j^2 \prod r_k^3$, and p_i, q_j, r_k are distinct primes, and $n = 0, 1, 2, 3$, $m = 0, 1$.

By the way, there exist 2-isogeny morphism between E_D and E_{-4D}:

$$\phi : E_D \longrightarrow E_{-4D}$$
$$(x,y) \longmapsto (\frac{y^2}{x^2}, \frac{y(D+x^2)}{x^2})$$
$$(0,0) \longmapsto \infty$$
$$\infty \longmapsto \infty$$

Without loss of generality, we can choose $n = 0,1$, then we assume that $D = (-1)^m 2^n \prod p_i \prod q_j^2 \prod r_k^3$, $n = 0,1$, $m = 0,1$. For simplicity, We denote E_D by E, and E_{-4D} by $\hat{E}$.

2.2 Torsion Subgroups

Theorem 3 *(see [12]). Let $D \in \mathbb{Z}$ be quartic-free, $E_D : y^2 = x^3 - Dx$ is defined over $\mathbb{Q}$, then*

$$E_{D,tors}(\mathbb{Q}) \cong \begin{cases} \mathbb{Z}/4\mathbb{Z} & if D = -4, \\ \mathbb{Z}_2 \oplus \mathbb{Z}_2 & if\ D\ is\ the\ square\ integer, \\ \mathbb{Z}_2 & otherwise, \end{cases} \tag{1}$$

where $E_{D,tors}$ is the torsion subgroup of E_D.

By Theorem 3, we know that the torsion subgroup of E_{Nr} is $\mathbb{Z}/2\mathbb{Z}$, two elements of which are ∞ and $(0,0)$. We will denote $(0,0)$ by T later.

2.3 Parity Conjecture

Let E be an elliptic curve defined over $\mathbb{Q}$ with conductor N_E. By the Modularity Theorem, the L-function can be analytically extended to the entire complex plane and satisfies the functional equation [5]

$$\Lambda_E(2 - s) = w_E \lambda_E(s), \text{ where } \lambda_E(s) = (2\pi)^{-s} N_E^{s/2} \Gamma(s) L_E(s) \tag{2}$$

and $w_E = \pm 1$ is called the global root number.

Let r_E^{an} and r_E be the analytic rank and arithmetic rank of E respectively, where r_E^{an} is the order of vanishing of $L_E(s)$ at $s = 1$ and r_E is the rank of the abelian group $E(\mathbb{Q})$. The famous BSD conjecture says that $r_E^{an} = r_E$.

Conjecture 1 (Birch-Swinnerton-Dyer, see [5]). Let E be an elliptic curve define over $\mathbb{Q}$, the algebraic rank r_E defined by Mordell's theorem is equal to the analytic rank r_E^{an}.

A weak but sufficient form of the known result is as following:

Theorem 4 *(Kolyvagin et al. see [5]). Let E be an elliptic curve defined over $\mathbb{Q}$. Then*

(1) *If the analytic rank is equal to 0, in other words if $L_E(1) \neq 0$, then $r_E = 0$.*
(2) *If the analytic rank is equal to 1, in other words if $L_E(1) = 0$ and $L'_E(1) \neq 0$, then $r_E = 1$.*
(3) *In both case, $\text{III}(E)$ is finite and the BSD conjecture is valid up to a controlled rational factor.*

Theorem 4 tell us that when analytic rank $r_E^{an} = 0$ or 1, BSD conjecture is true. On the other hand for the parity of r_E, there is another conjecture:

Conjecture 2. (Parity conjecture, see [1,7]). We have $(-1)^{r_E} = w_E$.

So assuming BSD conjecture is true, we obtain the following:

Corollary 1 *(see [1]). Let elliptic curve $E_D : y^2 = x^3 - Dx$ be defined over $\mathbb{Q}$ with $4 \nmid D$ and D quartic-free. We denote the rank of E_D by r_E. Then $(-1)^{r_E} = (-1)^{r_E^{an}} = w_E = w_\infty \cdot w_2 \cdot \prod_{p^2 \| D} w_p$, in which*

$$w_\infty = sgn(-D),$$

$$w_2 = \begin{cases} -1 & D \equiv 1,3,11,13 \bmod 16, \\ 1 & otherwise, \end{cases}$$

$$w_p = \left(\frac{-1}{p}\right) = \begin{cases} -1 & p \equiv 3 \bmod 4, \\ 1 & p \equiv 1 \bmod 4. \end{cases}$$

Remark 4. $(\frac{\cdot}{\cdot})$ is Jacobi symbol.

So when $w_E = -1$, we can infer that r_E is an odd number. At this point we can prove that the rank of the elliptic curve is equal or greater than 1. Then we can proof Theorem 1.

Proof. For the curve $E_{Nr} : y^2 = x^3 - Nrx$, where r is a suitable rational number with $(r, N) = 1$. We may normalise so that Nr is an integer, not divisible by 4 or by any fourth power. Let $D = Nr$, write E_{Nr} as $E_D : y^2 = x^3 - Dx$, where $D = (-1)^m 2^n \prod p_i \prod q_j^2 \prod r_k^3$, and p_i, q_j, r_k are distinct primes, and $n = 0, 1$, $m = 0, 1$.

Assume that the probability that D contains square factors is p_0, and the probability that the product of the square factors modulo 4 remaining 1 is A, while remaining 3 is B. Naturally, we have $A + B = 1$.

Case1: When $m = 0$, $n = 0$.

$$w_\infty = sgn(-D) = -1,$$

$$w_2 = \begin{cases} -1 & D \equiv 1,3,11,13 \bmod 16, \\ 1 & D \equiv 5,7,9,15 \bmod 16, \end{cases}$$

$$\prod_{p^2 \| D} w_p = \prod_{q_j} \left(\frac{-1}{q_j}\right) = \begin{cases} -1 & \prod q_j \equiv 3 \bmod 4, \\ 1 & \prod q_j \equiv 1 \bmod 4. \end{cases}$$

So $P(w_E = -1) = p_0[P(w_2 = -1)P(\prod_{p^2 \| D} w_p = -1) + P(w_2 = 1)P(\prod_{p^2 \| D} w_p = 1)] + (1 - p_0)P(w_2 = 1) = p_0[\frac{1}{2}B + \frac{1}{2}A] + (1 - p_0)\frac{1}{2} = \frac{1}{2}$.

Case2: When $m = 0$, $n = 1$.

$$w_\infty = sgn(-D) = -1,$$
$$w_2 = 1$$

$$\prod_{p^2 \| D} w_p = \prod_{q_j} (\frac{-1}{q_j}) = \begin{cases} -1 & \prod q_j \equiv 3 \ mod \ 4, \\ 1 & \prod q_j \equiv 1 \ mod \ 4. \end{cases}$$

So $P(w_E = -1) = p_0 P(\prod_{p^2 \| D} w_p = 1) + (1 - p_0) = 1 - Bp_0$.

Case3: When $m = 1$, $n = 0$.

$$w_\infty = sgn(-D) = 1,$$
$$w_2 = \begin{cases} -1 & D \equiv 1, 3, 11, 13 \ mod \ 16, \\ 1 & D \equiv 5, 7, 9, 15 \ mod \ 16, \end{cases}$$

$$\prod_{p^2 \| D} w_p = \prod_{q_j} (\frac{-1}{q_j}) = \begin{cases} -1 & \prod q_j \equiv 3 \ mod \ 4, \\ 1 & \prod q_j \equiv 1 \ mod \ 4. \end{cases}$$

So $P(w_E = -1) = p_0[P(w_2 = -1)P(\prod_{p^2 \| D} w_p = 1) + P(w_2 = 1)P(\prod_{p^2 \| D} w_p = -1)] + (1 - p_0)P(w_2 = -1) = p_0[\frac{1}{2}A + \frac{1}{2}B] + (1 - p_0)\frac{1}{2} = \frac{1}{2}$.

Case4: When $m = 1$, $n = 1$.

$$w_\infty = sgn(-D) = 1,$$
$$w_2 = 1$$

$$\prod_{p^2 \| D} w_p = \prod_{q_j} (\frac{-1}{q_j}) = \begin{cases} -1 & \prod q_j \equiv 3 \ mod \ 4, \\ 1 & \prod q_j \equiv 1 \ mod \ 4. \end{cases}$$

So $P(w_E = -1) = p_0 P(\prod_{p^2 \| D} w_p = -1) = Bp_0$.

In summary, $P(w_E = -1) = P(m = 0, n = 0) \cdot \frac{1}{2} + P(m = 0, n = 1) \cdot (1 - Bp_0) + P(m = 1, n = 0) \cdot \frac{1}{2} + P(m = 1, n = 1) \cdot Bp_0 = \frac{1}{4} \cdot \frac{1}{2} + \frac{1}{4} \cdot (1 - Bp_0) + \frac{1}{4} \cdot \frac{1}{2} + \frac{1}{4} \cdot Bp_0 = \frac{1}{2}$.

So $P(r_E \geq 1) > P(w_E = -1) = \frac{1}{2}$. This finish our proof.

3 Two-Descent Method and Integer Factorization

In this section we introduce how Pan and Li [11] reduce the problem of factoring integer to computing the Mordell-Weil group of $E_{Nr} : y^2 = x^3 - Nrx$. Considering the elliptic curve $E_{Nr} : y^2 = x^3 - Nrx$, where $N = pq$ and $r = (-1)^m 2^n \prod p_i \prod q_j^2 \prod r_k^3$, $n = 0, 1$, $m = 0, 1$. Denote it by E. And denote its dual curve $E_{-4Nr} : y^2 = x^3 + 4Nrx$ by $\widehat{E}$.

Definition 1 *(see [5]). Define the two-descent map*

$$\alpha : E(\mathbb{Q}) \longrightarrow \mathbb{Q}^\times / \mathbb{Q}^{\times^2}$$
$$(x, y) \longmapsto \bar{x}$$
$$\infty \longmapsto 1$$
$$T \longmapsto \overline{-Nr}$$

$$\hat{\alpha} : \hat{E}(\mathbb{Q}) \longrightarrow \mathbb{Q}^\times / \mathbb{Q}^{\times^2}$$
$$(\hat{x}, \hat{y}) \longmapsto \bar{\hat{x}}$$
$$\hat{\infty} \longmapsto 1$$
$$\hat{T} \longmapsto \overline{Nr}$$

where $\bar{x}$ means x with the square factors removed.

Proposition 1 *(see [5]). For α and $\hat{\alpha}$, we have the following properties:*

(1) *α and $\hat{\alpha}$ are group homomorphisms.*
(2) *$Im(\alpha) \subseteq < -1, b_i >$, where $b_i | Nr$.*
     $Im(\hat{\alpha}) \subseteq < -1, b_i' >$, where $b_i' | 4Nr$.
(3) *If $b \in Im(\alpha)$, then $\overline{\frac{-Nr}{b}} \in Im(\alpha)$.*
     If $b \in Im(\hat{\alpha})$, then $\overline{\frac{4Nr}{b}} \in Im(\hat{\alpha})$.
(4) *$\{1, \overline{-Nr}\} \subseteq Im(\alpha)$ and $\{1, \overline{Nr}\} \subseteq Im(\hat{\alpha})$.*
(5) *$|Im(\alpha)| \cdot |Im(\hat{\alpha})| = 2^{r_E+2}$.*

Let $S = \{\infty\} \bigcup \{b_i \mid b_i$ *is the prime factor of* $Nr\}$, $Q(S, 2)$ be the subgroup generated by -1 and S in $\mathbb{Q}^\times / \mathbb{Q}^{\times^2}$. Simultaneously, let $\hat{S} = \{\infty\} \bigcup \{b_i \mid b_i$ *is the prime factor of* $4Nr\}$, $\hat{Q}(\hat{S}, 2)$ be the subgroup generated by -1 and $\hat{S}$ in $\mathbb{Q}^\times / \mathbb{Q}^{\times^2}$.

Theorem 5 *(see [5]). (1) $\forall b \in Q(S, 2)$, $b \in Im\alpha \Leftrightarrow C_b' : w^2 = b - \frac{Nr}{b} z^4$ has solutions in $\mathbb{Q}$.*
     (2) $\forall b \in \hat{Q}(\hat{S}, 2)$, $b \in Im\hat{\alpha} \Leftrightarrow C_b : w^2 = b + \frac{4Nr}{b} z^4$ has solutions in $\mathbb{Q}$.

Theorem 5 gives the conditions to be satisfied by the elements in $Im\alpha$ and $Im\hat{\alpha}$. Because there are finitely many elements in $Q(S, 2)$ and $\hat{Q}(\hat{S}, 2)$, we only need to check both elements in $Q(S, 2)$ and $\hat{Q}(\hat{S}, 2)$ one by one. In fact, according to Proposition 1 (3), we only need to check half of the elements in $Q(S, 2)$ and $\hat{Q}(\hat{S}, 2)$. But deciding whether C_b and C_b' have solutions in $\mathbb{Q}$ is a difficult problem, so instead we consider whether they have solutions on local field $\mathbb{Q}_p$ $(p \leq \infty)$. Furthermore, according to [12], we only need to consider whether C_b and C_b' have solutions in $\mathbb{Q}_p$ $(p \mid 2Nr$ and $p = \infty)$. Now we give the definition of 2-Selmer group.

Definition 2 *(see [13]). (1) Define $S'(\phi) \triangleq \{b \in Q(S, 2) \mid C_b'(\mathbb{Q}_p) \neq \Phi, \forall p \in S\}$, it is an abelian group, called 2-Selmer group of $E(\mathbb{Q})$.*
     (2) Define $S(\phi) \triangleq \{b \in \hat{Q}(\hat{S}, 2) \mid C_b(\mathbb{Q}_p) \neq \Phi, \forall p \in \hat{S}\}$, it is an abelian group, called 2-Selmer group of $\hat{E}(\mathbb{Q})$.

From Definition 2, we know that $Im(\alpha) \subseteq S'(\phi)$ and $Im(\hat{\alpha}) \subseteq S(\phi)$, the opposite sides are not necessarily true. In order to measure the gaps between them, we give the following definition.

Definition 3 *(see [13])*. *(1) Define* $Ш'(\phi) \triangleq S'(\phi)/Im(\alpha)$, *called the 2-Shafarevich group of* $E(\mathbb{Q})$,
    (2) Define $Ш(\phi) \triangleq S(\phi)/Im(\hat{\alpha})$, *called the 2-Shafarevich group of* $\hat{E}(\mathbb{Q})$.

To illustrate the combination of the Mordell-Weil group and integer factors, we can consider the two-descent map under the special situation.

Theorem 6 *([11])*. *Suppose* $r_E \geq 1$, $|S'(\phi)| = 4$, $|S(\phi)| = 2$ *or* $|S'(\phi)| = 2$, $|S(\phi)| = 4 \Leftrightarrow Ш'(\phi) = Ш(\phi) = 1$ *and* $r_E = 1$.

When $Ш'(\phi) = Ш(\phi) = 1$, we can get that $Im(\alpha) = S'(\phi)$, $Im(\hat{\alpha}) = S(\phi)$, then we can write the two-decent map more clearly.

Proposition 2 *([11])*. *When* $r_E \geq 1$, *if* $S'(\phi) = \{1, d, \frac{\overline{-Nr}}{d}, \overline{-Nr}\}$, $S(\phi) = \{1, \overline{Nr}\}$, *then* $r_E = 1$. *At that time, the map* α *and* $\hat{\alpha}$ *can be written as:* •

$$\alpha : E(\mathbb{Q}) \longrightarrow \mathbb{Q}^{\times}/\mathbb{Q}^{\times^2}$$

$$\infty \longmapsto 1$$

$$T \longmapsto \overline{-Nr}$$

$$(2k+1)P \longmapsto d \text{ or } \frac{\overline{-Nr}}{d}$$

$$(2k+1)P + T \longmapsto \frac{\overline{-Nr}}{d} \text{ or } d$$

$$2kP \longmapsto 1$$

$$2kP + T \longmapsto \overline{-Nr}$$

$$\hat{\alpha} : \hat{E}(\mathbb{Q}) \longrightarrow \mathbb{Q}^{\times}/\mathbb{Q}^{\times^2}$$

$$\hat{\infty} \longmapsto 1$$

$$\hat{T} \longmapsto \overline{Nr}$$

$$k\hat{P} \longmapsto 1$$

$$k\hat{P} + \hat{T} \longmapsto \overline{Nr}$$

where P *and* $\hat{P}$ *are the generators of* $E(\mathbb{Q})$ *and* $\hat{E}(\mathbb{Q})$ *respectively.*

From the map α, we see that if d can only be divided by p (resp q), then $v_p(x((2k+1)P))$ is an odd number (resp even number) and the corresponding $v_q(x((2k+1)P))$ is an even number (resp odd number). It follows that $v_p(x((2k+1)P)) \neq v_q(x((2k+1)P))$, and then we can use $x((2k+1)P)$ to factor N. Moreover, we also find that N can be factored not only for points on a curve of rank 1, but also for curves of rank greater than 1.

So things become clear. According to Proposition 1 (2), there may have N's factors contained in $Im(\alpha)$ or $Im(\hat{\alpha})$. But we can't get $Im(\alpha)$ or $Im(\hat{\alpha})$ directly, we turns to compute $S(\phi)$ and $S'(\phi)$. From Definition 2, we know that the structure of $S(\phi)$ and $S'(\phi)$ are depended on the solutions of C_b and C_b' in local field.

Theorem 7 ([11]). Let $C_d : w^2 = d + \frac{D}{d}z^4$, where $D = (-1)^m 2^n \prod p_i \prod q_j^2 \prod r_k^3$, p_i, q_j, r_k are distinct primes, d is square-free and $d \mid D$, we have

(1) When $m = 0$, $C_d(\mathbb{Q}_\infty) \neq \Phi \Leftrightarrow d > 0$.
   When $m = 1$, $C_d(\mathbb{Q}_\infty) \neq \Phi$ holds for any d.
(2) 1) When $2 \nmid d$
     (i) If $n = 0$, $C_d(\mathbb{Q}_2) \neq \Phi \Leftrightarrow d \equiv 1 \bmod 8$ or $d + \frac{D}{d} \equiv 0 \bmod 16$ or $d + \frac{D}{d} \equiv 4 \bmod 32$ or $\frac{D}{d} \equiv 1 \bmod 8$.
     (ii) If $n = 1$, $C_d(\mathbb{Q}_2) \neq \Phi \Leftrightarrow d \equiv 1 \bmod 8$ or $d + \frac{D}{d} \equiv 1 \bmod 8$.
     (iii) If $n = 2$, $C_d(\mathbb{Q}_2) \neq \Phi \Leftrightarrow d \equiv 1 \bmod 8$ or $d + \frac{D}{d} \equiv 1 \bmod 8$ or $\frac{D}{4d} \equiv 1 \bmod 4$.
     (iv) If $n = 3$, $C_d(\mathbb{Q}_2) \neq \Phi \Leftrightarrow d \equiv 1 \bmod 8$.
   2) When $2 \mid d$
     (i) If $n = 1$, $C_d(\mathbb{Q}_2) \neq \Phi \Leftrightarrow d + \frac{D}{d} \equiv 1 \bmod 8$ or $\frac{D}{d} \equiv 1 \bmod 8$.
     (ii) If $n = 2$, $C_d(\mathbb{Q}_2) \neq \Phi \Leftrightarrow \frac{d}{2} + \frac{D}{2d} \equiv 0 \bmod 32$ or $\frac{d}{2} + \frac{D}{2d} \equiv 2 \bmod 16$ or $\frac{d}{2} + \frac{D}{2d} \equiv 8 \bmod 32$.
     (iii) If $n = 3$, $C_d(\mathbb{Q}_2) \neq \Phi \Leftrightarrow \frac{D}{4d} \equiv 1 \bmod 4$.
(3) $\forall t \mid d$, t is prime
   1) When $t = p_i$, $C_d(\mathbb{Q}_t) \neq \Phi \Leftrightarrow (\frac{D/d}{t}) = 1$.
   2) When $t = q_j$, $C_d(\mathbb{Q}_t) \neq \Phi \Leftrightarrow (\frac{-d^2/D}{t})_4 = 1$.
   3) When $t = r_k$, $C_d(\mathbb{Q}_t) \neq \Phi \Leftrightarrow (\frac{D/dt^2}{t}) = 1$.
(4) $\forall t \nmid d$, t is prime
   1) When $t = p_i$, $C_d(\mathbb{Q}_t) \neq \Phi \Leftrightarrow (\frac{d}{t}) = 1$.
   2) When $t = q_j$, $C_d(\mathbb{Q}_t) \neq \Phi \Leftrightarrow (\frac{d}{t}) = 1$ or $(\frac{D/dt^2}{t}) = 1$.
   3) When $t = r_k$, $C_d(\mathbb{Q}_t) \neq \Phi \Leftrightarrow (\frac{d}{t}) = 1$.

4   2-Selmer Group and Integer Factorization

We have known from Proposition 2 that if $Im(\alpha)$ and $Im(\hat{\alpha})$ have proper structure, we can use the points on E_{Nr} to factor N. And we may replace $Im(\alpha)$ and $Im(\hat{\alpha})$ by $S'(\phi)$ and $S(\phi)$ in the case of $\mathrm{III}'(\phi) = \mathrm{III}(\phi) = 1$.

We can infirm that N can be factored in the Proposition 2 condition. So our idea is compute the probability of condition occurred in Proposition 2 as our lower bound, i.e. P_2. So analytic the structure of $S'(\phi)$ and $S(\phi)$ are very important to us.

From Theorem 7, we can deduce that for $\forall d \in Q(S, 2)$ (resp $\hat{Q}(\hat{S}, 2)$), whether $d \in S'(\phi)$ (resp $S(\phi)$) or $d \notin S'(\phi)$ (resp $S(\phi)$) is determined by the factors of d.

We assume that the probabilities of prime number $p \equiv 1, 3, 5, 7 \bmod 8$ are the same, and for $\forall p$, q, the probabilities of $(\frac{q}{p}) = 1$ or -1 are also the same.

For the elliptic curve $E_D : y^2 = x^3 - Dx$ and its dual curve $E_{-4D} : y^2 = x^3 + 4Dx$, we define their Tawagama ratio $T_D = \frac{|S(\Phi)|}{|S'(\Phi)|}$ [8]. According to Birch [2], we have following proposition.

Proposition 3 *(see [2]).* $T_D = \prod_{p|2D\infty} \rho_p$, *in which*

$$\rho_\infty = \begin{cases} \frac{1}{2} & D > 0, \\ 1 & D < 0, \end{cases}$$

$$\rho_2 = \begin{cases} 1 & D \equiv 5,9 \bmod 16 \ or \ D \ is \ even, \\ 2 & D \equiv 1,3,11,13 \bmod 16, \\ 4 & D \equiv 7,15 \bmod 16, \end{cases}$$

$$\rho_p = (\frac{-1}{p}) = \begin{cases} 2 & p^2 \parallel D \ and \ p \equiv 3 \bmod 4 \ and \ {-}D \ is \ p\text{-}adic \ square, \\ \frac{1}{2} & p^2 \parallel D \ and \ p \equiv 3 \bmod 4 \ and \ {-}D \ is \ not \ p\text{-}adic \ square, \\ 1 & otherwise. \end{cases}$$

Corollary 2. *Let $E_{Nr} : y^2 = x^3 - Nrx$ be a family elliptic curves defined over $\mathbb{Q}$, where $N = pq$, $r \in \mathbb{Z}$. As r varies in $\mathbb{Z}$, $P(T_{Nr} = \frac{1}{2}) > \frac{1}{6}$.*

Proof. While r varies in $\mathbb{Z}$, we choose r be a positive even square-free integer. For E_{Nr}, $\rho_\infty = \frac{1}{2}$, $\rho_2 = 1$, $\prod_{p|D} \rho_p = 1$. At that time, $T_{Nr} = \frac{1}{2}$. So $P(T_{Nr} = \frac{1}{2}) > P(r$ is positive even square-free integer$) = \frac{1}{2} \cdot \frac{1}{2} \cdot \prod_{p \text{ is odd prime}} (1 - \frac{1}{p^2}) > \frac{1}{6}$.

For convenience, we will fix some symbols, see Table 1.

Table 1. Fix some events

Symbols	Events
H_0	The points on E_{Nr} can factor N
H_1	$r_E = 1$
H_2	$\text{III}'(\phi) = \text{III}(\phi) = 1$
H_3	$|S'(\phi)| = 4, |S(\phi)| = 2|$
H_4	$|S'(\phi)| = 2, |S(\phi)| = 4|$
H_d	$d \in S'(\phi)$
H_s	$(d,N) = p$ or q
H_{m_1,m_2,m_3}	$d = \prod_{x=1}^{m_1} p_{i_x} \prod_{y=1}^{m_2} q_{j_y} \prod_{z=1}^{m_3} r_{k_z} \in Q(S,2)$

Lemma 1. *If $d = \prod_{x=1}^{m_1} p_{i_x} \prod_{y=1}^{m_2} q_{j_y} \prod_{z=1}^{m_3} r_{k_z} \in Q(S,2)$, $d' = \prod_{x=1}^{m_1} p_{i'_x} \prod_{y=1}^{m_2} q_{j'_y} \prod_{z'=1}^{m_3} r_{k'_z} \in Q(S,2)$, in which $-1 \leq i_x, i'_x \leq n_1$, $1 \leq j_y, j'_y \leq n_2$, $1 \leq k_z, k'_z \leq n_3$, and $p_{-1} = p$, $p_0 = q$, then $P(H_d|H_1, H_3) = P(H_{d'}|H_1, H_3)$.*

Proof. Theorem 7 and symmetry give us an immediate conclusion.

Corollary 3. $P(H_d, H_s | H_1, H_2, H_3, H_{m_1, m_2, m_3}) = \dfrac{2\binom{n_1}{m_1-1}\binom{n_2}{m_2}\binom{n_3}{m_3}}{\binom{n_1+2}{m_1}\binom{n_2}{m_2}\binom{n_3}{m_3}} \geq \dfrac{2}{n_1+2}.$

Proof. A direct corollary of Lemma 1 using a small trick of permutation and combination.

Lemma 2. $P(H_1, H_2, H_3) > \frac{c}{6}.$

Proof. According to Theorem 6, $H_1, H_2 \Leftrightarrow H_1, H_3$ or H_4. According to Corollary 3, we can get that $P(H3|H1, H3$ or $H4) > \frac{1}{6}$. So we can conclude that: $P(H_1, H_2, H3) = P(H3|H1, H_2)P(H1, H_2) = P(H3|H1, H3$ or $H4)P(H_1, H_2) > \frac{c}{6}$

With the above preparation, then we can proof Theorem 2.

Proof. We randomly select $r = (-1)^m 2^n \prod_{i=1}^{n_1} p_i \prod_{i=j}^{n_2} q_j^2 \prod_{k=1}^{n_3} r_k^3 \in \mathbb{Z}$. We can compute $w_{E_{Nr}}$, $S'(\phi)$ and $S(\phi)$. If $w_{E_{Nr}} = -1$ and $|S'(\phi)| = 4$, $|S(\phi)| = 2$, moreover if the nontrivial element $d \in S'(\phi)$ only divided by p(resp q), then by Proposition 2 we can say the points on E_{Nr} can factor N. So we can get that:

$$P_2 > P(H_d, H_s, H_1, H_2, H_3)$$

$$= \sum_{m_1=1}^{n_1+1} \sum_{m_2=0}^{n_2} \sum_{m_3=0}^{n_3} P(H_d, H_s, H_1, H_2, H_3, H_{m_1, m_2, m_3})$$

$$\geq \frac{2}{n_1+2} \sum_{m_1=1}^{n_1+1} \sum_{m_2=0}^{n_2} \sum_{m_3=0}^{n_3} P(H_1, H_2, H_3, H_{m_1, m_2, m_3})$$

$$= \frac{2}{n_1+2} \Big(P(H_1, H_2, H_3) - \sum_{m_2=0}^{n_2} \sum_{m_3=0}^{n_3} P(H_1, H_2, H_3, H_{0, m_2, m_3}) -$$

$$\sum_{m_2=0}^{n_2} \sum_{m_3=0}^{n_3} P(H_1, H_2, H_3, H_{n_1+2, m_2, m_3}) \Big)$$

$$\geq \frac{2}{n_1+2} \Big(\frac{c}{6} - \frac{1}{2^{n_1+1}} \Big)$$

From Theorem 2, we can get that we can factor r by choosing a small number of r. So if we can find a efficient method to find points on E_{Nr}, N can be factored immediately. And moreover, Suppose we can find a method to compute the rational points on the elliptic surface $y^2 = X^3 - Nzx$, then N can also be factored.

5 Experiment

We also conduct some experiments to illustrate our result. We choose random $N = pq$. Once $N = pq$ is selected, then we choose 1000 random square-free r with $1, 2, \cdots, 11$ factors respectively. The following Fig. 1 is our result. The vertical axis is the number of r such that the points on E_{Nr} success factor N. The horizontal axis is the number of n_1.

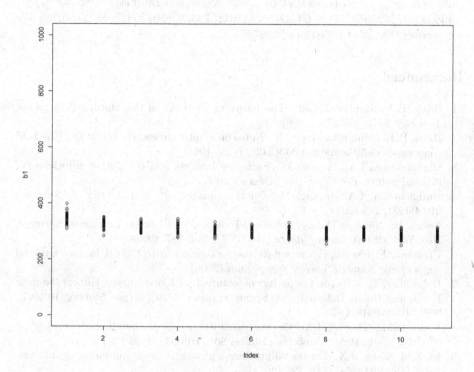

Fig. 1. The number of r that the points on E_{Nr} can factor N with 1000 random r

Finally, we use an example to illustrate the correctness of our Integer Factorization method.

Example 1. Suppose we want to factor $N = 2619143683493$, we select r in $[1, 1000]$ randomly, use Magma to compute its generator, then compute gcd with N. Our experiment result shows that after 3 times attempted we can choose the suitable r. Finally we choose $r = 859$, so the elliptic curve is $E : y^2 = x^3 - 2249844424120487x$ whose generator is $(-17863200496/5041, -31868177440670324/357911)$, GCD $(-17863200496, 2619143683493) = 1299709$. We can recover that $N = 1299709 * 2015177$.

There is another experiment we do for factoring $N = 2619143683493$. We select r in $[1, 100000]$ randomly. After 39 times attempted, we can choose the suitable $r = 71867$. The elliptic curve is $E : y^2 = x^3 - 188229999101591431x$ whose generator is $(-93406186703/576, -70839905838862121/13824)$, GCD $(-93406186703, 2619143683493) = 1299709$. We can recover that $N = 1299709 * 2015177$.

Example 2. Suppose we want to factor $N = 7971410115793$, we select r in $[1, 100000]$ randomly, after 2 times attempted, we choose $r = 93760$, the elliptic curve is $E : y^2 = x^3 - 747399412456751680x$ whose generator is $(-5085043991/81, -4980359372925653/729)$, $GCD(7971410115793, 5085043991) = 2750159$. We can recover that $N = 2750159 * 2898527$.

References

1. Birch, B.J., Stephens, N.M.: The parity of the rank of the Mordell-Weil group. Topology **5**(4), 295–299 (1966)
2. Birch, B.J., Swinnerton-Dyer, H.: Notes on elliptic curves. II. J. Für Die Rne Und Angewandte Mathematik **1963**(212), 7–25 (1963)
3. Burhanuddin, I.A., Huang, M.: Factoring integers and computing elliptic curve rational points. Bsc Computer Science (2012)
4. Burhanuddin, I.A., Huang, M.: On the equation $y^2 = x^3 - pqx$. J. Numbers **2014**(193), 1–5 (2014)
5. Cohen, H.: Number Theory: Volume I: Tools and Diophantine Equations. Springer, New York (2008). https://doi.org/10.1007/978-0-387-49923-9
6. Cremona, J.: The elliptic curve database for conductors to 130000. In: International Algorithmic Number Theory Symposium (2006)
7. Dokchitser, T.: Notes on the parity conjecture. In: Elliptic Curves, Hilbert Modular Forms and Galois Deformations. Springer, Basel (2010). https://doi.org/10.1007/978-3-0348-0618-3_5
8. Kane, D.M., Thorne, J.A.: On the ϕ-selmer groups of the elliptic curves $y^2 = x^3 - dx$. Math. Proc. Cambridge Philos. Soc. **163**(01), 1–23 (2016)
9. Li, X.M., Zeng, J.X.: On the elliptic curve $y^2 = x^3 - 2rdx$ and factoring integers. Sci. China **2014**(04), 719–728 (2014)
10. Miller, R.L.: Proving the Birch and Swinnerton-Dyer conjecture for specific elliptic curves of analytic rank zero and one. LMS J. Comput. Math. (2013)
11. Pan, Z., Li, X.: Elliptic curve and integer factorization. In: International Conference on Information Security and Cryptology (2021)
12. Silverman, J.H.: The Arithmetic of Elliptic Curves. GTM, vol. 106. Springer, New York (2009). https://doi.org/10.1007/978-0-387-09494-6
13. Washington, L.C.: Elliptic Curves: Number Theory and Cryptography, 2nd edn. CRC Press, Inc. (2008)

Embedded Systems Security, Security in Hardware

Towards a Black-Box Security Evaluation Framework

Mosabbah Mushir Ahmed[2], Youssef Souissi[2], Oualid Trabelsi[2],
Sylvain Guilley[2,3], Antoine Bouvet[1(✉)], and Sofiane Takarabt[2,3]

[1] Secure-IC S.A.S., Z.A.C. des Champs Blancs, 35510 Cesson-Sévigné, France
antoine.bouvet@secure-ic.com
[2] Secure-IC S.A.S., Tour Montparnasse, 75015 Paris, France
{mosabbah.mushirahmed,youssef.souissi,oualid.trabelsi,sylvain.guilley,
sofiane.takarabt}@secure-ic.com
[3] Télécom Paris, 91120 Palaiseau, France
{sylvain.guilley,sofiane.takarabt}@telecom-paris.fr

Abstract. Injection of faults has been studied in various research works since last decades. Several hardware targets have been studied with respect to the efficiency of fault injections. In this paper we address the security evaluation of embedded systems in constrained environments called black-box analyses. This is not considered by standards of evaluation as they require conducting the analysis in the most relaxed conditions, often called white-box analysis which focuses on specific security modules provided that the finer details are available. However, black-box analysis has a much larger view by focusing on all the system as potential target. It is closer to a real world attacker. This allows measuring the impact of real attack scenarios, and therefore thinking and building the most adequate protections. We put forward a six steps evaluation methodology along with a practical use-case on a real end-user device. This shall give a better understanding and also an evaluation framework of black-box analysis.

Keywords: Security evaluation · Black-box analysis · Embedded systems · Physical attacks · Methodology · Laboryzr™ tool

1 Introduction

Today, security of user data is becoming worth more than devices. Therefore, the evaluation of any device holding and manipulating sensitive data is mandatory before being used. Fortunately, international standards exist as testing frameworks to assess the robustness of security modules. We cite the Common Criteria [4], FIPS 140 [12] and ISO 17825 [19]. Even better, more strict regulation has been recently put in place thanks to GDPR [3] that is a regulation in European Union law on data protection and privacy. The methodologies proposed

A. Bouvet—Security Science Factory (SSF) Sponsor at Secure-IC Rennes, and corresponding author of this cybersecurity research paper.

P. Stănică et al. (Eds.): ICSP 2021, CCIS 1497, pp. 79–92, 2021.
https://doi.org/10.1007/978-3-030-90553-8_6

for the security evaluation of the embedded systems are usually conducted in a white-box context through comfortable analysis conditions. This often requires the maximum of details about the target of evaluation. Those details range from technical specifications, architecture implementations or source codes, to conception schemes and more [8]. Moreover, the scope of the analysis view is limited to a target module that can be for instance a cryptographic library run by some CPU or a secure element run by hardware. In addition to this, a white-box analysis is usually run on testing boards that are well prepared and conditioned to get a direct access to the target module. This approach has limitations: indeed, disclosing all the details might raise a problem of trust between the provider and certifications laboratories (because the former should describe all the security features in a document called a Protection Profile). Moreover, a white-box analysis focuses on a small piece of the puzzle that is the whole system, called the scope of analysis. All the inputs and outputs of that scope are provided for evaluation independently from the rest of pieces. In fact, security might be broken at the frontier of the analysis scope. The perimeter of that scope is sometimes confusing and complex specifically when it comes to a combination of software, hardware with storage requirements. Furthermore, a white-box analysis does not aim at assessing the robustness of devices against reverse-engineering as the access to the target is by default not considered or it should be opened and well documented anyways.

Contributions. In this context, we propose to push upward a testing framework to assess the security of a system in its integrity. We expose the so-called black-box methodology that is followed by advanced attackers to harm end-user devices:

- **Testing framework.** In the first phase of this study we have analyzed a high-level description about various modes of targets in terms of their accessibility by an attacker.
- **Practical use-case.** The second phase of this study elaborates a practical use-case scenario that shows the experimentation setup, results and analysis from the experiments. These experiments are carried out to assess the security of a black-box target against physical attacks like fault injection.

Our goal is to shed light on the danger around this practical and powerful analysis mode, and to put forward a black-box testing framework for standardization purposes. Explaining the ways an experienced attacker behaves should help to design better protections. Besides, it should guide manufacturers in testing their final products.

Outline. The rest of the paper is organized as follows. In Sect. 2, we present the black-box approach along with the other analyses modes as white and grey-box respectively, as well as the electro-magnetic (EM) fault injection (EMFI) method. In Sect. 3, we go through a detailed description of our proposed testing framework. One related use-case on a real end-user device is presented and discussed in Sect. 4. Section 5 discusses advantages and limitations of the Black-box

(Bbox) evaluation evaluation methodology. Eventually, general conclusions are derived in Sec. 6.

2 Background

2.1 Security Evaluation Modes

A security testing allows to avoid cybersecurity-related incidents that cause a loss to an organization or individual. Its aim is to demonstrate the possible ways of penetrating into a system. We generally distinguish three main security testing modes, depending on the level of knowledge and access that is granted to the security tester:

- **White-box mode.** The analysis is conducted in the best conditions, with a full knowledge about the target. Every detail should be accessible and documented, including the specification, architecture and implementation of the target module along with the ways to communicate and query it. The inputs and outputs of the target are controlled, which allows to perform all the possible assessment tests [17]. This mode of analysis is often required by certification laboratories, when seeking a certification label according to one standard as Common Criteria or FIPS 140.
- **Grey-box mode.** The analysis is performed with some knowledge about the target. This situation happens for instance when a circuit provider wants to make his product evaluated by some labs without necessarily disclosing all the details [17] (*e.g.* implementation and countermeasures are kept secret).
- **Bbox mode.** The analysis is made with the minimum knowledge about the target. The underlying systems are usually hidden from the end-user or attacker. Generally, the black-box security mode is chosen for reverse-engineering purposes, or when the device manufacturer wants to measure the extent of a real attacker. Another situation is purely defensive, by exploring the device for any hidden backdoor, or robustness testing before deployment in a company with sensitive activity and high security conditions.
  Obviously, there is no standard explaining how to assess and conduct such analysis. Therefore, the black-box mode puts the evaluator in the worst and toughest analysis conditions, even if there is dedicated team, with complementary skills, involved in the analysis.

2.2 Electro-Magnetic Fault Injection Attacks

We choose for our experiments the EM interference fault injection [7]. Considered for Radio-Frequency (RF) applications, the design of an EM probe is highly related to the generated EM interference. Therefore, the EMFI setup is characterized by several properties: pulse intensity, spatial distribution, injection time, pulse width, polarity and amplitude, number of pulses, etc. All these parameters need to be considered for a successful fault injection.

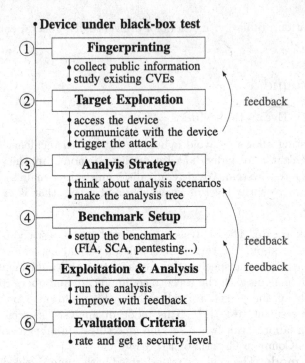

Fig. 1. Illustration of the proposed Bbox testing framework.

Many studies have been conducted to characterize embedded systems faulty behavior under EMFI [10,15,18]. Related results provide a clear evidence of the possibility to fault a system at the hardware or software level [6]. By the analysis of the fault model derived from the faulty behavior [15,18], recent works point out how the program flow of a running device can be disturbed (*i.e.* bypassing authentication process), and where the efficiency of countermeasures is to be reconsidered [9,21].

3   Proposed Testing Framework

It is clear that there is a need to elaborate the mechanisms with which a black-box mode of testing can be done. To accomplish so, we propose a black-box testing framework which consists of six main and generic steps, summarized in Fig. 1.

3.1   Fingerprinting

As the target is a Commercial Off-The-Shelf (COTS) device, the only input an attacker might have is the user product sheet. It is obvious that an attacker needs to find and explore more inputs. Publicly available information – documentation, datasheets, references and discussions available in the common and accessible web – are first explored. Advanced attackers might look at the deepest and darkest side of the web to extract non-public resources such as private datasheets or firmware specifications. Moreover, during this theoretical exploration phase, the attacker might check the existing Common Vulnerabilities and Exposures (CVEs), publicly available databases that disclose devices' vulnerabilities. This is a very important point as the goal of the attacker is to shorten the time-to-attack, involve affordable resources and perform the exploit in the more efficient way.

At this point, the attacker makes a synthesis of his knowledge about the target by trying to find answers. From the evaluator viewpoint, he should have the maximum possible knowledge that a best attacker can acquire during this phase:

- **Components enumeration.** Those are soldered on the target as CPUs, memories or System-on-Chip (SoC). In addition to this, the attacker shall be interested not only in the electrical part, but mechanical and maybe the optical parts should be considered too.
- **Information about components manufacturers.** This allows knowing about CPU's type, namely its frequency and architecture along with the internals of available memories, by having a precise exploration of their datasheets. A very basic example is to check the pads of a flash memory. This allows knowing the ground (GND) pad which itself is needed to identify the GND pad of the UART debugging port. After identifying all the UART pads, the debugging port will be used of course to access and interact with the target device. Other information can be the model of available MIPS or fingerprint sensors.
- **Availability of hardware or software sources.** Having the source code or even a binary form of it is always useful. Lets take for instance an Internet of Things (IoT) manufacturer that leaves the firmware of the main chip available on the Internet for upgrading purposes. This can be used by an attacker to reverse the code and explore sensitive information like user or even root passwords.
- **Existing vulnerabilities (CVEs).** The attacker often studies and explores the existing vulnerabilities looking for potential leakages. It is the shortest way to conduct an exploit. The CVEs are generally held in the public databases. That is different from zero-day vulnerabilities that exist but never made public. They can be intentionally created as backdoors by the manufacturer or its providers; or just a security flaw exploited by advanced attackers.
- **Possible security mechanisms.** The manufacturer might show some claims of security as certification labels which help the attacker to make a first view about implemented security. For instance, a FIPS 140 level-3 certification requires tamper resistant mechanisms as putting epoxy on the top of the circuit.

3.2 Target Exploration

The fingerprinting phase is complemented by a practical approach that is an active exploration. In other words, the attacker starts looking at how to access the device. For this purpose, several points can be addressed:

- **How to open the device?** Some devices do not present any difficulties, as for smart-cards of which the main circuit is totally exposed. In some other cases, only what an attacker has to do is to use a screwdriver to have a full access to the PCB board and all electronic components of the target like for hard drivers. In other situations, the target circuit is often hidden by a cooling fun system like for personal computers.
- **How to bypass anti-tamper protections?** More and more devices have anti-tamper mechanisms. It can be for instance a light sensor that detects that the device is opened; a coating (*e.g.* epoxy, acrylic or silicone) or encapsulation layer at the top of the SoC; a radiated sensor that detects an X-ray scanning or Focused Ions Beam (FIB) for probing, or also a fuse bit system for on-chip memories protection [1]. Another aspect can be a suicide kill activation process when the tamper action is detected.
- **How to communicate with the target?** Communication with the target can be time consuming as it might differ from one target to another. This depends on many factors as the availability of left debugging ports, the control of inputs and outputs (*e.g.* plaintexts and ciphertexts), the possibility to upload and download data from the device, or the number of possible iterations with the target before locking it. More precisely, the debugging ports such as JTAG and UART are considered as first option. Those ports are initially used for testing and verification purposes, but when left accessible after device production, then they would be exploited. With a UART port for instance, we can follow the boot process along with the interaction between the main process, the Flash and dynamic memories. Moreover, if not protected, then a root access might be obtained which allows a deeper penetration of the installed software. The JTAG could be more harmful as it allows a dynamic interaction with the processor and memory. For instance, with the JTAG, one may spy the internal registers, halt the processor and then dump a copy of the dynamic memory.
- **How to trigger the attack?** Irrespective of the targeted layer (hardware, software or network), triggering the attack consists in finding a short time window of opportunity to target some running sensitive process.

3.3 Analysis Strategy

After having properly gathered all the possible knowledge about the target, the evaluator starts thinking about an analysis strategy. The strategy is generally motivated by the attackers goals as finding a precise secret or getting an access with full privileges. It allows having a general picture with a top level view of the possible analysis paths and the time needed for each of them.

Basically, a strategy can be illustrated by a tree or a diagram. Whatever the illustration is, it should be complete by showing attack surfaces, each possible path and the analysis conditions. Obviously, there is no generic strategy. Actually, it depends on the device itself and the knowledge about it. Moreover, a full analysis strategy should address all the possible attacks. But this also depends on the experience and skills of the evaluator, that is why a dedicated team of evaluators with complementary skills is required.

3.4 Benchmark Setup

Performing a Bbox analysis is not an easy task which could be time consuming and expensive. Generally, the benchmark used for a Bbox analysis can mix between several platforms and tools as follows:

- **A Side-Channel Attack (SCA) platform.** SCA [14] allows the exploitation, during some sensitive running process like encryption or authentication, of a physical property such as the EM emanations, the power or current flows, or the acoustic waves. In fact, side-channel waves are able to disclose sensitive patterns directly related to the intermediate computations. More importantly, such attacks do not make brute force attacks on the entire secret, but split it and make assumptions on smaller chunks which is tricky and much more faster than a full brute force attack.
- **A Fault Injection Attack (FIA) platform.** Fault injections are powerful attacks that can be mounted easily. Their impact can be bypassing an authentication process, dumping a memory, secret key recovery, denial of service and more. A FIA is generally based on two phases: a fault injection phase and then an exploitation phase. The injection phase could be performed by several modes of injection as clock [13] or power [20] glitching, EM or Laser [16] injections. The exploitation phase often comes with statistical techniques to analyze the temporal and spatial location of the fault. Some techniques aim at recovering the secret key as Differential Fault Analysis (DFA) [5].
- **A scanning platform.** This platform aims at inspecting the PCB circuit looking for an abnormal manufacturing or behavior. Actually, a physical backdoor can be for example a tiny mounted surface component that is on the PCB to infiltrate connected devices [2]. For this purpose, techniques as thermal imaging, infra-red or X-ray can be used. Another aspect consists in scanning and analyzing the communication protocols with the target. Tools as spectrum analyzer or RF signals scanners might be used.
- **A pentesting platform.** This is useful especially to improve the target exploration phase as opening the device and accessing its components. It can be basically composed of a screwdriver kit, a heat gun, an optical microscope and a soldering material support. Pentesting is not a new topic. In fact, several tools exist in the literature as network sniffing, fuzzing, and data-bases testing. Moreover, we can find dedicated OS distributions to deal with security testing as Kali Linux or formerly Linux Backtrack. In addition to this, interfacing tools and boards might be needed to communicate with debugging ports as UART and JTAG.

3.5   Exploitation and Analysis

A full analysis strategy tree will allow the evaluator to gather all analysis paths including all possible attacks. Now the evaluator could run the analysis and improve it with a continuous feedback to the analysis strategy to precisely tune the exploitation benchmark. Analyzing a real device is not an easy task as the evaluator might play with several benchmarks and attacks in the same time. As a matter of fact, Fault Injection and Side-Channel Attacks can run hand in hand. Actually, a SCA can serve as signal trigger to activate the fault injection. The most commonly classes of analysis can be: scanning, probing, sniffing, fuzzing, web attacks, binary static and dynamic analyses, cache memory attacks, passwords recovery, malware analysis, SCA, FIA, unauthorized debugging and more.

3.6   Evaluation Criteria

After performing the exploitation and analysis phase, it is time to make a synthesis about the assessment results. As standards of evaluation, Common Criteria and FIPS 140, we propose to address a table to rate the black-box security level. As mentioned, we are interested in the whole system with all layers and not focusing on some parts or specific security modules. For this purpose, our framework comes with a rating table with a minimal list of evaluation actions. The more the number of successful actions is, the less the device is secure against black-box analysis. In fact, those phases allow gathering all the possible theoretical and practical actions to tamper with the device in a black-box context. The criteria table that we propose consists of four columns as follows:

1. **Bbox actions.** Defines the set of all possible actions and events in a Bbox analysis context. A minimal list can be addressed and that is common to most of embedded devices. The list can be extended depending on the fingerprinting, exploration and strategy phases.
2. **Tested (Te).** Is a rating column. Rate +1 if the test is performed successfully. It represents a high risk of exploitable leakage.
3. **Not tested (Nt).** Is a rating column. Rate +1 if the test is not performed but still theoretically and practically possible. It represents a potential exploitable leakage. It is likely to be successful in practice.
4. **Not possible (Np).** Is a rating column. Rate +1 if the test is not possible but still theoretically possible on similar devices. In other words a protection or countermeasure exists. It represents a low risk of exploitable leakage.

The way we propose to evaluate a device against Bbox attacks can be described by a generic table that covers most of possible Bbox actions. It can serve as a basis for the evaluation. However, the evaluator might refine the table by editing more or less actions depending on the three first phases of the methodology. We note that only theoretically possible actions are considered. For instance, if our target is standalone and does not have any connectivity with the outside world, then network attacks actions should not be considered by the evaluation table as they could not exist.

The Bbox testing framework criteria table is illustrated with real experiments in Sect. 4, Table 2.

4 Experiments on a Real Device: Door-Lock Unlock

We illustrate the discussion about the Bbox analysis with a practical use-case scenario. The proposed testing framework is used for assessing the security of a black-box target – namely, a smart Door-lock – against physical attacks like FIAs. Basically, the aim is to force the smart Door-lock to unlock without knowing the necessary Personal Identification Number (PIN) using EMFI. The obtained results highlight the possibility to break the security of a system without knowing the underlying features, structure or details of the system. Further, it validates the fact that EMFI is a potent technique against Bbox security also.

Fingerprinting. The knowledge of target's microcontroller has been accessed through the datasheet of the vendor. This assisted in estimating the type of software instructions that could be installed in the target. Establishing the knowledge of the existing setup, the further work has been made to determine if such targets are vulnerable to any type of implementation attacks such as fault injection.

Target Exploration. This phase is executed as part of the experimentation. Once the target details are determined, we physically access the target by removing the outer covering of the target without changing anything to the underlying hardware setup (or IC). More physical analysis details make it easier to inject faults at right spot over the microcontroller chip.

Analysis Strategy. This phase determines the strategy that is adopted in order to bypass the security mechanism of the Door-lock. For the implementation, we have regarded various types of attack scenarios which can be achieved with EMFI. Each scenario has been evaluated in terms of its ease of exploitation, repetition and effectiveness of the practical experimentation.

EMFI. The methodology of implementing the EMFI on the smart Door-lock depends upon the selection of the appropriate hardware setup and their parameters. The injection of faults through EM is based on coupling induction between the target and the injection source. The goal of the attack path is to bypass the checks so that any entered PIN is accepted as a valid one.

Fault Model. On microcontrollers primarily, fault injection is used to skip an assembly instruction set or subroutine calls. Moreover, in general a fault injection is useful in algorithm modification, by inducing safe errors, replacing or skipping instructions executed by the microcontroller [10,11]. As shown in Fig. 2, in order

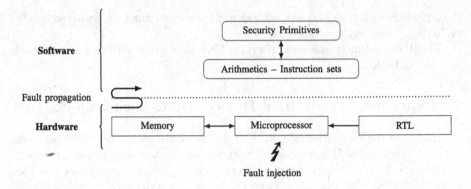

Fig. 2. Fault propagation between hardware and software layers.

to induce a fault into a Bbox setting it is very important to fix the fault model. The choice depends upon the attacker; he can induce the fault in either hardware or software flow. However, faults like EMFIs are induced in the hardware (bus, registers...), thus the faulty output propagates from the hardware to the software layer, and alters the execution of the instructions.

In order to bypass the authentication phase of the Door-lock PIN, a fault injection is required just after the PIN entry. It can cause the following effects:

– **Skipping instructions**, when an instructions comparison occurs;
– **Bit-flip** (*i.e.* 0 ⟶ 1, and vice-versa): if the entered value is wrong, it can still be coded as correct after the fault injection due to bits flipping.

Benchmark Setup. The setup for the attack has been developed with the EMFI setup (consisted of the equipments, tools, or softwares) effective in injecting the high powered EM signal that can disrupt the normal execution of the target. We have made some iterations in order to determine the best possible location of the probe over the target, or setting up of the target (undisturbed) by external disruptions.

To inject EM pulses, the basic hardware requirements are an EM pulse generator (including a RF amplifier and a delay generator), and probes. To perform the experimentation on the Door-lock provided as a Bbox, we have applied a gated pulse EM injection as a medium to disrupt the normal operation of the device (Fig. 3).

To operate an effective EM attack, we have removed the outer thick covering of the Door-lock such that we could gain good access to the microcontroller. No other modification has been made in the target.

Exploitation and Analysis. This phase determines how the faults injection strategy obtained can be exploited and improved upon. This part is performed experimentally by fine tuning the various parameters – such as the voltage level or the delay between the trigger and the injection – which are central to EMFI.

Fig. 3. Backside view of an opened doorlock (reference: SKY-001-RFPDA-Z) with an EM H-field probe.

For instance, the activation of the trigger is actually done by analyzing the chip activity through EM side-channel techniques.

During the preliminary experiments, some alterations have been observed in the functionality of the Door-lock. All of these may not be effective in bypassing its security feature but still can provide us with useful information about the potency of EMFI. Table 1 summarizes the results and thus highlights the robustness of the Bbox target against EMFI:

- **Crash.** The whole system crashes and the Door-lock beeps some alarms. A crash is not exploitable because it takes time to reset target.
- **Language setting access.** The attacker is able to change the language setting without accessing any vital functionality/software code.
- **Stop operation/Target freeze.** With the EM injection, the attacker can freeze the target that can result in causing the system to reset. Under this circumstance, the Door-lock can be left open until the system and access PIN is reset.
- **PIN bypass/Authentication failure.** Apart from these outcomes, on certain instances, we have been able to bypass the security completely, that is open the Door-lock with any PIN.

Evaluation Criteria. We have drawn the criteria Table 2 corresponding to our Door-lock unlock experiments. Since the percentage of high risk is about 36%, one-third of the time an attacker would be able to circumvent the security if the proposed approach is applied in a Bbox target.

The results obtained here validates the fact that EMFI can be useful or effective in breaking the security of a Bbox setup. Further, the basic security mechanisms of implementing PIN code are vulnerable to non-invasive fault attacks.

Table 1. Success rate and exploitability of fault injections on Door-lock.

Fault types	Exploitation	Frequency
Crash	Not exploitable (4 surfaces)	63%
Language setting access	Exploitable fault	5%
Stop operation/Target freeze	Exploitable fault	11%
PIN bypass/Authentication failure	Imperative fault	21%

Table 2. Door-lock black-box testing framework criteria table.

Bbox actions	Te	Nt	Np
Have one attack surface	+3 (3 surfaces)	–	–
Open the device	+1	–	–
Scanning	–	+1	–
Visually identify components	+1	–	–
Have one debug access	–	+1	–
Communicate with the device	–	+1	–
Get shell access	–	–	+1
Reverse operation sequence (e.g. boot process)	–	+1	–
Sniff the communication	–	+1	–
Fuzzing	–	–	+1
Control cryptographic I/O	–	–	+1
Find not public variables	–	+1	–
Exploit one CVE	–	+1	–
Extract the firmware binary	–	+1	–
Analyse the firmware binary	–	+1	–
Fault injection attacks	+1	–	–
Side-channel attacks	–	+1	–
Compromise authorization (user permission)	+1	–	–
Compromise integrity	+1	–	–
Brute force passwords	–	–	+1 (limited trials)
Bypass authentication	+1 (only for PIN)	–	+1 (fingerprint module)
Attacks combination	+1 (FIA + SCA)	–	–
Secret keys recovery	–	+1	–
Dumping memories	–	+1	–
Protocol attacks	–	+1 (on NFC)	–
Total	10	13	5
Percentage	36%	46%	18%

5   Discussion

Bbox security evaluations are obviously not enough to guarantee the security of a device against physical attacks, that is why we do recommend to perform both the usual white-box security evaluation, and the Bbox one following the framework introduced in this paper. Indeed the former method aims at assessing some known vulnerabilities on specific parts of a design, whereas the latter aims at reproducing a more realistic attack on the end-user device. In both cases, there are multiple analysis paths and all of them can not be followed: therefore evaluators have to make choices which obviously have an impact on the final evaluation reports.

6   Conclusion

This study has come with the first initiative to push upward an evaluation framework for end-user devices security testing. By contrast to Common Criteria, FIPS-140 and ISO standards that focus only on analysis performed in the best conditions, known also as white-box analysis, our framework deals with the whole system by considering all its layers and complexity. It is a high level security view of the target which matches with a real impact caused by a real attacker. Our testing framework comes with a six steps-based methodology along with a criteria rating of the security level. Moreover, we have illustrated our study with a real use-case on a real end-user device. This study is a starting point to consider and democratize Bbox analysis in a more elaborated evaluation context as the case for current standards.

References

1. Anti-tamper techniques. Elena Dubrova Royal Institute of Technology, Stockholm, Sweden. https://docplayer.net/79391807-Anti-tamper-techniques-elena-dubrova-royal-institute-of-technology-stockholm-sweden.html
2. The big hack. https://www.bloomberg.com/news/features/2018-10-04/the-big-hack-how-china-used-a-tiny-chip-to-infiltrate-america-s-top-companies
3. General Data Protection Regulation GDPR. https://gdpr-info.eu/
4. Common Criteria (2020). https://www.commoncriteriaportal.org/
5. Biham, E., Shamir, A.: Differential fault analysis of secret key cryptosystems. In: Kaliski, B.S. (ed.) CRYPTO 1997. LNCS, vol. 1294, pp. 513–525. Springer, Heidelberg (1997). https://doi.org/10.1007/BFb0052259
6. Dehbaoui, A., Dutertre, J., Robisson, B., Tria, A.: Electromagnetic transient faults injection on a hardware and a software implementations of AES. In: 2012 Workshop on Fault Diagnosis and Tolerance in Cryptography, pp. 7–15, September 2012
7. Dumont, M., Lisart, M., Maurine, P.: Electromagnetic fault injection: how faults occur. In: 2019 Workshop on Fault Diagnosis and Tolerance in Cryptography (FDTC), pp. 9–16 (2019)
8. Ehmer, M., Khan, F.: A comparative study of white box, black box and grey box testing techniques. Int. J. Adv. Comput. Sci. Appl. 3 (2012). https://doi.org/10.14569/IJACSA.2012.030603

9. Laurent, J., Beroulle, V., Deleuze, C., Pebay-Peyroula, F., Papadimitriou, A.: On the importance of analysing microarchitecture for accurate software fault models. In: 2018 21st Euromicro Conference on Digital System Design (DSD), pp. 561–564, August 2018

10. Moro, N., Dehbaoui, A., Heydemann, K., Robisson, B., Encrenaz, E.: Electromagnetic fault injection: towards a fault model on a 32-bit microcontroller. In: 2013 Workshop on Fault Diagnosis and Tolerance in Cryptography, pp. 77–88 (2013)

11. Moro, N., Dehbaoui, A., Heydemann, K., Robisson, B., Encrenaz, E.: Electromagnetic fault injection on microcontrollers. In: Chip-to-Cloud Security Forum 2013, Nice, France, September 2013. https://hal-emse.ccsd.cnrs.fr/emse-00871686

12. Morris, J.: Understanding FIPS 140–2 Validation (2000). https://csrc.nist.rip/nissc/2000/proceedings/papers/901slide.pdf

13. Ning, B., Liu, Q.: Modeling and efficiency analysis of clock glitch fault injection attack. In: 2018 Asian Hardware Oriented Security and Trust Symposium (AsianHOST), pp. 13–18 (2018)

14. Oswald, E., Mangard, S., Pramstaller, N., Rijmen, V.: A side-channel analysis resistant description of the AES S-box. In: Gilbert, H., Handschuh, H. (eds.) FSE 2005. LNCS, vol. 3557, pp. 413–423. Springer, Heidelberg (2005). https://doi.org/10.1007/11502760_28

15. Proy, J., Heydemann, K., Berzati, A., Majéric, F., Cohen, A.: A first ISA-level characterization of EM pulse effects on superscalar microarchitectures: a secure software perspective. In: Proceedings of the 14th International Conference on Availability, Reliability and Security, ARES 20D19, pp. 7:1–7:10 (2019)

16. Roscian, C., Dutertre, J., Tria, A.: Frontside laser fault injection on cryptosystems - application to the AES' last round. In: 2013 IEEE International Symposium on Hardware-Oriented Security and Trust (HOST), pp. 119–124 (2013)

17. Sasdrich, P., Moradi, A., Güneysu, T.: White-box cryptography in the gray box, pp. 185–203 (03 2016). https://doi.org/10.1007/978-3-662-52993-5_10

18. Trouchkine, T., Bouffard, G., Clédière, J.: Fault injection characterization on modern CPUs: from the ISA to the micro-architecture, pp. 123–138 (2019)

19. Whitnall, C., Oswald, E.: A critical analysis of ISO 17825 ('testing methods for the mitigation of non-invasive attack classes against cryptographic modules'). Cryptology ePrint Archive, Report 2019/1013 (2019). https://eprint.iacr.org/2019/1013

20. Yanci, A.G., Pickles, S., Arslan, T.: Characterization of a voltage glitch attack detector for secure devices. In: 2009 Symposium on Bio-Inspired Learning and Intelligent Systems for Security, pp. 91–96 (2009)

21. Yuce, B., Ghalaty, N.F., Santapuri, H., Deshpande, C., Patrick, C., Schaumont, P.: Software fault resistance is futile: effective single-glitch attacks. In: 2016 Workshop on Fault Diagnosis and Tolerance in Cryptography (FDTC), pp. 47–58, Aug 2016

Multi-source Fault Injection Detection Using Machine Learning and Sensor Fusion

Ritu-Ranjan Shrivastwa[1,2]([✉]) [iD], Sylvain Guilley[1,2], and Jean-Luc Danger[2]

[1] Secure-IC S.A.S., Rennes, France
{ritu-ranjan.shrivastwa,sylvain.guilley}@secure-ic.com
[2] LTCI, Télécom Paris, Institut Polytechnique de Paris, Paris, France
{ritu.shrivastwa,sylvain.guilley,jean-luc.danger}@telecom-paris.fr

Abstract. Fault attacks have raised serious concern with the growing amount of connected devices. Even a small vulnerability might compromise a complete network. It is therefore important to secure all the devices in the connected architecture. A solution to this problem is presented in this paper where we provide a hardware framework, called Smart Monitor, that utilizes a set of sensors (digital or physical) placed on the chip alongside the security target to be protected. The framework continuously monitors the status of the sensors and its Artificial Intelligence (AI) core produces two outputs viz. presence of a fault and type of detected perturbation. The types of attack sources can be electromagnetic, clock-glitch, laser, temperature, etc. In this work we utilize Electro-Magnetic (EM) and Clock-Glitch (CG) as sources of fault injections. Both attacks are performed in multiple settings to increase attack diversity. The framework is able to detect the presence of an attack with 92% accuracy for mixed or multiple attack sources, and further classify the type of perturbation with 78% accuracy keeping the false positive rate at 0%. Overall, this two-stage detection framework is a cost-effective countermeasure that can be deployed easily in any integrated circuit to safeguard against multiple fault attacks. The AI core is further evaluated for consistency in performance on hardware using High Level Synthesis (HLS), as a proof-of-concept, emulating real-world scenario.

Keywords: Internet of Things (IoT) · Artificial Intelligence (AI) · Machine Learning (ML) · Threat detection · Cyber-protection · Decision making process · Naive Bayes Classifier · Embedded security · Cyber-physical attacks · High-Level Synthesis (HLS)

1 Introduction

1.1 Motivation

The growth rate of connected devices is on a fast pace and soon the Internet-of-things might be as huge as the Internet itself. This draws massive attention,

© Springer Nature Switzerland AG 2021
P. Stănică et al. (Eds.): ICSP 2021, CCIS 1497, pp. 93–107, 2021.
https://doi.org/10.1007/978-3-030-90553-8_7

in terms of security, towards all the devices that form the nodes of this network including the end-devices. The breach can be made through these nodes via active or passive attacks [26]. Passive attacks include Side-Channel Attacks (SCA) that is well researched, to break even the complex cryptosystems, where mostly the device vulnerabilities are exploited to obtain the security parameters [24]. Active (fault) injections like laser, EM, CG, etc. can be performed to disrupt the normal functions of the device and eventually forcing the system to malfunction in order to bypass security [8,11]. Precise attacks can be made to execute targeted operations inside the chips, like skip or replace instructions, to perform undesired operations [9]. In this paper we focus on the active attacks and provide a countermeasure that is able to detect multiple such attacks. In other words, a single solution to detect fault injection attacks from multiple sources on the same target.

1.2   Our Contribution

We present a two-stage detection framework to detect active fault attacks. This Machine Learning (ML) based system is able to detect the presence of multiple types of attack. The first stage reports the presence of an attack and the next stage predicts its type. ElectroMagnetic Fault Injection (EMFI) and Clock-Glitch Fault Injection (CGFI) are performed on a chip that runs a standard encryption algorithm. The same chip is also mounted with precise digital sensors (DS) that are the core components used for the detection. The ML based controller, called Smart Monitor, continuously monitors the statuses of the sensors and generates two outputs viz. attack status and perturbation type. In this work we utilize two attack sources, however, other sources can be added to the same framework. We validate the design using HLS by performing benchmark testing with the test vectors used to derive the classification results at the software level.

The rest of the paper is organized as follows: Sect. 2 provides a background of Fault Injection attacks and Machine Learning, Sect. 3 presents the entire framework structure and HLS evaluation with hardware performance and utilization, Sect. 4 provides the results of various stages of detection, and conclusion in Sect. 5.

2   Background

2.1   Fault Injection Attacks

Fault Injection Attacks (FIA) have been around for quite some time and have been extensively used to cause glitches in the Integrated Circuits (IC) to eventually extract the secret parameters or cause malfunction to the system. One of the early fault analysis was done in [3]. Several vulnerabilities exposed due to fault attacks have been reported along with their countermeasures like in [2] and [4]. A new class of fault attack was introduced in 2017 by Tang et al. in [23], known as CLKSCREW, where they exposed the vulnerabilities of the energy management mechanisms, basically the Dynamic Voltage and Frequency Scaling (DVFS), to break security without the need for physical access to the devices or any equipment to inject fault by overclocking at the software level in ARM processors thereby compromising the Trusted Execution Environment (TEE). More recent attacks, targeting the DVFS, have been proposed such as Plundervolt [15] and VoltJockey [17]. In [7] the authors illustrate the use of Laser fault injection ease the process of syndrome decoding of code-based public-key cryptosystems. A background on Electromagnetic and Clock-Glitch fault injections, considered for this work, is detailed as follows.

Electromagnetic based EMFI has several implications in retrieving secret data using fault analysis. There have also been works to tamper the control flow of a program by causing instructions skip [18] with high precision. Another detailed study of EMFI impact on Instruction Set Architecture (ISA) was done in [16]. A recent work on the effect of data transfer due to EMFI was done in [12] with a byte-level precision.

Clock-Glitch based CGFI is relatively easier to perform as compared to EMFI. The technique can be in temporarily increasing the clock frequency to either cause some flip-flops to sample their inputs before the new state is reached [1] or reduce the processor's time to write a jump address and prevent the branch execution [14].

2.2 Detecting Fault Attacks with Machine Learning

The use of Machine Learning (ML) in the security domain is relatively new. Major works have been done in the Side Channel Analysis [10,22,25]. In [20], the authors provide a ML-assisted technique to explore and characterize the fault attack space and use the knowledge of a known fault attack on a cipher in understanding new attack instances. Regarding detection of fault attacks, a recent work [19] is presented that evaluates fault induced leakages from non-cryptographic peripheral components of a security module, targeting cipher implementations, using a Deep Neural Network (DNN) test. From the defensive side, while most fault analyses are based on the characterized faults from known attacks (like [6]), our work is based on a completely different approach of online identification of attacks using real-time sensors. To the best of the knowledge of the authors, our work is the premiere in providing a hardware based framework to dynamically detect FIA from multiple sources.

3 Proposed Methodology and Design Idea

3.1 Digital Sensor

Digital Sensor (DS) is a light weight delay chain unit that can be placed anywhere on the chip fabric. The DSs have delay chains longer than the critical path and thereby detecting delay faults before they affect the user logic [21] (Fig. 14, page 189). The Digital Sensor is designed to detect various FIAs, such as clock glitch, power glitch, underfeeding, heating, laser attack and electromagnetic. A DS converts all observed stresses into a timing stress for measurement. It is extremely sensitive to variations in temperature and voltage as well as to internal activities of the Device-Under-Test (DUT) which makes it a generic sensor that can detect multiple perturbation types. For a UMC design kit with 28 nm HPC (High Performance Computing), with a frequency of 100 MHz, each Digital Sensor is 2.93 kGE (kilo Gate Equivalent), which means 730 μm^2 for this technology node.

3.2   Smart Monitor

Smart Monitor (SM) is a customizable framework that utilizes a fleet of DSs (aggregating their values) along with the capability of having other physical precision sensors attached to it to analyze and synthesize appropriate outcome. The core of the SM is an AI engine that accumulates all the statuses and evaluates them to produce a meaningful response. We call this method of using all sensor data Sensor Aggregation strategy (see Fig. 1).

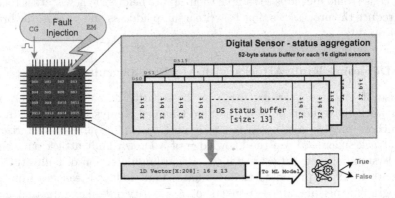

Fig. 1. Illustration of data acquisition from multiple sensors (sensor aggregation) for EM and CG fault injections and their formatting for ML algorithms

Sensor aggregation is important to prevent single DS saturation, a condition in which all the status bits are true/high, which cannot determine the difference between the sources of attacks i.e. the perturbation type, since there is no resolution left to differentiate. Multiple sensors placed at different locations on the chip can have varied impacts based on the type of perturbation and, thus, produce different statuses that can contain information (features) of the attack type and can be easily learnt by the AI engine. This helps to classify among the types of attack using a ML classifier.

3.3 Dataset Information

The EM and CG fault injections are recorded with sixteen Digital Sensors placed inside a Sakura-G FPGA (Field Programmable Gate Array) board, running a standard AES algorithm. In each of the sessions for EM and CG data recording, for every setting, traces have been recorded for both the nominal (without injection) condition and the injected (with fault injection) condition.

A status buffer is associated with each DS. The buffer can store thirteen sensor values and works as a shifting queue i.e., every time (N cycles, depending upon the implementation) a new status is pushed on the top of the stack, the bottom status pops out. The EMFI is performed at four random locations on the chip surface.

A similar session has been carried for the CG fault injection trace acquisition with different CG parameters with varying delay between 379 nanoseconds (ns) to 511 ns with a pulse width of 5 ns, 8 ns and 1.5 ns.

3.4 Machine Learning Based Evaluation Using Two-Stage Detection Framework

Recall the motive of the evaluation, which is to identify if there is any fault injection being performed on the DUT. Conventionally, a single sensor (physical or digital) is enough to detect any kind of unusual activity inside the chip like in [5] and [13] and produce acceptable accuracy. However, most works have been conducted on single type of Fault Injection scenarios (like EMFI) and the detection algorithm relies upon statistical and mathematical models. In this work, we propose a generic framework that is capable of taking multiple types of fault injection scenarios as inputs and deduce whether the DUT is in nominal condition or it is experiencing a fault injection attack attempt. Since the problem reduces to classification of the state of the DUT, it can easily be modelled on a ML classification algorithm. The core engine of the framework is, thus, based on ML algorithms that are trained with example scenarios of nominal and attack conditions.

Another extended aspect of the proposed framework is in its capability of predicting the type of attack. The modalities of operation of the two-stage detection framework can be understood from the simple illustration in Fig. 2. The first stage is responsible for detecting the presence of an attack and the second stage is responsible for detecting the type of the attack. This splitting of the functionality in two stages keeps the ML models in binary detection mode[1] which in turn speeds up the process of injection detection to make the system more responsive and also gives the user flexibility to disregard the second stage if not required.

---

[1] The output classes in second stage will be same as the expected number of attack sources i.e. multi-class classification scenario. However, in our case since we are utilizing only EMFI and CGFI sources, the second stage can also be served by a binary classifier.

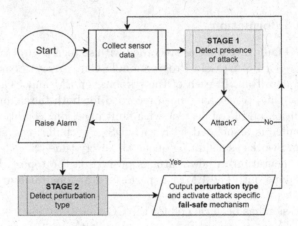

Fig. 2. Proposed framework's modalities of operation. A high level control and data flow diagram of the multi-sourced attack detection with two-stage detector results.

ML Classification Algorithms. The choice of ML classifiers is kept to a minimalistic model to enhance latency of detection while maintaining lower footprint on the silicon fabric for the interests of space and power. The popular binary classifier for Gaussian data is the Gaussian Naive Bayes Classifier (GNBC). Given that the sensor data has limited features and does not require non-linear ML algorithms to form a separation, we proceed with the idea that linear models such as GNBC and Logistic regression classifier (LRC) might be able to produce acceptable accuracy. To verify this idea, we perform classification over two linear and two non-linear ML models. Among the non-linear models we choose the popular Support Vector Machines (SVM) and a simple Multi-Layered Perceptron (MLP) neural network.

Modes of Evaluation of FIA. To describe the detection capabilities (with scores) of the ML models with the EM and CG fault injection datasets, multiple modes of evaluation are performed. Primarily, the classifier should be able to differentiate between nominal and injection classes (labelled as: 0 and 1 respectively). Additionally, the model should be able to detect the source of attack based on selected features from the training datasets. Since the sensors currently used have status saturation directly proportional to the strength of the attack, the problem of classifying the type of attack becomes harder. This is due to the fact that at highest saturation levels of the sensors, it becomes difficult to differentiate between the types of attack. This is why we resort to the sensor-aggregation strategy where multiple sensors are placed at different locations and, even though some sensors might be saturated, some sensors might not be. However, there may be a case where even all the sensors get fully saturated, diminishing the class difference boundary of the attack sources which results in predicting wrong classes.

Therefore, we propose the sensor aggregation strategy where we place multiple (in our case 16) sensors across the entire chip. The placement of the sensors is left upon the discretion of the embedded developer since the critical boundary can vary from device to device. The sensors are placed randomly on the chip such as to receive more general statuses and not to localise the sensors to a particular area on the chip. The status values of the 16 DSs in nominal, clock-glitch fault injection and electro-magnetic fault injection case is presented in Fig. 3. Please note that each sensor has a buffer depth of 13 which is represented in the x-axis for all the 16 DSs.

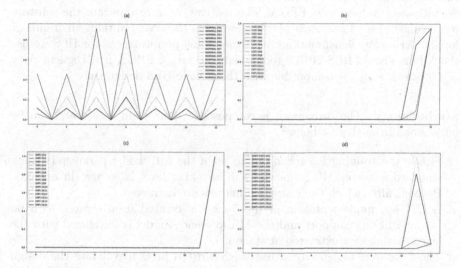

Fig. 3. Comparison between states of 16 DSs for nominal as well CGFI and EMFI cases. The x-axis is the status buffer for each DS. (a) represents the nominal state of the DSs when no injection is performed, (b) represents the state of the DSs when CGFI is performed, (c) represents the state of the DSs when EMFI is performed, and (d) represents the difference in values of the DSs from CGFI and EMFI cases. It can be seen that some DSs behave similarly in both EMFI and CGFI cases (for example DS12). In case of one DS based system, it would not have been possible to differentiate between the type of attack. Therefore, sensor aggregartion provides more features which can be utilized by a classification algorithm to differentiate between the type of attack.

The classification task is divided into four parts, as mentioned below, and each of them is inferred separately over the same ML models.

 i. Detection of EMFI by performing binary classification between nominal and injected classes of EMFI dataset
ii. Detection of CGFI by performing binary classification between nominal and injected classes of CGFI dataset

iii. Combining the FI datasets of both EMFI and CGFI and classification between the combined FI datasets and nominal dataset from both EMFI and CGFI sessions

iv. Classification between EMFI and CGFI datasets to detect the perturbation type (by combining both FI datasets and classifying between them)

3.5 Hardware Testing of the Design Using HLS

The performance of the design is validated on hardware. To achieve this, the authors utilize the HLS methodology for a quick design evaluation with real digital sensor values on a FPGA. The motivation is to replicate the software results on the target hardware platform, which is the actual working environment for the design, by benchmarking with the offline performance. For HLS we use the Xilinx Vivado HLS 2019.2 tool where the target FPGA is a Digilent Arty S7-50 board, which is compatible with the Vivado HLS design suite.

Methodology. The framework is composed of four main stages and can be understood from the list below:

i Firstly the training is carried out to train the ML model parameters using standard software ML frameworks in any high level language (in our case Python) after which the learnt parameters are extracted.

ii A C/C++ implementation of the design is created from scratch with no external library support and the ML inference model is initialized with the learnt parameters extracted at stage **i**.

iii The C source, along with a testbench written in C to validate the design performance at simulation level, is used to perform HLS using Vivado HLS design platform to generate RTL (Register Transfer Level) without any additional optimization, such as the usage of HLS pragmas, other than the ones already integrated in the design flow, thereby having no control upon the generated HDL (Hardware Description Language) code structure.

iv The generated RTL is packed into an IP and imported in the Vivado HLX suite where a controller program is written in Verilog to interface with the IP. Real DS test dataset for the ML IP is stored in a RAM block which is used by the controller program to segment and test the IP for classification accuracy (please see Fig. 4).

Experimental Setup. The setup is simply composed of a computer connected to the target FPGA board. The target board, Digilent Arty S7-50, is a Vivado compatible FPGA board. The design is run at a clock-cycle of 10 nanoseconds (ns) with on-board clock running at 100 MHz frequency. Other features of the FPGA include 52,160 logic cells, 8,150 slices, 65,200 Flip-Flops, 2,700 Kbits of Block RAM, and 120 DSP slices.

Hardware Performance. The test dataset (test vectors) used to validate the classification accuracy of the ML IP created using HLS is same as used at the software level in the ML testing phase. Upon evaluation, the classification capability remains unaltered at the hardware level. The resource utilization report for the current HLS implementation is shown in Table 1.

Table 1. Post-implementation resource utilization of the FPGA for the whole design including the controller module and test data

Resource	Utilization	Available	Utilization (%)
LUT	8898	32600	27.29
LUTRAM	266	9600	2.77
FF	8478	65200	13.00
BRAM	1.50	75	2.00
DSP	43	120	35.83
IO	6	210	2.86
BUFG	1	32	3.13

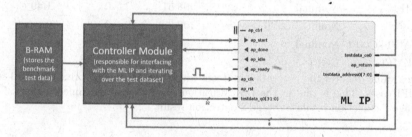

Fig. 4. High level block diagram of the test setup with a controller module interfacing the ML HLS IP with the benchmark test data stored in a B-RAM

Each DS consumes ≅ 400 LUT slices. In this design we chose the minimum number of DSs required to achieve sensor aggregation and improved accuracy fo the classification. We use 16 DSs which is approximately 6400 LUT slices. The SM consumes 8898 LUT slices which is 39% greater than the total consumption of all the deployed DSs. However, it is to note that the SM design is not optimized and an optimized design can be similar in area of the total number of DSs deployed. In terms of throughput, the total number of cycles required to perform sensor aggregation and one classification, with a DS buffer length of 13 statuses, is 38275 cycles. It is the first time an online integrable sensor aggregation strategy and ML based classification for fault injection detection is showcased.

The FPGA test is performed to justify the use-case and establish a proof of concept. However, the next task would be to optimize the HLS output such that the footprint on the hardware fabric is further reduced and throughput is enhanced.

4   Results

In this section we present all the results of the four classification categories at the software level. Table 2 shows the accuracy percentages of the various classifications performed. Since all the classifications are binary, two datasets are used for all cases. The attack diversity column of the table refers to the different conditions in which the data were recorded viz. four chip locations for EMFI and two different conditions for CGFI. If both the datasets are used for either classification from nominal condition or between both the attack conditions, the diversity is indicated as 6. For classification between the types of perturbation the DS saturation leads to class overlapping and, thus, the ML model tends to predict incorrect classes.

Table 2. Detection accuracy of the best performing ML model in various classification tasks

Classification between		Attack diversity	Detection accuracy (%)		
Data A	Data B		True detection	False pos.	False neg.
EMFI	Nominal	4	98.51	0	1.49
CGFI	Nominal	2	100.00	0	0
*EMFI+CGFI	Nominal	6	91.98	0	8.02
**EMFI	CGFI	6	77.25	22.74†	0

†This value denotes the percentage of tests where the ML model predicts CGFI for EMFI cases. This is due to the DS saturation phenomenon explained in Sect. 3.4. *Stage 1 detection result, **Stage 2 detection result

The evaluation is extended to compare the ML based methods with the classical sensor threshold based method where a sensor is tuned to set a threshold value that defines the class boundary. The disadvantage of this method is in choosing the threshold value, which is often chosen empirically over multiple test cases, therefore leading to non-generic coarse-tuned setting which may fail due to lack of sufficient test cases. To overcome this, we train the threshold for each individual DS and use the collective result to predict the class i.e. if ≥ 8 (half of total number of sensors involved) DSs predict positive, the result is taken as FI, else nominal. The result comparison and gain of ML method over classical threshold based method is provided in the following subsections.

4.1   Threshold Optimization of Every DS

To optimize the thresholds for each DS, the buffer data (13×4 bytes) is converted to an average form as shown below in Eq. 1, where X is the input vector (of size 13) and X' is the vector obtained after the averaging process:

$$\forall i \in \{0, 1, ..., 12\} \text{ and,}$$
$$X = \{V_i\} \text{ and } X' = \{V_i'\}, \text{ where,} \tag{1}$$
$$V_i' = V_i \text{ if } i = 0, \text{ else } V_i' = (V_i + V_{i-1})/2.$$

Thereafter the bounds (Lower/Upper for class Zero/One) of both the classes (0: Non-injection/Nominal, 1: Injection) are calculated by running a linear search over 80% (similar to training set ratio in ML methods) of the dataset. These bounds are used as threshold for the test set to detect FI states.

4.2   Classification Between EMFI and Nominal Condition

The EMFI is performed with a very low power. The aggregated sensor method enables high precision detection of FI. The detection performance of all the ML models is shown in Table 3 along with a comparison with the classical threshold based method. The accuracy fluctuation between the different datasets corresponds to the DSs' behavior based on the locality of EMFI.

4.3   Classification Between CGFI and Nominal Condition

The best performing ML model (GNBC: see Table 3) is chosen for further evaluation to maintain symmetry along all the evaluations. Similar comparison of performance between the ML and Threshold method, shown in Table 4, is made for the CGFI datasets. The ML method produces 100% accurate predictions over the test dataset since the FI case produces nearly full saturation in the DSs' statuses.

Table 3. Detection accuracy of different ML models over the EMFI datasets. (EM1–EM4 correspond to the different recording sessions with varying injection location on the XY plane of the DUT). (Note: All values in the table are in %)

Dataset	ML models				Threshold
	MLP	SVM	LRC	GNBC	
EM1	94.75	92.25	81.50	97.50	60.92
EM2	95.71	92.93	88.64	97.98	81.17
EM3	98.90	98.90	90.63	99.72	91.23
EM4	100.00	100.00	100.00	100.00	100.00
Combined (EM1–EM4)	96.25	96.18	88.49	**98.51**	82.82

4.4   Classification Between Combined EMFI and CGFI Against Nominal Condition

In this case the attack datasets from both EMFI and CGFI sessions are combined to form the attack class. Similarly, the nominal class is also created for training/inference of the binary classifiers. The evaluation is also performed with the

Table 4. Detection accuracy comparison of CGFI between ML and Threshold methods over CGFI datasets

Dataset	Detection accuracy (%)	
	ML (GNBC)	Threshold
CG1	100	98.64
CG2	100	99.27
CG1&CG2 combined	100	98.24

threshold method and the results are compared as shown in Table 5. The combination of diverse datasets increases the linear classification complexity manifold which can be observed from the performances of the ML and Threshold models over the hybrid datasets.

Table 5. Detection accuracy of FI from nominal case with combined EMFI and CGFI attack case. (The EMFI and CGFI columns contain results of combined dataset of all sessions)

Method	Classification accuracy (%) of nominal dataset from		
	EMFI	CGFI	EMFI+CGFI
ML (GNBC)	98.51	100	91.98
Threshold	82.82	98.24	89.36

4.5 Classification Based on Attack Type Between EMFI and CGFI

Finally, for perturbation detection, the results are presented in Table 6. It is important to note that this classification is performed with just the attack case (injection datasets only) and the DSs, as mentioned earlier, have linear saturation directly proportional to attack strength. Thus, in the attack dataset with the two classes being CGFI and EMFI, the difference is minimal where the linear classifiers tend to fail in precisely optimizing the separation plane.

Table 6. Accuracy comparison of perturbation detection between EMFI and CGFI of ML and Threshold methods

Method	Values in %		
	Accuracy	False pos.	False neg.
ML (GNBC)	77.25	22.75	0
Threshold	39.61	0	60.39

5   Conclusion

In this work we introduce a two-stage fault injection detection framework for EMFI and CGFI while opening doors to more attack sources. Furthermore, we provide analysis of fault detection for individual attacks of EM and CG while comparing the ML based model with a classic threshold based method where the threshold is trained instead of manually choosing a value. The ML model is evaluated on a FPGA with benchmark testing, using the same test dataset from the software evaluation, to record the classification accuracy of the ML model on hardware. The ML model performs very well in detecting individual attacks with accuracies of 98.51% and 100.00% for EMFI and CGFI respectively, and 92% in detecting both CGFI and EMFI combined. Furthermore, to detect the perturbation type, classification is performed between CGFI and EMFI fault dataset only with 77.25% detection accuracy. We finally combine all the methods to form a two-stage FI detector where the stage one predicts the existence of an attack when the DSs input can either be nominal, EMFI or CGFI. The second stage is enabled if the first stage detects an attack and, thus, it predicts the perturbation type.

References

1. Bar-El, H., Choukri, H., Naccache, D., Tunstall, M., Whelan, C.: The sorcerer's apprentice guide to fault attacks. Proc. IEEE **94**(2), 370–382 (2006)
2. Barthe, G., Dupressoir, F., Fouque, P.A., Grégoire, B., Zapalowicz, J.C.: Synthesis of fault attacks on cryptographic implementations. In: Proceedings of the 2014 ACM SIGSAC Conference on Computer and Communications Security, pp. 1016–1027. ACM (2014)
3. Biham, E., Shamir, A.: Differential fault analysis of secret key cryptosystems. In: Kaliski, B.S. (ed.) CRYPTO 1997. LNCS, vol. 1294, pp. 513–525. Springer, Heidelberg (1997). https://doi.org/10.1007/BFb0052259
4. Boneh, D., DeMillo, R.A., Lipton, R.J.: On the importance of checking cryptographic protocols for faults. In: Fumy, W. (ed.) EUROCRYPT 1997. LNCS, vol. 1233, pp. 37–51. Springer, Heidelberg (1997). https://doi.org/10.1007/3-540-69053-0_4
5. Breier, J., Bhasin, S., He, W.: An electromagnetic fault injection sensor using Hogge phase-detector. In: 2017 18th International Symposium on Quality Electronic Design (ISQED), pp. 307–312, March 2017
6. Breier, J., Hou, X., Bhasin, S. (eds.): Automated Methods in Cryptographic Fault Analysis. Springer, Cham (2019). https://doi.org/10.1007/978-3-030-11333-9
7. Cayrel, P.-L., Colombier, B., Drăgoi, V.-F., Menu, A., Bossuet, L.: Message-recovery laser fault injection attack on the *Classic McEliece* cryptosystem. In: Canteaut, A., Standaert, F.-X. (eds.) EUROCRYPT 2021. LNCS, vol. 12697, pp. 438–467. Springer, Cham (2021). https://doi.org/10.1007/978-3-030-77886-6_15
8. Claudepierre, L., Péneau, P.Y., Hardy, D., Rohou, E.: TRAITOR: a low-cost evaluation platform for multifault injection. In: ASIACCS 2021–16th ACM ASIA Conference on Computer and Communications Security, pp. 1–6. ACM, Virtual Event Hong Kong, Hong Kong SAR China, June 2021

9. Dottax, E., Giraud, C., Rivain, M., Sierra, Y.: On second-order fault analysis resistance for CRT-RSA implementations. In: Markowitch, O., Bilas, A., Hoepman, J.-H., Mitchell, C.J., Quisquater, J.-J. (eds.) WISTP 2009. LNCS, vol. 5746, pp. 68–83. Springer, Heidelberg (2009). https://doi.org/10.1007/978-3-642-03944-7_6
10. Hospodar, G., Gierlichs, B., De Mulder, E., Verbauwhede, I., Vandewalle, J.: Machine learning in side-channel analysis: a first study. J. Cryptogr. Eng. **1**(4), 293 (2011)
11. Joye, M., Tunstall, M.: Fault Analysis in Cryptography, vol. 147. Springer, Heidelberg (2012). https://doi.org/10.1007/978-3-642-29656-7
12. Menu, A., Bhasin, S., Dutertre, J.M., Rigaud, J.B., Danger, J.L.: Precise spatio-temporal electromagnetic fault injections on data transfers. In: 2019 Workshop on Fault Diagnosis and Tolerance in Cryptography (FDTC), pp. 1–8. IEEE (2019)
13. Miura, N., et al.: PLL to the rescue: a novel EM fault countermeasure. In: 2016 53nd ACM/EDAC/IEEE Design Automation Conference (DAC), pp. 1–6, June 2016
14. Moore, S.W., Anderson, R.J., Kuhn, M.G.: Improving smartcard security using self-timed circuit technology. In: Fourth ACiD-WG Workshop, Grenoble (2000)
15. Murdock, K., Oswald, D., Garcia, F.D., Van Bulck, J., Gruss, D., Piessens, F.: Plundervolt: software-based fault injection attacks against intel SGX. In: Proceedings of the 41st IEEE Symposium on Security and Privacy (S&P 2020) (2020)
16. Proy, J., Heydemann, K., Majéric, F., Cohen, A., Berzati, A.: Studying EM pulse effects on superscalar microarchitectures at ISA level. arXiv preprint arXiv:1903.02623 (2019)
17. Qiu, P., Wang, D., Lyu, Y., Qu, G.: VoltJockey: breaching TrustZone by software-controlled voltage manipulation over multi-core frequencies. In: Proceedings of the 2019 ACM SIGSAC Conference on Computer and Communications Security, pp. 195–209 (2019)
18. Riviere, L., Najm, Z., Rauzy, P., Danger, J.L., Bringer, J., Sauvage, L.: High precision fault injections on the instruction cache of ARMv7-M architectures. In: 2015 IEEE International Symposium on Hardware Oriented Security and Trust (HOST), pp. 62–67. IEEE (2015)
19. Saha, S., Alam, M., Bag, A., Mukhopadhyay, D., Dasgupta, P.: Leakage assessment in fault attacks: a deep learning perspective. Cryptology ePrint Archive, Report 2020/306 (2020). https://ia.cr/2020/306
20. Saha, S., Jap, D., Patranabis, S., Mukhopadhyay, D., Bhasin, S., Dasgupta, P.: Automatic characterization of exploitable faults: a machine learning approach. IEEE Trans. Inf. Forensics Secur. **14**(4), 954–968 (2018)
21. Selmane, N., Bhasin, S., Guilley, S., Danger, J.L.: Security evaluation of application-specific integrated circuits and field programmable gate arrays against setup time violation attacks. IET Inf. Secur. **5**(4), 181–190 (2011)
22. Swaminathan, S., Chmielewski, L., Perin, G., Picek, S.: Deep learning-based side-channel analysis against AES inner rounds. IACR Cryptol. ePrint Arch 2021, 981 (2021)
23. Tang, A., Sethumadhavan, S., Stolfo, S.: {CLKSCREW}: exposing the perils of security-oblivious energy management. In: 26th {USENIX} Security Symposium ({USENIX} Security 2017), pp. 1057–1074 (2017)
24. Taouil, M., Aljuffri, A., Hamdioui, S.: Power side channel attacks: where are we standing? In: 2021 16th International Conference on Design & Technology of Integrated Systems in Nanoscale Era (DTIS), pp. 1–6. IEEE (2021)

25. Zaid, G., Bossuet, L., Dassance, F., Habrard, A., Venelli, A.: Ranking loss: maximizing the success rate in deep learning side-channel analysis. IACR Trans. Cryptogr. Hardw. Embed. Syst. 25–55 (2021)
26. Zankl, A., Seuschek, H., Irazoqui, G., Gulmezoglu, B.: Side-channel attacks in the internet of things. In: Research Anthology on Artificial Intelligence Applications in Security, pp. 2058–2090. IGI Global (2021)

Authentication, Key Management, Public Key (Asymmetric) Techniques, Information-Theoretic Techniques

Secure Multi-Party Computation Using Pre-distributed Information from an Initializer

Amirreza Hamidi$^{(\boxtimes)}$ and Hossein Ghodosi

James Cook University, Townsville, Australia
amirreza.hamidi@my.jcu.edu.au, hossein.ghodosi@jcu.edu.au

Abstract. Secure Multi-Party Computation (MPC) is a concept that includes a system of n participants communicating each other securely such that the participants want to compute any given function using their private inputs without giving any information about their inputs. The matter of computing a multiplication gate has raised a security concern. That is, because the multiplication gate rises the degree of the resulted polynomial while there is a limited number of required participants to reconstruct and compute the outcome. In this study, we propose a MPC protocol using a server or a remote computer as an initializer, which has become popular these days to conduct a probabilistic functionality in the circuit. The initializer does not get involved in the actual online computation and it can just share some random pre-computed information at any time prior to it. Our protocol needs only one round of online secret sharing, and the online computation of both the inputs addition and multiplication gates can be executed in parallel. The extension of our protocol can be used for the multiplication gates with different multiplicative depths (intermediate levels). The proposed protocol is information-theoretic secure against a coalition of t passive adversaries with the presence of at least $n \geq t + 1$ participants. The communication complexity of a multiplication gate is linear.

Keywords: Multi-party computations protocol · Pre-processed information · Information-theoretic security

1 Introduction

Secure Multi-Party Computation (MPC) has been a prominent area of research since it was introduced by Yao [23] in 1982. In this field, two or more parties, in a distributed system, want to collaborate and compute any given function using their private inputs without revealing any information about the inputs except what they can get from the actual output. It was first introduced for the case of two party computation [23,24] and, later, was extended to a system with n participants [18]. In the threshold MPC, t out of n parties are enough to compute any function using their inputs.

© Springer Nature Switzerland AG 2021
P. Stănică et al. (Eds.): ICSP 2021, CCIS 1497, pp. 111–122, 2021.
https://doi.org/10.1007/978-3-030-90553-8_8

Definition 1. *In a (t, n) threshold Multi-Party Computation, a set of t-out-of-n participants $P_1, \ldots, P_n$, with their private inputs $x_1, \ldots, x_n$, are able to compute any given function $f(x_1, \ldots, x_n)$ without revealing their inputs or any other information, except what the input holders can obtain from the actual outcome.*

The two major types of adversaries in any MPC system are semi-honest (passive) and malicious (active) adversaries. A passive adversary is a coalition of participants who follows the protocol but tries to learn more information about the inputs as much as possible. An active adversary is a coalition of the participants who can deviate from the protocol in an arbitrary fashion using the messages it shares to the protocol [15]. Note that considering a passive adversary is more realistic and may be assumed in many MPC settings. That is because recording the contents of some communication registers through standard activities while following the protocol is easier than deviating from the protocol [14]. Furthermore, a semi-honest participant more likely wants to obtain the correct outcome at the end of the protocol while learning more information about the honest participants' inputs. In terms of computational boundary assumptions, the MPC protocols are generally divided into two categories: computationally bounded and unbounded protocols [15]. The security of an unconditionally secure protocol is stronger as it doesn't depend on the assumptions of the computational intractability meaning that an adversary can have unlimited computing power and time [19].

Any secure MPC protocol must satisfy the security conditions *Correctness* and *Privacy*. *Correctness* means that the participants compute the correct outcome at the end of the protocol. *Privacy* is that an adversary learns no information about the inputs and the protocol, except what he can obtain from the computation outcome after running the protocol. It is analogous with the definition of zero-knowledge in cryptography [14]. Hence, the correctness condition of a protocol is preserved in the presence of passive adversaries; however, the protocol must hold a level of privacy condition against a number of maximum passive adversaries. This defines the security level of a MPC protocol with n participants, where there is a maximum number (t) out of the participants that can be corrupted by a passive adversary while the privacy of the honest participants and the actual protocol outcome is preserved [13]. These protocols which tolerate up to t passive adversaries are called t *private*.

Definition 2. *A MPC protocol is t-private, if any subset of up to t passive adversaries in the protocol cannot gain any information about the private inputs of honest participants and the actual outcome after running the protocol.*

1.1 Background

Secure MPC has been a prominent subject of research by many studies. After the introduction of the secure two-party computation by [23], a computationally bounded protocol [18] extended it to n- party computation with a major set

of honest participants $n \geq 2t + 1$. The case of online computing a share of
two or more inputs addition can be conducted using linear feature of secret
sharing with no interaction [5]. Furthermore, multiplying an input by a constant
number is another form of the addition. However, a problem arises when n
parties want to compute a share of a inputs multiplication gate by employing
secret sharing as it decreases the security level. Let P_i and P_j $(1 \leq i,j \leq n,$
$i \neq j)$ distribute their inputs, x_i and x_j, to n participants using the polynomials
$g(x)$ and $h(x)$, respectively, of degree t where $n \leq 2t$. To compute a share of their
multiplication $f(x_i, x_j) = x_i \times x_j$ which is the constant term of the polynomial
$f(x) = g(x) \times h(x)$, each participant P_k calculates the new share $f_k = g_k \times h_k$
where g_k and h_k are his corresponding shares such that $g_k = g(k)$ and $h_k = h(k)$. Thus, the new polynomial $f(x)$ is of degree $2t$ while, based on Lagrange
interpolation, a number of at least $2t + 1$ parties are required to reconstruct the
outcome which is beyond the security threshold condition. Moreover, the free
coefficients of the resulted polynomial $f(x)$ are not random which contradicts
the information-theoretic security definition [4].

Some methods have been proposed to deal with this problem. degree reduction methods were presented by [4,8]. [4] conducted the first information-
theoretic secure study of using verifiable secret sharing in a MPC system including $n \geq 3t + 1$ players and the major honest participants with zero probability
of errors. [12] and, later, [16] suggested another method for reducing degree of
a polynomial using linear feature of secret sharing to redistribute new shares of
the truncated polynomial such that the new shares result the same old secret.
Beaver proposed a protocol with an offline pre-processing phase and probabilistic functionality by introducing random pre-shared values, called triples [1]. The
interesting idea of distributing random triples before running the actual computation phase opened a new efficient solution in MPC systems. The Protocols
employing this idea have two different phases:

- **Pre-Processing/Offline Phase**: In this phase, the participants receive random pre-processed information which is used in the next online phase. The
  information can be distributed by initializers/servers which can be considered
  as selling random information to the participants. Note that the idea of generating random information in this phase leads to a probabilistic functionality
  that ensures preserving the inputs privacy in the actual online computation.
- **Computation/Online Phase**: In this phase, the participants implement
  actual computation of the protocol using the random numbers they hold
  which result higher efficiency. Here, the important challenge is that the process of using the pre-distributed information must not reveal any information
  about the private inputs and their privacy condition must be preserved.

The online phase of the Beaver's scheme is linear with a passive adversary;
however, generating triples, as pre-computed information, in the offline phase
in an efficient way has been a challenging subject of some studies which can be
improved. This efficiency can be in terms of either the communication complexity
or the required number of participants. [16] and [3] proposed different methods

for generating the triples with the communication upper bound $O(n^2)$ and the number of $2t + 1$ required participants.

Some studies have utilized the idea of random pre-processed information before the actual computation in their protocols. It has been employed in both boolean circuit [7,17] and arithmetic circuit [6,10,11] to improve efficiency and security of their protocols. [9] suggested an online protocol using Oblivious Linear Evaluation, and pre-computed information distributed by an initializer with passive security. The idea of employing more than one server was first suggested by Beaver [2]. In this study, several non-cooperating severs, called commodity-based MPC, were utilized in the circuit with passive security. [22] proposed a MPC protocol where a set of raw triples is distributed by cloud service providers in a pre-processing phase. An important drawback of using more than one server is that it causes much higher communication complexity in the pre-processing phase since the participants must communicate with multiple servers to receive the required information.

1.2   Our Contribution

In this paper, we present an information-theoretic secure MPC protocol which computes a share of inputs addition and multiplication gates with the same multiplicative depth in parallel with no interaction. It also can be extended to compute a share of multiplication gates with different multiplicative levels. We employ an initializer, as a semi-honest third party, to perform pseudo-random probabilistic functionality in a pre-processing phase. An initializer is a type of server which doesn't get involved in the actual computation and it was first suggested by Rivest to improve the efficiency of his 1-out of-2 $\binom{1}{2}$ Oblivious Transfer protocol [20]. Its main task is to provide some random pre-computed values and the shares in an offline mode before the actual protocol making MPC protocols more efficient and cheaper to run. Our protocol needs only $n \geq t + 1$ participants in the both offline and online phases and it is unconditionally secure against a coalition of t participants controlled by an adversary. Our protocol requires only one round of secret sharing in the online phase that is common for both the inputs addition and the same-level multiplication gates. Hence, both of these computation gates can be conducted in parallel. Furthermore, the share of multiplication gates with different multiplicative depths can be computed by implementing it in different communication rounds.

1.3   Outline

The rest of this paper is devised as follows: Sect. 2 presents an overview and preliminaries of our protocol. It also contains required conditions of the secure MPC protocols with a pre-processing phase. Sections 3 describes our proposed protocol including the offline and online phases, and the discussion of the security evaluation. Finally, Sect. 4 gives the conclusion of this paper.

2   Model

Our protocol employs an independent initializer in the pre-processing phase, to distribute random values among the participants in a probabilistic functionality. Suppose, two input holders P_i and P_j with their corresponding inputs, x_i and x_j, are given two random numbers r_i and r_j, respectively. The idea is that P_i can calculate two numbers, α_{i1} and α_{i2}, such that $f(\alpha_{i1}) \simeq r_i$ and $f(\alpha_{i2}) \simeq r_i$ while $f(x_i) \not\simeq r_i$. The same method can be proved for P_j with his corresponding random number r_j such that $f(x_j) \not\simeq r_j$. Thus, their multiplication gate $f(x_i, x_j) \leftarrow x_i \times x_j$ can be expressed as $f(x_i, x_j) \not\simeq r_i, r_j$ meaning that the outcome doesn't depend on the pseudo-random numbers. In fact, the random numbers just ensure the privacy condition of our protocol. Using this trick achieves the possibility of computing a share of the both addition and multiplication gates in parallel. Moreover, this computation phase can be conducted using just one common round of online secret sharing by the input holders. Our protocol has a linear communication upper bound and it is secure against a coalition of at most t participants corrupted by a passive adversary. Since we employ Shamir's secret sharing as a secure method of threshold secret distribution in our protocol, we briefly explain it in the next section.

2.1   Shamir's Secret Sharing Scheme

This scheme consists of n participants and a secret holder (dealer) who distributes his secret s among all the players using a random polynomial ($f(x) = s + a_1 x + a_2 x^2 + \ldots + a_t x^t \mod q$). In the sharing phase, he privately sends the share f_i to each player P_i, based on its value $x = i$. The coefficients $a_1, a_2, \ldots, a_t$ are randomly chosen by the secret holder and this scheme is operated over a field $\mathbb{F}_q$ where q is a prime number and $q > n$ [21].

In the reconstruction phase, a set of at least $t + 1$ participants pools their shares and utilizes Lagrange interpolation method to compute the polynomial with the constant term s. It can be seen that a set of up to t participants cannot reconstruct the secret which means that this is a (t, n) threshold secret sharing scheme unconditionally secure against t passive adversaries. This method is linear and any linear function of shared values (including addition and a multiplication by a constant number) can be computed locally, such that each shareholder simply applies the same linear function to the shares.

2.2   Security Conditions

To evaluate the security of our protocol, we describe the security condition requirement in this section. Suppose n participants P_i (for $i = 1, \ldots, x_n$), with their private inputs x_i, want to compute the given function $f(x_1, \ldots, x_n)$. The security requirements are as follows:

- **Correctness**: After running the protocol, each participant P_k obtains the correct result of the function $f(x_1, \ldots, x_n)$.

– **Privacy**: After completion of the protocol, a coalition of t participants (not including P_i) controlled by a passive adversary can gain no information about the input of P_i except what they can obtain from the output.

3   The Protocol

Our proposed protocol is synchronous and consists of one offline pre-processing phase and an online phase. This protocol can be executed in parallel for addition gates and multiplication gates with the same multiplicative depth, with the capability of being extended to the multiplication gates with intermediate levels as well, in any given function $f(x_1, \ldots, x_n)$. It is assumed that private channels between the players are secure.

3.1   Pre-processing Phase

This offline phase can be executed by an initializer T at any time before the online computation phase and it is operated in a probabilistic assumption. Note that this pre-computed information can be given to the players before the actual computation. Let there exist a two-inputs multiplication gate, $x_i x_j$, belonging to the two input holders, P_i and P_j, and also a n-inputs addition gate $\sum_{i=1}^{n} x_i$ in a circuit. Suppose n participants want to compute a share of these gates in parallel. Figure 1 illustrates the detail of this phase.

– The initializer T generates n random numbers r_i (for $i = 1, \ldots, n$) and random polynomials of degree t with the free term r_i as:

$$r_i(x) = r_i + \gamma_1 x + \gamma_2 x^2 + \ldots + \gamma_t x^t$$

and distributes the shares r_{ik} among the participants P_k ($1 \le k \le n$)
– For the multiplication gate $x_i x_j$, T calculates the value $R = r_i r_j$ and generates a random polynomial of degree t with the free term R as follows:

$$R(x) = R + c_1 x + c_2 x^2 + \ldots + c_t x^t$$

and distributes the shares R_k among the participants P_k .
– T leaves the protocol and takes no step further.

Fig. 1. The offline pre-processing phase of our proposed protocol

The communication upper bound of this phase for each multiplication gate $x_i x_j$ is $O(n)$.

3.2 Computation Phase

This is a deterministic online phase where the input holders and the participants are involved to compute the desired gate outcome. They employ the random pre-computed information distributed by the initializer in the previous offline phase. This phase is divided into two sub-phases: *sharing* and *actual computation*.

Sharing

This sub-phase is common for both addition and multiplication gates. Figure 2 illustrates the online sharing sub-phase.

***

Inputs: Each input holder P_i (for $i = 1, \ldots, n$) has the input x_i.

- Each input holder P_i generates a polynomial $g_i(x)$ of degree t with the free term x_i and distributes the shares g_{ik} among the participants P_k ($1 \leq k \leq n$).
- Each participant P_k computes two new shares, using the corresponding random share r_i distributed by T in the pre-processing phase, as follows:

$$A_{ik} = g_{ik} + r_{ik}$$

$$B_{ik} = g_{ik} - r_{ik}$$

Where the t-sharings A_{ik} and B_{ik} belong to two polynomials with the free terms $\alpha_i = x_i + r_i$ and $\beta_i = x_i - r_i$, respectively.

***

Fig. 2. The online sharing in the computation phase

Addition

Here, the actual online computation of the addition gate takes place where each participant is able to compute a share of an inputs addition gate with no inter-action. This is as efficient as the homomorphic secret sharing method for the addition gate. Figure 3 presents the online computation of the inputs addition gate.

***

Output: Each participant P_k among a set of $t + 1$ participants ($1 \leq t + 1 \leq n$) computes a share of $f(x_1, \ldots, x_n) = x_1 + \ldots + x_n = \sum_{i=1}^{n} x_i$

- Each participant P_k computes the new share of the inputs addition as follows:

$$f_k = \frac{\sum_{i=1}^{n}(A_{ik} + B_{ik})}{2}$$

***

Fig. 3. Online computation sub-phase of the inputs addition gate

Now, we assess the security conditions of the proposed inputs addition gate.

Correctness

Theorem 1. *At the end of the inputs addition sub-phase, each participant P_k ($1 \leq k \leq n$) has the correct share of the function $F = f(x_1, \ldots, x_n) = \sum_{i=1}^{n} x_i$.*

Proof. Based on homomorphic nature of the Shamir's secret sharing, if a set of $n \geq t+1$ participants pools their shares f_k, they can reconstruct the function F with the following free term:

$$f = \frac{\sum_{i=1}^{n}[(x_i + r_i) + (x_i - r_i)]}{2}$$

$$= x_1 + \ldots + x_n$$

Privacy

Theorem 2. *At the end of the inputs addition, a coalition of up to t participants (not including P_i) cannot gain any information about the input of P_i, except the information they can obtain from the outcome after computing it.*

Proof. Without loss of generality, let x_1 be the input of the player P_1. The view of at most t participants corrupted by a passive adversary (not including P_1), denoted by $VIEW_{\mathcal{A}}$, would include the following shares:

$$f_2 = \frac{\sum_{i=1}^{n}(A_{i2} + B_{i2})}{2}$$

$$f_3 = \frac{\sum_{i=1}^{n}(A_{i3} + B_{i3})}{2}$$

$$\vdots$$

$$f_{t+1} = \frac{\sum_{i=1}^{n}(A_{i(t+1)} + B_{i(t+1)})}{2}$$

Where, based on the threshold feature of the Shamir's secret sharing discussed in Sect. 2.1, the adversary cannot gain any information about the free term $(\alpha_1 + \beta_1) \leftarrow [(x_1 + r_1) + (x_1 - r_1)]$. Thus, the value x_1 is t-private.

Multiplication

In this online computation gate each participant computes a correct share of a two-inputs multiplication gate. Note that the protocol can be employed for computing a share of all the multiplication gates with the same multiplicative depth at the same time in parallel. In other words, in a circuit with m multiplication gates with the same multiplicative level, it can be executed m times in parallel.

Output: Each participant P_k among a set of $t+1$ participants ($1 \leq t+1 \leq n$) computes a share of $f(x_i, x_j) = x_i \times x_j$ in the given function $f(x_1, \ldots, x_n)$.

- A set of at least $t+1$ participants pools their shares A_{jk} and B_{ik}, and reconstructs the values α_j and β_i, respectively.
- Each participant P_k computes a share of the inputs multiplication gate using the corresponding share R_k, sent by T in the pre-processing phase, as follows:

$$f_k = \frac{\alpha_j A_{ik} + \beta_i B_{jk}}{2} - R_k$$

Fig. 4. Online computation sub-phase of the inputs multiplication gate

Moreover, the protocol can be extended to compute a share of the multiplication gates with different multiplicative levels such that it must be implemented for each intermediate gate separately. As an example, suppose each participant P_k wants to compute a share of the function $f(x_1, x_2, x_3) = x_1 x_2 x_3$. First, the participants obtain two sets of the pre-distributed information (r_{1k}, r_{2k}, R_{1k}) and $(r_{12k}, r_{3k}, R_{2k})$ where $R_1 \leftarrow r_1 r_2$ and $R_2 \leftarrow r_{12} r_3$. The participants compute a share of the multiplication gate $x_1 x_2$ denoted by $(x_1 x_2)_k$ using the protocol in one communication round with replacing the shares $g_{ik} \leftarrow x_{1k}$, $g_{jk} \leftarrow x_{2k}$, $r_{ik} \leftarrow r_{1k}$, $r_{jk} \leftarrow r_{2k}$ and $R_k \leftarrow R_{1k}$ denoted in our protocol. Then, similarly, they execute the protocol in another communication round re-assigning the shares $g_{ik} \leftarrow (x_1 x_2)_k$, $g_{jk} \leftarrow x_{3k}$, $r_{ik} \leftarrow r_{12k}$, $r_{jk} \leftarrow r_{3k}$ and $R_k \leftarrow R_{2k}$. Thus, in a circuit with n multiplication gates with different multiplicative depths, the protocol must be executed in n separate rounds of communication.

The communication complexity of a multiplication gate is linear $O(n)$. The security condition of the each multiplication gate is evaluated in following section.

Correctness

Theorem 3. *At the end of the inputs multiplication sub-phase, each participant P_k ($1 \leq k \leq n$) has the correct share of the multiplication gate $f = x_i \times x_j$.*

Proof. After reconstructing the values α_j and β_i, the share f_k of the participant P_k can be written as:

$$f_k = \frac{(x_j + r_j)A_{ik} + (x_i - r_i)B_{jk}}{2} - R_k$$

If a set of at least $t+1$ participants pools their shares f_k, and based on the linear feature of the secret sharing, the constant free term is computed as:

$$f = \frac{(x_j + r_j)(x_i + r_i) + (x_i - r_i)(x_j - r_j)}{2} - r_i r_j$$

$$= \frac{2x_i x_j + 2r_i r_j}{2} - r_i r_j$$

$$= x_i \times x_j$$

Privacy

Theorem 4. *At the end of the inputs multiplication gate, a coalition of t participants including P_j/P_i, corrupted by an adversary, cannot gain any information about the input of P_i/P_j, except the information they can obtain from the outcome after computing it.*

Proof. Without loss of generality, let assume $P_1 \leftarrow P_i$ and $x_1 \leftarrow x_i$. The view of the adversary, $VIEW_{\mathcal{A}}$, would include the following shares:

$$f_2 = \frac{\alpha_j A_{12} + \beta_1 B_{j2}}{2} - R_k$$

$$f_3 = \frac{\alpha_j A_{13} + \beta_1 B_{j3}}{2} - R_k$$

$$\vdots$$

$$f_{t+1} = \frac{\alpha_j A_{1(t+1)} + \beta_1 B_{j(t+1)}}{2} - R_k$$

Where, based on the threshold feature of the Shamir's secret sharing, the adversary cannot gain any information about the free terms $A_1 \leftarrow (x_1 + r_1)$ and R which is t-shared in the pre-processing phase. Furthermore, the input is masked by the value $\beta_1 \leftarrow (x_1 - r_1)$ where the t-sharings of r_1 is distributed in the pre-processing phase. Thus, $VIEW_{\mathcal{A}}$ can obtain no information about the input x_1 and and it is t-private.

4   Conclusion

In this paper, we propose a MPC protocol using an initializer. The initializer is involved in an offline pre-processing phase which can be conducted at any time before running the actual online protocol. It can be considered as a server which generates and distributes some random pre-computed information among the participants in a probabilistic functionality such that the information can be utilized in the actual online computation phase. Our protocol presents a solution for the problem of inputs multiplication with linear communication complexity $O(n)$ and the presence of only $n \geq t + 1$ participants in both offilne and online phases. It is unconditionally secure against a coalition of t participants corrupted by a passive adversary. The online sharing phase of our protocol can be employed to execute both the inputs addition and multiplication gates, with the same multiplicative depth, in parallel. Also, It can be extended to the case of multiplication gates with different multiplicative levels at the cost of separate communication rounds.

References

1. Beaver, D.: Efficient multiparty protocols using circuit randomization. In: Feigenbaum, J. (ed.) CRYPTO 1991. LNCS, vol. 576, pp. 420–432. Springer, Heidelberg (1992). https://doi.org/10.1007/3-540-46766-1_34
2. Beaver, D.: Commodity-based cryptography. In: Proceedings of the twenty-ninth annual ACM symposium on Theory of computing, pp. 446–455 (1997)
3. Beerliová-Trubíniová, Z., Hirt, M.: Perfectly-secure MPC with linear communication complexity. In: Canetti, R. (ed.) TCC 2008. LNCS, vol. 4948, pp. 213–230. Springer, Heidelberg (2008). https://doi.org/10.1007/978-3-540-78524-8_13
4. Ben-Or, M., Goldwasser, S., Wigderson, A.: Completeness theorems for non-cryptographic fault-tolerant distributed computation. In: Providing Sound Foundations for Cryptography: On the Work of Shafi Goldwasser and Silvio Micali, pp. 351–371 (2019)
5. Benaloh, J.C.: Secret sharing homomorphisms: keeping shares of a secret secret (Extended Abstract). In: Odlyzko, A.M. (ed.) CRYPTO 1986. LNCS, vol. 263, pp. 251–260. Springer, Heidelberg (1987). https://doi.org/10.1007/3-540-47721-7_19
6. Bendlin, R., Damgård, I., Orlandi, C., Zakarias, S.: Semi-homomorphic encryption and multiparty computation. In: Paterson, K.G. (ed.) EUROCRYPT 2011. LNCS, vol. 6632, pp. 169–188. Springer, Heidelberg (2011). https://doi.org/10.1007/978-3-642-20465-4_11
7. Blier, H., Tapp, A.: A single initialization server for multi-party cryptography. In: Safavi-Naini, R. (ed.) ICITS 2008. LNCS, vol. 5155, pp. 71–85. Springer, Heidelberg (2008). https://doi.org/10.1007/978-3-540-85093-9_8
8. Chaum, D., Crépeau, C., Damgard, I.: Multiparty unconditionally secure protocols. In: Proceedings of the twentieth annual ACM symposium on Theory of computing, pp. 11–19 (1988)
9. Cianciullo, L., Ghodosi, H.: Efficient information theoretic multi-party computation from oblivious linear evaluation. In: Blazy, O., Yeun, C.Y. (eds.) WISTP 2018. LNCS, vol. 11469, pp. 78–90. Springer, Cham (2019). https://doi.org/10.1007/978-3-030-20074-9_7
10. Damgård, I., Keller, M., Larraia, E., Pastro, V., Scholl, P., Smart, N.P.: Practical covertly secure MPC for dishonest majority – Or: breaking the SPDZ limits. In: Crampton, J., Jajodia, S., Mayes, K. (eds.) ESORICS 2013. LNCS, vol. 8134, pp. 1–18. Springer, Heidelberg (2013). https://doi.org/10.1007/978-3-642-40203-6_1
11. Damgård, I., Pastro, V., Smart, N., Zakarias, S.: Multiparty computation from somewhat homomorphic encryption. In: Safavi-Naini, R., Canetti, R. (eds.) CRYPTO 2012. LNCS, vol. 7417, pp. 643–662. Springer, Heidelberg (2012). https://doi.org/10.1007/978-3-642-32009-5_38
12. Gennaro, R., Rabin, M.O., Rabin, T.: Simplified vss and fast-track multiparty computations with applications to threshold cryptography. In: Proceedings of the Seventeenth Annual ACM Symposium on Principles of Distributed Computing, pp. 101–111 (1998)
13. Ghodosi, H., Pieprzyk, J.: Multi-party computation with omnipresent adversary. In: Jarecki, S., Tsudik, G. (eds.) PKC 2009. LNCS, vol. 5443, pp. 180–195. Springer, Heidelberg (2009). https://doi.org/10.1007/978-3-642-00468-1_11
14. Goldreich, O.: Secure multi-party computation. Manuscript. Preliminary version 78 (1998)
15. Goldwasser, S.: Multi party computations: past and present. In: Proceedings of the sixteenth annual ACM symposium on Principles of distributed computing, pp. 1–6 (1997)

16. Hirt, M., Maurer, U., Przydatek, B.: Efficient secure multi-party computation. In: Okamoto, T. (ed.) ASIACRYPT 2000. LNCS, vol. 1976, pp. 143–161. Springer, Heidelberg (2000). https://doi.org/10.1007/3-540-44448-3_12

17. Lindell, Y., Pinkas, B., Smart, N.P., Yanai, A.: Efficient constant round multi-party computation combining BMR and SPDZ. In: Gennaro, R., Robshaw, M. (eds.) CRYPTO 2015. LNCS, vol. 9216, pp. 319–338. Springer, Heidelberg (2015). https://doi.org/10.1007/978-3-662-48000-7_16

18. Micali, S., Goldreich, O., Wigderson, A.: How to play any mental game. In: Proceedings of the Nineteenth ACM Symp. on Theory of Computing, STOC, pp. 218–229. ACM (1987)

19. Rabin, T., Ben-Or, M.: Verifiable secret sharing and multiparty protocols with honest majority. In: Proceedings of the Twenty-first Annual ACM Symposium on Theory of Computing, pp. 73–85. ACM (1989)

20. Rivest, R.: Unconditionally secure commitment and oblivious transfer schemes using private channels and a trusted initializer. Unpublished manuscript (1999)

21. Shamir, A.: How to share a secret. Commun. ACM **22**(11), 612–613 (1979)

22. Smart, N.P., Tanguy, T.: Taas: Commodity mpc via triples-as-a-service. In: Proceedings of the 2019 ACM SIGSAC Conference on Cloud Computing Security Workshop, pp. 105–116 (2019)

23. Yao, A.C.: Protocols for secure computations. In: 23rd Annual Symposium on Foundations of Computer Science (SFCS 1982), pp. 160–164. IEEE (1982)

24. Yao, A.C.C.: How to generate and exchange secrets. In: 27th Annual Symposium on Foundations of Computer Science (SFCS 1986), pp. 162–167. IEEE (1986)

Evolving Secret Sharing in Almost Semi-honest Model

Jyotirmoy Pramanik[1]($\boxtimes$) and Avishek Adhikari[2]

[1] Taki Government College, Taki 743429, India
jyotirmoy@tgc.ac.in
[2] Presidency University, 86/1 College Street, Kolkata 700073, India
avishek.maths@presiuniv.ac.in
https://sites.google.com/view/jyotirmoypramanik
https://www.isical.ac.in/~avishek_r/

Abstract. Evolving secret sharing is a special kind of secret sharing where the number of shareholders is not known beforehand, i.e., at time $t = 0$. In classical secret sharing such a restriction was assumed inherently i.e., the number of shareholders was given to the dealer's algorithm as an input. Evolving secret sharing relaxes this condition. Pramanik and Adhikari left an open problem regarding malicious shareholders in the evolving setup, which we answer in this paper. We introduce a new cheating model, called the almost semi-honest model, where a shareholder who joins later can check the authenticity of share of previous ones. We use collision resistant hash function to construct such a secret sharing scheme with malicious node identification. Moreover, our scheme preserves the share size of Komargodski et al. (TCC 2016).

Keywords: Secret sharing · Evolving · Malicious · Collision resistance

1 Introduction

Secret sharing, initially introduced to safekeep cryptographic keys, has now evolved to have numerous applications in other protocols like multiparty computation, private information retrieval etc. The main motto of such a protocol is to *share* an information (usually encoded as a field element) among few *shareholders* so that some *qualified* combinations can recover it back whereas the other *forbidden* combinations may not. Few interesting articles and references on secret sharing are [1–4,6,7,9,12,13,17,19,21,24,37].

In simple words, evolving secret sharing [25] covers the special case of secret sharing where the number of shareholders is not known beforehand, i.e., at time $t = 0$. In classical secret sharing such a restriction was assumed inherently i.e., the total set of shareholders (or, at least the number of them) was given to the dealer's algorithm (the ShareGen algorithm) as an input. Evolving secret sharing

The research of the second author is partially supported by DST-SERB Project MATRICS vide Sanction Order: MTR/2019/001573 and DST-FIST project.

P. Stănică et al. (Eds.): ICSP 2021, CCIS 1497, pp. 123–131, 2021.
https://doi.org/10.1007/978-3-030-90553-8_9

relaxes this condition. This is a budding research direction that has attracted a good amount of researchers such as [10,11,16,18,20,23,26,30].

In secret sharing, be it classical (bounded set of shareholders) or evolving, the context of *cheating* varies. For example, in *semi-honest* setup, shareholders follow the protocol but try to learn more information than their entitlement. On the other hand, *malicious* cheaters may deviate from the protocol according to their whim. In this manuscript, now onwards, we shall abuse the word 'cheater' to mean malicious cheaters only. In literature there exist many schemes which address cheaters such as [5,8,14,15,22,27–29,31–35].

Open Problem: Despite some good amout of research in evolving secret sharing, to the best of our knowledge no work on malicious node detection or the so called *cheater identification* has been done yet. This question was asked by Pramanik and Adhikari in [30]. We answer this question in this paper using collision resistant hash functions and assumption of a trusted public bulletin board. To the best of our knowledge, evolving schemes preserve qualified sets, i.e., once qualified, a set always remains so. We maintain this assumption in this work.

Organization: In Sect. 1.1, we discuss threshold evolving secret sharing. In Sect. 2, we breifly discuss hash functions. In Sect. 3, we define a new model of cheating called the almost semi-honest model. We present our construction in Sect. 4. In Sect. 5, we leave two open problems.

Notations: In this work, we use the following notations.

Symbol	Meaning
t	time
l	bit length of secret value
ShareGen	share distribution protocol
Reconst	secret recovery protocol
k	secret recovery threshold
g	generation number
$a \leftarrow X$	sampling an element a from the set X
$\oplus$	addition modulo 2
$size(g)$	size of the gth generation
$\mathcal{C}$	centralized malicious cheater
$\mathcal{L_C}$	shareholders under control of $\mathcal{C}$
Π_k	the (k, ∞) secret sharing due to [25]
$\mathcal{H}$	collision resistant hash
$\mathcal{A}_t$	restriction of access structure at time t
$\mathcal{R}_t$	reconstructing shareholders from $\mathcal{A}_t$
P_t	t^{th} shareholder

1.1 Threshold Evolving Secret Sharing

For completion, allow us to summarize how a threshold evolving secret sharing scheme, also known as (k, ∞) secret sharing scheme works. A shareholder, when he arrives, is assigned to a generation by the dealer. To be specific, $t \in \mathbb{N}$ is assigned to generation $g = \log_k t$. Naturally, the generations grow in size: For $g = 0, 1, 2, \ldots$ the g-th generation begins with the arrival of the k^g-th party. Hence, the size of the g-th generation is $size(g) = k^{g+1} - k^g = (k-1).k^g$. We state the evolving secret sharing on threshold access structure by [25] in Fig. 1.

Evolving Secret Sharing in the Threshold Setup

Let s be an l-bit secret. During the beginning of a generation g, the dealer stores k^g many l-bit strings s_A for all $A = (u_0, \ldots, u_{g-1}) \in \{0, \ldots, k\}^g$ (where if $g = 0$ it preserves only s). Each such s_A is an l-bit string that we share to the shareholders in generation g assuming that in generation $i \in \{0, \ldots, g-1\}$, u_i parties arrived.

(k, ∞) Secret Sharing

The owner of the secret sets the value of s_A where $A = (u_0, \ldots, u_g)$ as follows:
(Notation: let $s_{prev(A)} = s$ if $g = 0$ and $s_{prev(A)} = s_{(u_0, \ldots, u_{g-1})}$ otherwise.)

1. If $u_g = 0$, then set $s_A = s_{prev(A)}$ and HALT.
2. If $u_0 + \cdots + u_g < k$, then the owner of the secret:
   (a) samples $r_A \leftarrow \{0, 1\}^l$ uniformly at random.
   (b) sets $s_A = s_{prev(A)} \oplus r_A$.
   (c) shares the l-bits r_A among the shareholders in the g-th generation using any ideal $(u_g, size(g))$-threshold secret sharing scheme (for example, Shamir's [37]).
3. If $u_0 + \cdots + u_g = k$, then the dealer shares the l-bit string $s_{prev(A)}$ among the parties in the g-th generation using using any ideal $(u_g, size(g))$-threshold secret sharing scheme.

Fig. 1. Construction of (k, ∞) secret sharing due to [25].

2   Hash Functions

Cryptographic hash functions or simply hash functions play an important role in efficiently 'hiding' an information. To be specific, a hash function $\mathcal{H}$ takes as input an arbitrary bit string x and outputs a fixed length output $\mathcal{H}(x)$. A hash function $\mathcal{H} : \mathcal{X} \to \mathcal{Y}$ is called *one way* or *pre-image resistant* if for given $y \in \mathcal{Y}$ there is no efficient algorithm to find $x \in \mathcal{X}$ such that $\mathcal{H}(x) = y$. $\mathcal{H}$ is called *second pre-image resistant*, if for $x \in \mathcal{H}$, there is no efficient algorithm to find $x'(\neq x) \in \mathcal{X}$ such that $\mathcal{H}(x) = \mathcal{H}(x')$. In case of *collision resistant* hash function, there is no efficient algorithm to find distinct $x, x' \in \mathcal{X}$ such that $\mathcal{H}(x) = \mathcal{H}(x')$.

It can be shown that collision resistance implies second pre-image resistance, which further implies onewayness. For further reading on the same one may refer [36,38].

3   The 'Almost' Semi-honest Model

We introduce a new cheating model in (evolving) secret sharing, called the almost semi-honest model. In this model, in short, a malicious shareholder may choose to submit incorrect (arbitrary) shares for reconstruction of the shared bit(s) but with a very high probability, will be detected by the *latter* shareholders, if so. Let us explain the same by the following game (Fig. 2).

Game between the scheme and a centralized cheater $\mathcal{C}$

1. A centralized cheater $\mathcal{C}$ chooses a *last* cheating shareholder.
2. $\mathcal{C}$ may corrupt at most c shareholders arrived before him. Let their collection be denoted by $\mathcal{L}_{\mathcal{C}}$.
3. Reconst round takes place, strictly consisting of at least one shareholder who has arrived after the last cheating shareholder.
4. In the reconstruction round Reconst, some of the shareholders in $\mathcal{L}_{\mathcal{C}}$ submit false shares.

Fig. 2. Cheating model

Let $\mathcal{C}^{(r)}_{success}$ denote the probability that all the honest shareholders participating in Reconst accept share submitted by at least one $P_r \in \mathcal{L}_{\mathcal{C}}$. We call an evolving secret sharing scheme ϵ-secure if $\mathcal{C}^{(r)}_{success} < \epsilon$, $\forall P_r \in \mathcal{L}_{\mathcal{C}}$. We call this model *almost semi-honest*, because the latter shareholders' authenticity cannot be verified by prior shareholders, as, once distributed, refreshing of shares are not allowed.

4   Our Construction

Let Π_k denote the (k, ∞) scheme described above, for some positive integer $k > 1$. Also, let $\mathcal{H}$ denote a collision resistant hash function. $\mathcal{H}$ is made public. Moreover, let c denote the maximum number of corruptions possible, where $k \geq 2c + 1$, i.e., we assume honest majority. We describe our construction in Fig. 3.

A construction for (k, ∞) secret sharing with cheater identification

Dealer's Algorithm: The dealer shares a bit secret as follows.

1. When the tth shareholder arrives, the dealer calls the share generation protocol of Π_k and outputs a share v_t.
2. Moreover, the dealer calculates the hash $\mathcal{H}(v_t)$, and publishes it on a trusted public bulletin board.
3. The tth shareholder is handed over his share v_t.

Reconstructing Shareholders' Algorithm: Suppose at some point of time t, a set of shareholders $\mathcal{R}_t \subset \mathcal{A}_t$, the latest access structure, wish to recover the secret bit(s).

1. If the reconstructing shareholders do not form a qualified set, ABORT.
2. If they form a qualified set:
   (a) (Round-1): Every shareholder announces his share.
   (b) (Local computation): Every shareholder P_i checks if v_s where $s \in \{j : P_j \in \mathcal{R}_t\} \setminus \{i\}$ matches its hash from the public bulletin. If it doesn't match for some shareholder, he marks him as a cheater.
   (c) If a shareholder gets marked as a cheater by at least $c + 1$ shareholders, he is put in a list $\mathcal{L}$ of cheaters. If $\mathcal{R} \setminus \mathcal{L}$ remains a qualified set, they reconstruct using the reconstruction algorithm of Π_k and output the secret bit(s) and $\mathcal{L}$, else they output a symbol $\perp$ and $\mathcal{L}$.

Fig. 3. The construction

The scheme described above is an instance of (k, ∞) secret sharing with cheater identification property. To support our claim, we study the scheme case by case.

External View: An external shareholder with no shares can only view the hash function $\mathcal{H}$ and the digest of shares. Due to properties of hash function, it hides the shares. Similar arguments apply for a forbidden set.

Qualified Set with No Cheaters: In this case, whenever a qualified set of shareholders wish to recover the secret, they use the reconstruction algorithm of Π_k and recover the secret bit(s). Moreover, they cannot guess the shares of the other shareholders from their digest.

Cheaters' View: The c colluding cheaters can, before the secret reconstruction phase takes place, see c of their shares and the public digests of other shares, the latter of which doesn't aid them. Moreover, c shares in a k threshold scheme, is not enough to learn the secret bit(s).

Semi-honest Shareholders' View: The honest shareholders may easily check the authenticity of modified shares by verifying using the public digest. Suppose the security parameter of the hash $\mathcal{H}$ is δ, then the probability that at least one of the cheaters modifies share but does not get caught is bounded above by $c \cdot 2^{-\delta}$. In other words, our construction is $c \cdot 2^{-\delta}$-secure.

Note that our construction preserves the share size of the underlying (k, ∞) scheme, namely that of [25]. Based on the case by case discussion above, we may restate the following result from [25], modified to suit our context.

Theorem 1. *For every $k, l \in \mathbb{N}$ our construction gives a secret sharing scheme for the evolving (k, ∞) access structure with cheater identification and an l-bit secret in which for every $t \in \mathbb{N}$ the share size of the tth party is bounded by $kt \cdot \max\{l, \log kt\}$. The construction is $c \cdot 2^{-\delta}$ secure.*

The share size may be further modified to $(k-1)\log t + 6k^4 l \log \log t \cdot \log \log \log t + 7k^4 l \log k$.

5 Concluding Remarks

In this paper, we answer the open problem from [30] regarding cheating shareholders in the evolving setup. For the same, we introduce a new cheating model, called the almost semi-honest model, where a shareholder who joins later can check the authenticity of share of previous ones. We use collision resistant hash function to construct such a secret sharing scheme with malicious node identification. Moreover, our scheme preserves the share size of [25].

The kind of model that we introduce here probably does the best that can be done in the evolving setup, since refreshing shares is not allowed. However, the authors are hopeful that the use of public bulleting board may not be mandatory and leave that as an open problem. In this regard, use of some decentralized mechanism like blockchain might be of interesting, and demands more research in this direction. Moreover, since, evolving secret sharing schemes are, as it is, expensive, use of hash function, yielding computational security instead of information theoretic security, is probably a better option. Constructing information theoretically secure cheater identifiable evolving secret sharing scheme is left as another open problem.

Acknowledgment. In the end, the authors would like to thank the anonymous reviewers who have suggested constructive modifications, rectifications and amplifications, resulting in the current form of manuscript.

References

1. Adhikari, A.: Linear algebraic techniques to construct monochrome visual cryptographic schemes for general access structure and its applications to color images. Des. Codes Crypt. **73**(3), 865–895 (2014)
2. Adhikari, A., Bose, M.: A new visual cryptographic scheme using Latin squares. In: IEICE Transactions on Fundamentals of Electronics, Communications and Computer Sciences, pp. 1198–1202 (2004)
3. Adhikari, A., Bose, M., Kumar, D., Roy, B.K.: Applications of partially balanced incomplete block designs in developing $(2,n)$ visual cryptographic schemes. IEICE Trans. **90**(5), 949–951 (2007)
4. Adhikari, A., Dutta, T.K., Roy, B.: A new black and white visual cryptographic scheme for general access structures. In: Canteaut, A., Viswanathan, K. (eds.) INDOCRYPT 2004. LNCS, vol. 3348, pp. 399–413. Springer, Heidelberg (2004). https://doi.org/10.1007/978-3-540-30556-9_31
5. Adhikari, A., Morozov, K., Obana, S., Roy, P.S., Sakurai, K., Xu, R.: Efficient threshold secret sharing schemes secure against rushing cheaters. In: Information Theoretic Security of the 9th International Conference, ICITS 2016, 9–12 August 2016, Tacoma, pp. 3–23 (2016)
6. Adhikari, A., Sikdar, S.: A new $(2,n)$-visual threshold scheme for color images. In: Johansson, T., Maitra, S. (eds.) INDOCRYPT 2003. LNCS, vol. 2904, pp. 148–161. Springer, Heidelberg (2003). https://doi.org/10.1007/978-3-540-24582-7_11
7. Adhikari, M.R., Adhikari, A.: Basic Modern Algebra with Applications. Springer, India (2014)
8. Araki, T.: Efficient *(k, n)* threshold secret sharing schemes secure against cheating from n-1 cheaters. In: Information Security and Privacy, 12th Australasian Conference, ACISP 2007, 2–4 July 2007, Townsville, pp. 133–142 (2007)
9. Beimel, A.: Secret-sharing schemes: a survey. In: Chee, Y.M., Guo, Z., Ling, S., Shao, F., Tang, Y., Wang, H., Xing, C. (eds.) IWCC 2011. LNCS, vol. 6639, pp. 11–46. Springer, Heidelberg (2011). https://doi.org/10.1007/978-3-642-20901-7_2
10. Beimel, A., Othman, H.: Evolving ramp secret-sharing schemes. In: Security and Cryptography for Networks of the 11th International Conference, SCN 2018, 5–7 September 2018, Amalfi, pp. 313–332 (2018)
11. Beimel, A., Othman, H.: Evolving ramp secret sharing with a small gap. In: Advances in Cryptology - EUROCRYPT 2020 - 39th Annual International Conference on the Theory and Applications of Cryptographic Techniques, 10–14 May 2020, Zagreb, pp. 529–555 (2020)
12. Blakley, G.R.: Safeguarding cryptographic keys. In: Managing Requirements Knowledge, International Workshop on (AFIPS), pp. 313–317 (1979)
13. Brickell, E.F.: Some ideal secret sharing schemes. In: Quisquater, J.-J., Vandewalle, J. (eds.) EUROCRYPT 1989. LNCS, vol. 434, pp. 468–475. Springer, Heidelberg (1990). https://doi.org/10.1007/3-540-46885-4_45
14. Cabello, S., Padró, C., Sáez, G.: Secret sharing schemes with detection of cheaters for a general access structure. Des. Codes Crypt. **25**(2), 175–188 (2002)
15. Carpentieri, M.: A perfect threshold secret sharing scheme to identify cheaters. Des. Codes Crypt. **5**(3), 183–187 (1995)
16. Chaudhury, S.S., Dutta, S., Sakurai, K.: AC^0 constructions for evolving secret sharing schemes and redistribution of secret shares. IACR Cryptol. ePrint Arch. **2019**, 1428 (2019)

17. Cramer, R., Damgård, I.B., Döttling, N., Fehr, S., Spini, G.: Linear secret sharing schemes from error correcting codes and universal hash functions. In: Oswald, E., Fischlin, M. (eds.) EUROCRYPT 2015. LNCS, vol. 9057, pp. 313–336. Springer, Heidelberg (2015). https://doi.org/10.1007/978-3-662-46803-6_11
18. D'Arco, P., Prisco, R.D., Santis, A.D., del Pozo, A.L.P., Vaccaro, U.: Probabilistic secret sharing. In: 43rd International Symposium on Mathematical Foundations of Computer Science, MFCS 2018, 27–31 August 2018, Liverpool, pp. 64:1–64:16 (2018)
19. Das, A., Adhikari, A.: An efficient multi-use multi-secret sharing scheme based on hash function. Appl. Math. Lett. **23**(9), 993–996 (2010)
20. Desmedt, Y., Dutta, S., Morozov, K.: Evolving perfect hash families: a combinatorial viewpoint of evolving secret sharing. In: Cryptology and Network Security of the 18th International Conference, CANS 2019, 25–27 October 2019, Fuzhou, pp. 291–307 (2019)
21. Dutta, S., Bhore, T., Sardar, M.K., Adhikari, A., Sakurai, K.: Visual secret sharing scheme with distributed levels of importance of shadows. In Proceedings of the Fifth International Conference on Mathematics and Computing of the ICMC 2019, 6–9 February 2019, Bhubaneswar, pp. 19–32 (2019)
22. Dutta, S., Roy, P.S., Adhikari, A., Sakurai, K.: On the robustness of visual cryptographic schemes. In: Digital Forensics and Watermarking of the 15th International Workshop, IWDW 2016, Beijing, 17–19 September 2016, pp. 251–262 (2016)
23. Dutta, S., Roy, P.S., Fukushima, K., Kiyomoto, S., Sakurai, K.: Secret sharing on evolving multi-level access structure. In: Information Security Applications of the 20th International Conference, WISA 2019, 21–24 August 2019, Jeju Island, pp. 180–191 (2019)
24. Dutta, S., Sardar, M.K., Adhikari, A., Ruj, S., Sakurai, K.: Color visual cryptography schemes using linear algebraic techniques over rings. In: Information Systems Security of the 16th International Conference, ICISS 2020, 16–20 December 2020, Jammu, pp. 198–217 (2020)
25. Komargodski, I., Naor, M., Yogev, E.: How to share a secret, infinitely. In: Theory of Cryptography of the 14th International Conference, TCC 2016-B, October 31 - November 3 2016, Beijing, pp. 485–514 (2016)
26. Komargodski, I., Paskin-Cherniavsky, A.: Evolving secret sharing: dynamic thresholds and robustness. In: Theory of Cryptography of the 15th International Conference, TCC 2017, 12–15 November 2017, Baltimore, pp. 379–393 (2017)
27. Kurosawa, K., Obana, S., Ogata, W.: t-cheater identifiable (k, n) threshold secret sharing schemes. In: Coppersmith, D. (ed.) CRYPTO 1995. LNCS, vol. 963, pp. 410–423. Springer, Heidelberg (1995). https://doi.org/10.1007/3-540-44750-4_33
28. Ogata, W., Eguchi, H.: Cheating detectable threshold scheme against most powerful cheaters for long secrets. Des. Codes Crypt. **71**(3), 527–539 (2012). https://doi.org/10.1007/s10623-012-9756-5
29. Pramanik, J., Adhikari, A.: Ramp secret sharing with cheater identification in presence of rushing cheaters. Groups Complexity Crypt. **11**(2), 103–113 (2019)
30. Pramanik, J., Adhikari, A.: Evolving secret sharing with essential participants. In: Bhattacharjee, D., Kole, D.K., Dey, N., Basu, S., Plewczynski, D. (eds.) Proceedings of International Conference on Frontiers in Computing and Systems. AISC, vol. 1255, pp. 691–699. Springer, Singapore (2021). https://doi.org/10.1007/978-981-15-7834-2_64

31. Pramanik, J., Dutta, S., Roy, P.S., Adhikari, A.: Cheating detectable ramp secret sharing with optimal cheating resiliency. In: Information Systems Security of the 16th International Conference, ICISS 2020, December 16–20 2020, Jammu, pp. 169–184 (2020)
32. Pramanik, J., Roy, P.S., Dutta, S., Adhikari, A., Sakurai, K.: Secret sharing schemes on compartmental access structure in presence of cheaters. In: Information Systems Security of the 14th International Conference, ICISS 2018, 17–19 December 2018, Bangalore, pp. 171–188 (2018)
33. Roy, P.S., Adhikari, A., Xu, R., Morozov, K., Sakurai, K.: An efficient robust secret sharing scheme with optimal cheater resiliency. In: Chakraborty, R.S., Matyas, V., Schaumont, P. (eds.) SPACE 2014. LNCS, vol. 8804, pp. 47–58. Springer, Cham (2014). https://doi.org/10.1007/978-3-319-12060-7_4
34. Roy, P.S., Adhikari, A., Xu, R., Morozov, K., Sakurai, K.: An efficient t-cheater identifiable secret sharing scheme with optimal cheater resiliency. IACR Crypt. ePrint Arch. **2014**, 628 (2014)
35. Roy, P.S., et al.: Hierarchical secret sharing schemes secure against rushing adversary: cheater identification and robustness. In: Information Security Practice and Experience of the 14th International Conference, ISPEC 2018, 25–27 September 2018, Tokyo, pp. 578–594 (2018)
36. Sanadhya, S.K., Sarkar, P.: New collision attacks against up to 24-step SHA-2. In: Progress in Cryptology of the INDOCRYPT 2008, 9th International Conference on Cryptology in India, 14–17 December 2008, Kharagpur, pp. 91–103 (2008)
37. Shamir, A.: How to share a secret. Commun. ACM **22**(11), 612–613 (1979)
38. Song, L., Liao, G., Guo., J.: Non-full sbox linearization: applications to collision attacks on round-reduced keccak. In: Advances in Cryptology of the CRYPTO 2017 of the 37th Annual International Cryptology Conference, 20–24 August 2017, Santa Barbara, pp. 428–451 (2017)

Traceable and Verifier-Local Revocable Attribute-Based Signature with Constant Length

Syed Taqi Ali$^{(\boxtimes)}$ (iD)

Visvesvaraya National Institute of Technology, Nagpur 440010, India
`sta@cse.vnit.ac.in`

Abstract. Attribute-based signature (ABS) allows an authorised user to anonymously produced a signature on the document with satisfiable predicate. The predicate can be a threshold predicate, which supports only AND operator or can be a monotone predicate, which has AND and OR operator or can be a non-monotone predicate, which also includes NOT operator. Traceable ABS scheme additionally allows a designated authority to trace the identity of the real signer of ABS, whenever need arise. To make ABS more realistic a revocation feature need to be incorporated, which enables the designated authority to expel the user when found her signature on disputed document. There is one ABS scheme by J. Wei et al. supports traceability and revocability but with threshold predicate. Moreover, his signature length is variable in terms of the number of attributes. There are few more ABS schemes which either supports traceability or revocability, but not both. In this paper, we proposed a constant-size traceable ABS scheme with verifier-local revocation (VLR) feature and it supports monotone predicate. The scheme is secure in the standard model under well-known cryptographic assumptions.

Keywords: Attribute-based signature · Monotone access structure · Traceability · Verifier-local revocation · Constant-length signature

1 Introduction

In attribute-based signature (ABS), a user with private key associated with certain attributes produces an anonymous signature on a document which is associated with certain *predicate*, so that the user attributes satisfies that predicate. Then the verifier can verifies the signature without revealing the signer's identity but only proves that some user with valid attributes, which obeys the underlying predicate, has produced the signature. We call this type as signature-policy attribute-based signature. The predicate (can also be view as an *access structure*) is represented by an *access tree*, in which *leaves* are the attributes. Consider the example, where the predicate for the message M, $\Upsilon = \{ \textit{(University = U1) AND (TH2((Dept = Mathematics), (Age = 40's), (Gender = Female)) OR (Designation = Prof))} \}$, here *TH2* denoting the threshold gate with threshold 2 (i.e. any 2

© Springer Nature Switzerland AG 2021
P. Stănică et al. (Eds.): ICSP 2021, CCIS 1497, pp. 132–146, 2021.
https://doi.org/10.1007/978-3-030-90553-8_10

attributes has to satisfy from that set of attributes). Suppose that the attributes with Alice are, Λ_{alice} =((University := U1), (Dept := Mathematics), (Age := 30), (Designation := Postdoc), (Gender := Female)), and attributes with Bob are, Λ_{bob} = ((University := U1), (Dept := Biology), (Age := 45), (Designation := Professor), (Gender := Male)). Even their attributes, Λ_{alice} and Λ_{bob}, are different but satisfies the given predicate Υ, i.e. $\Upsilon(\Lambda_{allice}) = \Upsilon(\Lambda_{bob}) = 1$ hold, and similarly there can be many such attribute sets which will satisfy this predicate. Therefore, Alice and Bob are able to generate an ABS on M with the above predicate Υ, and as per the requirement of anonymity, an ABS should not reveal any partial information but only reveals that the signer (i.e. a valid possession of the private key) satisfies the given predicate Υ, with their attributes. If there exist few signatures on some disputed documents and we require to reveal the identity of that signers then the *traceability* feature will help to do so. Traceability feature in ABS scheme allows a designated authority with some special *tracing key* to reveal the signer's identity for the given signature. In some situations, a culprit signer's private key need to be *revoked*, in order to disallow her to produce further such signatures. To enable this a *revocation* feature need to be incorporated in ABS. A *verifier-local revocation* (VLR) [17] is a kind of revocation mechanism where a designated authority holding some special *revocation key* can revoke the user's private key without need of updating the unrevoked user's private keys, but only by updating the *revocation list* at the public repository. The VLR feature saves the unrevoked user's private key updation cost but increases the verification processing cost by linear times in terms of the number of revoked users.

1.1 Motivation

We considered the application scenario from [18]. Alice, being a finance manager in a big corporation, has decided to defame the corporation before leaving the job and gone through her company's financial records. She then decides to send some modified financial records (to blame the major scandal in their corporation) to a largely circulated newspaper, preserving her anonymity, but with a proof that she really has access to those documents. It was known that the several people, by some reasons, has access to those records: for example, those in the London, New York or Tokyo office who are either internal auditors or finance managers attached with a common project. As usual, Alice sends those records by endorsing it with ABS using her attribute keys. Later, when it came to know that the news were false then the corporation head wants to revel the identity of signer and expel all her attribute keys. This requires an ABS scheme to have both traceable and revocable features. Moreover, the scheme with monotone predicate and constant length signature is desirable.

1.2 Related Work

Maji et al. [18] first introduced an ABS scheme. Many ABS schemes were proposed in the literature [6,9,14,18–20], among which the scheme presented by [14] has constant-size signature but supports only threshold predicates. The scheme by Escala et al. [9] supports monotone predicate with revocation feature but has its signature size linear in the size of the predicate. The ABS scheme by Okamoto et al. [19] supports non-monotone predicates (i.e. with AND, OR and NOT operators), but it does not have traceability and revocation features. The ABS scheme is said to be practical if it supports traceability as well as revocability. And it was first pointed out and achieved by J. Wei et al. in [21]. But their scheme supports only a single threshold predicate. Apart from these, there are many other schemes which either supports traceability [9,12] or revocability [16], but not both.

Lian et al. [16] proposed the first revocable ABS scheme supporting monotone predicates. Here the revocation complexity is depends on the number of unrevoked users and has communication overhead. Few ABS schemes proposed by El Kaafraani et al. [7], which introduces a feature called *user-controlled linkability*. This feature allows signer to make a choice to make some of his signatures directed at the same verifier are linkable without compromising anonymity. This is to reduce the single bottle neck traceability to designated authority. But these schemes does not have constant-length signature and have no revocation feature. Gu et al. [12] have proposed a traceable ABS scheme for monotone predicates, but the signature size is depends on the number of attributes and the scheme does not support revocation feature. The traceability feature in signature schemes is extensively used in group signature schemes [1,5,8] as a primary feature, where the member of a group will produce an anonymous signature on behalf of the whole group and later on in case of any dispute the group manager can revoke the anonymity of that member.

1.3 Contribution and Strategy

- For achieving constant-size signature we adopt the modified version of the bottom-up approach [8] from [1], where the author accumulates all the attribute values along with the corresponding Lagranges coefficients into single component and all the dummy attributes values into another component.
- To achieve *traceability* we use user private key format from the group signature scheme by Boyen et al. [5], which is developed under the composite order group settings under subgroup decision assumption. They devised a two-level hierarchical signature scheme to build their group signature scheme.
- To achieve security in the standard model we commit our signature elements using Groth Sahai proof system [11] under subgroup decision assumption settings. We show how to extract the committed values in Sect. 4.
- The security of anonymity is reducible to the Groth Sahai proof under Subgroup decision (SD) and Decisional Tripartite Diffie-Hellman (DTDH) assumptions. The security of the traceability is reducible to unforgeability of two-level hierarchical signature scheme [5], which in turn depends on $\ell-$Hidden Strong Diffie Hellman Assumption ($\ell-$HSDH) assumption. Finally, we reduce the security of attribute-unforgeability to Knowledge of Exponent Assumption (KEA) and DL assumption.

– For incorporating *revocation* feature, we use verifier-locals revocation (VLR) concept from [17]. It increases the verification cost to linear in terms of the number of revoked users. In this at every time period, the revocation list gets updated with some partial information of the revoked users, if any.

1.4 Outline

Preliminaries are given in Sect. 2. And the proposed ABS scheme formal model with security definitions are depicted in Sect. 3. The cryptographic tools used is given in Sect. 4 followed by construction in Sect. 5. Security analysis and comparison is in Sect. 6 followed by the conclusion in Sect. 7.

2 Preliminaries

2.1 Bilinear Maps and Number Theoretic Assumptions

Common Parameters: k denotes the security parameter, $\mathbb{G}$ and $\mathbb{G}_T$ denotes a cyclic groups of order $n = pq$ where, p and q are primes of $O(k)$ bits length, and $p \neq q$. We use g to denotes a generator of $\mathbb{G}$. The $\mathbb{G}_p$ and $\mathbb{G}_q$ denotes subgroups of $\mathbb{G}$ of respective orders p and q.

Definition 1 (Bilinear Map). *An efficiently computable map, $e : \mathbb{G} \times \mathbb{G} \to \mathbb{G}_T$ having following properties,*

– *Bilinearity : For any $u \in \mathbb{G}$, and $x, y \in \mathbb{Z}_n$, $e(g^x, u^y) = e(g, u)^{xy}$.*
– *Non-degeneracy: $e(g, u) \neq 1_{\mathbb{G}_T}$ whenever $g, u \neq 1_{\mathbb{G}}$.*
  Such pairings are implementable due to [3, 4].

Definition 2 (Subgroup Decision assumption [3]). *For all PPT $\mathcal{A}$ the advantage, $\mathbf{Adv}_{\mathbb{G}, \mathcal{A}}^{\text{SD}}(k) = |Pr[\mathcal{A}(n, \mathbb{G}, \mathbb{G}_T, e, g, h) = 1 | h = g^x] - Pr[\mathcal{A}(n, \mathbb{G}, \mathbb{G}_T, e, g, h) = 1 | h = g^{px}]|$, is a negligible function in k and $x \in_R \mathbb{Z}_n^*$.c*

Definition 3 (ℓ-Hidden Strong DH assumption (ℓ-HSDH) [5]). *For all PPT $\mathcal{A}$ the advantage, $\mathbf{Adv}_{\mathbb{G}, \mathcal{A}}^{\ell - \text{HSDH}}(k) = Pr[\mathcal{A}(\tilde{g}, u, \tilde{g}^\omega, \tilde{g}^{\frac{1}{\omega + c_1}}, \tilde{g}^{c_1}, u^{c_1}, ...,$ $\tilde{g}^{\frac{1}{\omega + c_{\ell-1}}}, \tilde{g}^{c_{\ell-1}}, u^{c_{\ell-1}}) = (\tilde{g}^{\frac{1}{\omega + c}}, \tilde{g}^c, u^c) \wedge c \neq c_i$, for $i = 1, ..., \ell - 1]$, is a negligible function in k, where $u, \tilde{g}$ are the generators of $\mathbb{G}_p$, $\omega \in_R \mathbb{Z}_p^*$ and $c, c_i \in_R \mathbb{Z}_p$ for $i = 1, ..., \ell - 1$.*

Definition 4 (Decisional Tripartite DH (DTDH) Assumption [15]). *For all PPT $\mathcal{A}$ the advantage, $\mathbf{Adv}_{\mathbb{G}, \mathcal{A}}^{\text{DTDH}}(k) = |Pr[\mathcal{A}(Z_1 = g^{z_1}, Z_2 = g^{z_2}, Z_3 = g^{z_3}, \eta = g^{z_1 z_2 z_3}) = 0] - Pr[\mathcal{A}(Z_1, Z_2, Z_3, g^u) = 0]|$, is a negligible function in k, where $z_1, z_2, z_3, u \in_R \mathbb{Z}_n^*$.*

Definition 5 (Knowledge of Exponent Assumption 1 (KEA1) [2,13]). *If there exists an adversary $\mathcal{A}$ which takes q, v, v^a as input, where v is a generator of $\mathbb{G}_q$ and outputs a pair of elements v', v'^a from $\mathbb{G}_q$, then there exists an extractor $\bar{\mathcal{A}}$, which given the same inputs returns ξ such that $v^\xi = v'$.*

Definition 6 (DL Assumption). *For all PPT $\mathcal{A}$ the advantage, $\mathbf{Adv}_{\mathbb{G}, \mathcal{A}}^{\text{DL}} = Pr[\mathcal{A}(v, v' = v^\xi) = \xi]$, is a negligible function in k, where $v \in_R \mathbb{G}_p$ and $\xi \in_R \mathbb{Z}_p^*$.*

2.2   Access Structure [10]

Let $UAtt = \{at_1, at_2, ..., at_m\}$ denotes the set of attributes. We say a monotone property is satisfied by the Γ ($\Gamma \subseteq 2^{UAtt}\backslash\{\emptyset\}$) if $\forall C, D \subseteq UAtt, C \in \Gamma$ and $C \subseteq D$, then $D \in \Gamma$ is true. Then, the *access structure* is a collection set of such $\{\Gamma\}$.

A *predicate* Υ represents a boolean function with attributes as its literals. If ζ satisfies the predicate Υ then we write it as $\Upsilon(\zeta) = 1, \zeta \subset UAtt$. The *access structure* Γ_Υ *of a predicate* Υ is a set of subset of attributes $\zeta \subset UAtt$ for which $\Upsilon(\zeta) = 1$. That is, $\Gamma_\Upsilon = \{\zeta_i\}_{i=1}^k : \zeta_i \subseteq UAtt \wedge \Upsilon(\zeta_i) = 1, 1 \leq i \leq k$.

Access Tree. An access structure for the predicate Υ is represented by an access tree T_Υ, in a tree structure form. It consists of attributes as a leaves and threshold gates as internal nodes. Let denote the number of branches of node y as l_y, and k_y ($0 < k_y \leq l_y$) denotes the value of the threshold gate at node y. Here, the threshold gate shows that the number k_y of l_y branches of the node y should get satisfied in order to say that the parent node is satisfied. Note that, $k_y = l_y$ indicates an AND gate and $k_y = 1$ indicates an OR gate. If any leaf owns the attribute then it says that the leaf satisfies that attribute. $\Upsilon(Leaves) = 1$ denotes that the *Leaves*, set of attributes, satisfies the predicate Υ. Thus, any predicate can be expressed as access tree, easily.

3   Traceable and Verifier-Local Revocable Attribute-Based Signature Scheme ($\mathcal{TVLR} - \mathcal{ABS}$): Definitions and Security

In this section, we give basic model and security definitions of the $\mathcal{TVLR} - \mathcal{ABS}$. The model is similar to the one given by [21]. Our model supports verifier local revocation feature [17], i.e. whenever user get revoked the other users need not update their private keys. Verifier itself verifies whether the signature is generated by an unrevoked user. Thus it does not require $\mathtt{DeriveKey}$ algorithm, as use in [21]. Accordingly we modify the syntax of $\mathcal{TRABS}$ to incorporate all these features. The notations used in the scheme is given in the Table 1.

Intuition. The user U_{id} can generates a signature on a message M associated by predicate Υ during the interval t if $\exists \zeta \subseteq \Lambda_{id}$ with the user : $\Upsilon(\zeta) = 1$ and $grt[id][t] \notin RL_t$. The vector of tokens $\vec{grt}$, are precomputed at the time of issuing key and stores with the managing authority.

Definition 7 (Syntax of $\mathcal{TVLR} - \mathcal{ABS}$). *It consists six algorithms as follows,*

- $(params, pp, ik, tk) \xleftarrow{\$} \mathtt{Setup}(1^k)$
- $k_{id} \xleftarrow{\$} \mathtt{Extract}(pp, ik, id, \Lambda_{id})$
- $\sigma \xleftarrow{\$} \mathtt{Sign}(pp, k_{id}, \zeta, M, \Upsilon, t)$
- $0/1 \leftarrow \mathtt{Verify}(pp, M, \Upsilon, \sigma, t)$

Table 1. Notations

Symbols	Denotes	Symbols	Denotes
k	security parameter	k_{id}	user U_{id}'s private key
$UAtt$	universal set of attributes	Λ_{id}	attributes of the user U_{id}, $\Lambda_{id} \subseteq UAtt$
Υ	predicate'	$\Upsilon(\zeta) = 1$	Υ is satisfiable by the attribute set ζ
T_Υ	access tree of the predicate Υ	$\mathbb{T}$	total no. of time intervals ($= O(k)$)
$\mathcal{T}_\Upsilon$	set of public values of the T_Υ	RL_t	set of revocation tokens at interval t
pp	public parameters of ABS	$grt[id][t]$	token of the user U_{id} at interval t
MA	Managing authority	$\vec{grt}$	$\vec{grt} = \{grt[1][1], ..., grt[N][\mathbb{T}]\}$,
ik	issuing key		a ($N \times \mathbb{T}$)-vector of revocation tokens
tk	tracing key	$(.) \xleftarrow{\$} A(.)$	\$ the algorithm A is probabilistic,
N	total no. of users ($= O(k)$)		otherwise it is deterministic
id	user identity, id $\in [1, N]$	p, q	primes

- id$/\perp \leftarrow$ Trace(pp, tk, σ)
- $RL_t \leftarrow$ Revoke$(\vec{grt}, t, \{id_k\}_{k=1}^{\ell})$

There are following entities in $\mathcal{TVLR} - \mathcal{ABS}$ scheme:

- The *managing authority* MA , who runs the Setup algorithm. MA keeps issuing key ik and tracing key tk secret (may give it to *issuing authority* and *Tracer*, to delegate the task). Using issuing key MA (or issuing authority) issues private keys k_{id} to the user with identity id, by associating it with some attributes (in terms of attributes) say $\Lambda_{id} \subseteq UAtt$, by running the Extract algorithm. Using tk, MA (or Tracer, if separate) runs Trace algorithm to reveal the signer's identity from the signature. MA (or the issuing authority) runs Revoke algorithm to revoke the users at certain time intervals (t $\leq \mathbb{T}$).
- *Signers*, run Sign algorithm to produce an ABS on a document M with predicate Υ; assuming they possess a valid attribute set $\zeta \subseteq \Lambda_{id} : \Upsilon(\zeta) = 1$.
- *Verifier*, checks the signature using pp and also checks the revocation status using publicly available RL_t list.

Definition 8 (Correctness). *We say $\mathcal{TVLR} - \mathcal{ABS}$ is correct if for all honestly generated* $(params, pp, ik, tk) \leftarrow$ Setup(1^k), *for all* $k_{id} \leftarrow$ Extract$(pp, ik, id, \Lambda_{id})$ *the following equations hold.*

$$1 \leftarrow \text{Verify}(pp, M, \Upsilon, \text{Sign}(pp, k_{id}, \zeta, M, \Upsilon, t), t) : \zeta \subseteq \Lambda_{id}, \Upsilon(\zeta) = 1 \& grt[id][t] \notin RL_t$$
$$\text{id} \leftarrow \text{Trace}(pp, tk, \text{Sign}(pp, k_{id}, \zeta, M, \Upsilon))$$

3.1 Oracles and Security Experiments

- We use following notations for security analysis. Sign$(pp, ik, id, \zeta, M, \Upsilon, t)$ (as compare to original inputs, here in place of user private key k_{id}, we use ik and id) which denotes that, pick the corresponding k_{id} from the list (the list $L = \{(id, k_{id})\}$ which is already maintained) then returns the signature as $\sigma \leftarrow$ Sign$(pp, k_{id}, \zeta, M, \Upsilon, t)$, and suppose if k_{id} not exists (i.e. not generated yet) then selects $\Lambda_{\mathrm{id}} \subseteq UAtt$ randomly in which $\exists \zeta \in \Lambda_{\mathrm{id}} : \Upsilon(\zeta) = 1$ and retrieve $k_{\mathrm{id}} \leftarrow \mathsf{Extract}(pp, ik, \mathrm{id}, \Lambda_{\mathrm{id}})$, stores in the list L and outputs the suitable signature $\sigma \leftarrow \mathsf{Sign}(pp, k_{\mathrm{id}}, \zeta, M, \Upsilon, t)$.

- $\mathsf{Sign}(pp, ik, ., ., ., ., .)$ - Denotes *sign oracle*, invokes upon query (id, M, Υ, t).
- $\mathsf{Extract}(pp, ik, ., .)$ - Denotes *extract oracle* invokes upon query (id, Λ_{id}).
- $\mathsf{Revoke}(pp, ik, ., .)$ - Denotes *revoke oracle*, it revokes the user with identities $\{\mathrm{id}_k\}_{k=1}^{\ell}$ upon query $(\{\mathrm{id}_k\}_{k=1}^{\ell}, t)$.
- $z \xleftarrow{\$} \mathcal{A}(x, y, \ldots : O_1, O_2, \ldots)$- It denote that algorithm $\mathcal{A}$ with inputs $x, y, \ldots$ and access to oracles $O_1, O_2, \ldots$, outputs z.

Experiment $\mathbf{Exp}_{\mathcal{TVLR}-\mathcal{ABS}, \mathcal{A}}^{\mathrm{CPA-anon}-b}(k)$

    $(params, pp, ik, tk) \xleftarrow{\$} \mathsf{Setup}(1^k), L = \phi$

    $(M^*, \Upsilon^*, ID_0, ID_1) \xleftarrow{\$} \mathcal{A}(pp : \mathsf{Extract}(pp, ik, ., .), \mathsf{Sign}(pp, ik, ., ., ., ., .))$

            $: \exists \zeta_0 \subseteq \Lambda_{ID_0}, \zeta_1^1 \subseteq \Lambda_{ID_1} \wedge \Upsilon^*(\zeta_0) = \Upsilon^*(\zeta_1) = 1$

    $b \in_R \{0, 1\}, \sigma^* \xleftarrow{\$} \mathsf{Sign}(pp, k_{ID_b}, \zeta_b, M^*, \Upsilon^*, t^*)$

    $b' \xleftarrow{\$} \mathcal{A}(pp, \sigma^* : \mathsf{Extract}(pp, ik, ., .), \mathsf{Sign}(pp, ik, ., ., ., ., .))$

    If $b = b'$, **return** 1 **else return** 0

Experiment $\mathbf{Exp}_{\mathcal{TVLR}-\mathcal{ABS}, \mathcal{A}}^{\mathrm{trace}}(k)$

    $(params, pp, ik, tk) \xleftarrow{\$} \mathsf{Setup}(1^k), L = \phi$

    $(M^*, \Upsilon^*, \sigma^*) \xleftarrow{\$} \mathcal{A}(pp, tk : \mathsf{Extract}(pp, ik, ., .), \mathsf{Sign}(pp, ik, ., ., ., ., .))$

    If $\mathsf{Verify}(pp, M^*, \Upsilon^*, \sigma^*, t) = 1 \wedge \mathsf{Trace}(pp, tk, \sigma^*) = \bot$

        then return 1 **else return** 0

Experiment $\mathbf{Exp}_{\mathcal{TVLR}-\mathcal{ABS}, \mathcal{A}}^{\mathrm{att-unforge}}(k)$

    $(params, pp, ik, tk) \xleftarrow{\$} \mathsf{Setup}(1^k), L = \phi$

    $(M^*, \Upsilon^*, \sigma^*) \xleftarrow{\$} \mathcal{A}(pp : \mathsf{Extract}(pp, ik, ., .), \mathsf{Sign}(pp, ik, ., ., ., ., .))$

    If $\mathsf{Verify}(pp, M^*, \Upsilon^*, \sigma^*, t) = 1 \wedge \mathsf{Trace}(pp, tk, \sigma^*) = \mathrm{id} \wedge$

        $\nexists \zeta \in \Lambda_{\mathrm{id}} : \Upsilon^*(\zeta) = 1$ **then return** 1 **else return** 0

Fig. 1. Defines anonymity, traceability and attribute unforgeability of $\mathcal{TVLR}-\mathcal{ABS}$ ($^1 \zeta_1$ can be equal to ζ_0).

$$\mathbf{Adv}_{\mathcal{TVLR}-\mathcal{ABS}, \mathcal{A}}^{\mathrm{CPA-anon}}(k) = \Pr\left[\mathbf{Exp}_{\mathcal{TVLR}-\mathcal{ABS}, \mathcal{A}}^{\mathrm{CPA-anon}-b}(k) = 1\right] - \frac{1}{2}$$

$$\mathbf{Adv}_{\mathcal{TVLR}-\mathcal{ABS}, \mathcal{A}}^{\mathrm{trace}}(k) = \Pr\left[\mathbf{Exp}_{\mathcal{TVLR}-\mathcal{ABS}, \mathcal{A}}^{\mathrm{trace}}(k) = 1\right]$$

$$\mathbf{Adv}_{\mathcal{TVLR}-\mathcal{ABS}, \mathcal{A}}^{\mathrm{att-unforge}}(k) = \Pr\left[\mathbf{Exp}_{\mathcal{TVLR}-\mathcal{ABS}, \mathcal{A}}^{\mathrm{att-unforge}}(k) = 1\right]$$

Definition 9 (Anonymity (CPA)). *The TVLR-ABS scheme preserves Anonymity if the advantage,* $\mathbf{Adv}_{\mathcal{TVLR}-\mathcal{ABS}, \mathcal{A}}^{\mathrm{CPA-anon}}(k)$, *is negligible for all PPT $\mathcal{A}$.*

Definition 10 (Traceability). *We say that the* $\mathcal{TVLR} - \mathcal{ABS}$ *preserves* Traceability *if* $\mathbf{Adv}^{\text{trace}}_{TVLR-ABS,\mathcal{A}}(k)$ *is negligible for all PPT* $\mathcal{A}$.

Definition 11 (Attribute Unforgeability). *The* $\mathcal{TVLR} - \mathcal{ABS}$ *preserves* Attribute Unforgeability *if* $\mathbf{Adv}^{\text{att-unforge}}_{TVLR-ABS,\mathcal{A}}(k)$ *is negligible for all PPT* $\mathcal{A}$.

4 Cryptographic Tools

4.1 Two-Level Hierarchical Signature Scheme [5]

In this signature, the certificate get endorsed in the first level by the manager and a short signature is produced on message M in the second level.

Scheme: k denotes the security parameter and $m' = |M|$.

Setup(1^k): $(p, q, n, e, \mathbb{G}, \mathbb{G}_T)$ denotes the bilinear map setup of composite order groups. $g \in \mathbb{G}_p$, a generator. All group elements in this scheme have **order** p from $\mathbb{G}$ and $\mathbb{G}_T$. Finally output the public parameters, $PP = \{g, Z = g^z, u = g^y, v' = g^{z'}, \{v_i = g^{z_i}\}_{i=1}^{m'}, A = e(g,g)^\alpha\} \in \mathbb{G}^{m'+4} \times \mathbb{G}_T$ and the master key, $MK = (z, g^\alpha)$. Note that PP includes k, m', and $(p, \mathbb{G}, \mathbb{G}_T, e)$.

Extract(PP, MK, id): Output $k_{\text{id}} = (k_{\text{id},1}, k_{\text{id},2}, k_{\text{id},3}) = ((g^\alpha)^{\frac{1}{z+s_{\text{id}}}}, g^{s_{\text{id}}}, u^{s_{\text{id}}}) \in \mathbb{G}^3$, a private key, using randomly choosen $s_{\text{id}} \in \mathbb{Z}_p$.

Sign(PP, k_{id}, M): Message M, represented as a bit string $M = (\mu_1, ..., \mu_{m'}) \in \{0,1\}^{m'}$. Selects a random $s \in \mathbb{Z}_p$ and computes $\mathcal{F}(M) = v'\Pi_{j=1}^{m'}v_j^{\mu_j}$. Finally output $\sigma = (\sigma_1, \sigma_2, \sigma_3, \sigma_4) = (k_{\text{id},1}, k_{\text{id},2}, k_{\text{id},3}.\mathcal{F}(M)^s, g^{-s}) \in \mathbb{G}^4$.

Verify(PP, M, σ): The signature σ is valid if the following holds, $e(\sigma_1, \sigma_2 Z) \stackrel{?}{=} A$, and $e(\sigma_2, u) \stackrel{?}{=} e(\sigma_3, g).e(\sigma_4, \mathcal{F}(M))$.

This scheme is proven to be secure against existential forger with chosen message attack under ℓ–HSDH assumption, in [5].

4.2 Access Tree Secret Values Assigned

To construct the access tree for the given predicate we follow the *Bottom-up Approach* given by [8], which includes the following three functions:

1. DummyNodeAdd(T_Υ): Here dummy nodes are added to the access tree T_Υ and returns the *extended access tree* T_Υ^{ext}. Let D_{T_Υ} be a set of dummy nodes added. Let $s_j \in \mathbb{Z}_n^*$ denotes the attribute $\text{att}'_j s \in U Att$ secret value. Let $S = \{s_j\}_{\text{att}_j \in U Att}$.
2. AssignedValue(S, T_Υ^{ext}): It returns a dummy nodes' secret values $\{s_{d_j}\}_{d_j \in D_{T_\Upsilon}}$ and a root secret s_{T_Υ}.
3. MakeSimplifiedTree($Leaves, T_\Upsilon^{ext}$): Returns the product of Lagranges coefficients $\Delta_{leaf}(\forall leaf \in Leaves \cup D_{T_\Upsilon}^{Leaves})$, Such that

$$\sum_{\text{att}_j \in Leaves} \Delta_{\text{att}_j} s_j + \sum_{d_j \in D_{T_\Upsilon}^{Leaves}} \Delta_{d_j} s_{d_j} = s_{T_\Upsilon} \tag{1}$$

where $D_{T_\Upsilon}^{Leaves} \subseteq D_{T_\Upsilon}$ contains the *Leaves* associated dummy nodes.

For more details we refer readers to [1,8].

4.3   GS Non-interactive Proof Systems

In [11], Groth and Sahai gave a non-interactive witness-indistinguishable (NIWI) proof system for the following paring product equations,

$$\prod_{i=1}^{\hat{n}} e(\mathcal{A}_i, \mathcal{Y}_i) \left(\prod_{i=1}^{\hat{n}} \left(\prod_{j=1}^{\hat{n}} e(\mathcal{Y}_i, \mathcal{Y}_j)^{\gamma_{ij}} \right) \right) = t_T \tag{2}$$

for the variables $\mathcal{Y}_1, ..., \mathcal{Y}_{\hat{n}} \in \mathbb{G}$ and constants $t_T \in \mathbb{G}_T, \mathcal{A}_1, ..., \mathcal{A}_{\hat{n}} \in \mathbb{G}, \gamma_{ij} \in \mathbb{Z}_n$, for $i, j \in \{1, ..., \hat{n}\}$.

The prover in a GS proof system, proves that the secret values $\{\mathcal{Y}_i\}_{i=1}^{\hat{n}}$, (which knows to him only) satisfy the above equations. Based on the Subgroup Decision (SD) Assumption instantiation under the setup $(n, G, G_T, e, g), (p, q)$ for $n = pq, p$ and q being primes, the common reference string (CRS) denoted by h, where $h = g^{rp}$ is used in the *soundness setting* and $h = g^r$ used in the *witness-indistinguishable setting*, for some $r \in_R \mathbb{Z}_n^*$, and $Com(\mathcal{Y}_i) = \mathcal{Y}_i h^{t_i}$ are the commitments for $\{\mathcal{Y}_i\}_{i=1}^{\hat{n}} \in \mathbb{G}$, for randomly chosen $t_i \in \mathbb{Z}_n$.

$\text{Extract}_{GS}(\mathcal{Y}_i)$: If one knows the factors of n in the soundness setting, one can extract the committed value $\mathcal{Y}_i$ as follows, $Com(\mathcal{Y}_i)^q \mod n = (\mathcal{Y}_i h^{t_i})^q = \mathcal{Y}_i^q (h^{rpt_i})^q = \mathcal{Y}_i^q$, then $\mathcal{Y}_i = (\mathcal{Y}_i^q)^{\hat{q}}$, where $\hat{q} \in \mathbb{Z}_{\phi(n)}^* : \hat{q}q \equiv 1 \mod \phi(n)$ and $\phi(n) = (p-1)(q-1)$. It is computable.

The **proof** for each pairing product Eq. (2) is

$$\pi = \prod_{i=1}^{\hat{n}} \mathcal{A}_i^{t_i} \prod_{i=1}^{\hat{n}} \prod_{j=1}^{\hat{n}} \mathcal{Y}_j^{t_i(\gamma_{ij} + \gamma_{ji})} \prod_{i=1}^{\hat{n}} \prod_{j=1}^{\hat{n}} h^{t_i t_j \gamma_{ij}} \tag{3}$$

After receiving $\{Com(\mathcal{Y}_i)\}_{i=1}^{\hat{n}}, \pi$, by the verifier, checks that

$$\prod_{i=1}^{\hat{n}} e(\mathcal{A}_i, Com(\mathcal{Y}_i)) \prod_{i=1}^{\hat{n}} \prod_{j=1}^{\hat{n}} e(Com(\mathcal{Y}_i), Com(\mathcal{Y}_j))^{\gamma_{ij}} \overset{?}{=} t_T e(h, \pi). \tag{4}$$

The **proof** computed in Eq. (3) is proven to have perfect completeness, composable witness-indistinguishability and perfect L_{guilt}-soundness.

Similarly, the multi-exponentiation equations proofs follows,

$$\prod_{i=1}^{\hat{n}} \mathcal{Y}_i^{a_i} \cdot \prod_{i=1}^{\hat{m}} \mathcal{B}_i^{x_i} \cdot \left(\prod_{i=1}^{\hat{n}} \left(\prod_{j=1}^{\hat{m}} \mathcal{Y}_i^{x_j \gamma_{ij}} \right) \right) = T \tag{5}$$

the secret variables are $\mathcal{Y}_1, ..., \mathcal{Y}_{\hat{n}} \in \mathbb{G}$ and $x_1, ..., x_{\hat{m}} \in \mathbb{Z}_n^*$, where $\{\mathcal{B}_i, T\} \in \mathbb{G}$ and $\{a_i, \gamma_{ij}\} \in \mathbb{Z}_n$ are the constants. Here, the NIWI proof cost 1 element in $\mathbb{G}$. Similarly, the following Linear multi-exponentiation equations

$$\prod_{i=1}^{\hat{n}} \mathcal{Y}_i^{a_i} = T \tag{6}$$

demand 1 element in $\mathbb{G}$. Moreover, the Multi-exponentiation equation enables non-interactive zero-knowledge (NIZK) proofs with no additional cost. It is possible to simulate the proofs without knowing witness due to a trapdoor present in the simulated CRS (as in WI setting). It is proven that the distribution of simulated proofs are indistinguishable to real proofs. When $t_T = 1_{\mathbb{G}_T}$ in Eq. (2), the NIZK simulator can use $\mathcal{Y}_i = 1_\mathbb{G}$ as satisfactory witnesses. And in another case, when $t_T = \prod_{j=1}^{n'} e(g_j, h_j)$ for known group elements $\{g_i\}_{i=1}^{n'}, \{h_i\}_{i=1}^{n'} \in \mathbb{G}$, the simulator can prove that

$$\prod_{i=1}^{\hat{n}} e(\mathcal{A}_i, \mathcal{Y}_i) \prod_{i=1}^{\hat{n}} \prod_{j=1}^{\hat{n}} e(\mathcal{Y}_i, \mathcal{Y}_j)^{\gamma_{ij}} = \prod_{j=1}^{n'} e(g_j, \mathcal{Z}_j) \tag{7}$$

and that introduces the variables $\mathcal{Z}_j$ (which need to be committed) satisfy the linear equations of type (6), $\mathcal{Z}_j = h_j$ for $j \in \{1, ..., n'\}$, i.e. $e(\mathcal{Z}_j = h_j)$ and it can have NIZK proofs. The proof for the Eq. (7) can be simulated using witnesses $\mathcal{Y}_i = \mathcal{Z}_i = 1_\mathbb{G}$ and the proof cost one group element in $\mathbb{G}$.

5   Construction of $\mathcal{TVLR} - \mathcal{ABS}$

– Setup(1^k):
   1. Choose $p, q : |p| = |q| = O(k)$. Define $(n = pq, \mathbb{G}, \mathbb{G}_T, e, g)$, a bilinear map setup. $\mathbb{G}_p$ and $\mathbb{G}_q$ are the subgroups of $\mathbb{G}$ of respective orders p and q. Define $UAtt = \{att_1, ..., att_m\}$.
   2. Select the generators $u, h, \{u_t\}_{i=1}^T \in \mathbb{G}$, where u_t denotes the respective interval revocation generators. Also initialize the empty vector $\vec{grt}$.
   3. Select attribute secrets $s_i \in \mathbb{Z}_n^*$ for $att_i \in UAtt$. Let $S = \{s_i\}_{att_i \in UAtt}$.
   4. Set $\{h_{att_i} = h^{s_i}\}_{att_i \in UAtt}$, are the attributes public values.
   5. Choose $\alpha, z \in_R \mathbb{Z}_n^*$ and set $Z = g^z$.
   6. Choose the generators $v', v_1, ..., v_{m'} \in \mathbb{G}$ and suitably set the Waters function, $\mathcal{F}(M) = v' \Pi_{j=1}^{m'} v_j^{\mu_j}$, where $m' = O(k)$.
   7. Finally, returns the system parameters, $params = (n, \mathbb{G}, \mathbb{G}_T, e, UAtt)$, the public parameters, $pp = (g, u, Z, h, \{u_t\}_{i=1}^T, \mathcal{F}, \{h_{att_i}\}_{att_i \in UAtt}) \in \mathbb{G}^{4+T+m'+m}$, the issuing key ik and the opening key tk, $ik = (g^\alpha, z, S, \vec{grt}), tk = q \in \mathbb{Z}$
– Extract(pp, ik, id, Λ_{id}): It returns k_{id}, the user private key.
   1. Initially, selects $s_{id} \in \mathbb{Z}_n^*$, the unique identifier and compute enrollment certificate, $g_{id} = (g^\alpha)^{\frac{1}{z+s_{id}}}$. and Attribute certificates, $\{g_{id,i} = g_{id}^{s_i}\}_{att_i \in \Lambda_{id}}$.
   2. Compute revocation tokens, $\{grt[id][t] = u_t^{s_{id}}\}_{t=1}^T$ and adds it to $\vec{grt}$.
   3. Outputs $k_{id} = (k_{id,1}, k_{id,2}, k_{id,3}, k_{id,4}) = (g_{id}, g^{s_{id}}, u^{s_{id}}, \{g_{id,i}\}_{att_i \in \Lambda_{id}}) \in \mathbb{G}^{3+|\Lambda_{id}|}$
– BuildTree(pp, ik, Υ): The predicate Υ public values are generated here,
   1. Get extension tree $T_\Upsilon^{ext} \leftarrow$ DummyNodeAdd(T_Υ), T_Υ represents Υ in tree.
   2. Get $(\{s_{d_j}\}_{d_j \in D_{T_\Upsilon}}, s_{T_\Upsilon}) \leftarrow$ AssignedValue(S, T_Υ^{ext}).
   3. Output the public values $T_\Upsilon = (\{s_{d_j}\}_{d_j \in D_{T_\Upsilon}}, A_{T_\Upsilon} = e(g^\alpha, g^{s_{T_\Upsilon}}), T_\Upsilon^{ext})$

- $\text{Sign}(pp, k_{\text{id}}, \zeta, M, \Upsilon, t)$: Using k_{id} such that $\exists \zeta \subseteq \Lambda_{\text{id}}$ for which $\Upsilon(\zeta) = 1$, the signature on message $M \in \{0,1\}^{m'}$ is generated,
  1. Retrieve the public values of Υ from the public repository[1].
  2. Next a random $s \in \mathbb{Z}_n^*$ is selected and finds $\rho = (\rho_1, \rho_2, \rho_3, \rho_4) = (k_{\text{id},1}^{s_T}, k_{\text{id},2}, k_{\text{id},3}.\mathcal{F}(M)^s, g^{-s})$ where $\rho_1 = k_{\text{id},1}^{s_T}$ is computed as follows,
     - Select suitable $\zeta \subseteq \Lambda_{\text{id}} : \Upsilon(\zeta) = 1$.
     - Get $(\{\Delta_{\text{att}_j}\}_{(\forall \text{att}_j \in \zeta)}, \{\Delta_{d_j}\}_{(\forall d_j \in D_{T_\Upsilon}^\zeta)}) \leftarrow \texttt{MakeSimplifiedTree}(\zeta, T_\Upsilon^{ext})$
     - Then, $\rho_1 = \Pi_{\text{att}_i \in \zeta} g_{\text{id},i}^{\Delta_{\text{att}_i}} g_{\text{id}}^{(\Sigma_{d_j \in D_{T_\Upsilon}^\zeta} \Delta_{d_j} s_{d_j})} = g_{\text{id}}^{\Sigma_{\text{att}_i \in \zeta} \Delta_{\text{att}_i} s_j}$ $g_{\text{id}}^{\Sigma_{d_j \in D_{T_\Upsilon}^\zeta} \Delta_{d_j} s_{d_j}} = g_{\text{id}}^{s_{T_\Upsilon}}$.
  3. Compute $\rho_5 = u_t^\delta$, $T_1 = g^\delta$ and $T_2 = e(g^{s_{\text{id}}}, u_t)^\delta$.
  4. Commitments are computed, i.e. $\{\sigma_i = Com(\rho_i)\}_{i=1}^5$.
  5. Compute the NIWI proofs (as per the proof in Eq. (3)) for the committed variables $\{\rho_i\}_{i=1}^4$ satisfying the following equations,

$$e(Z, \rho_1)e(\rho_2, \rho_1) = A_{T_\Upsilon} \tag{8}$$

$$e(g, \rho_3)e(\mathcal{F}(M), \rho_4)e(u^{-1}, \rho_2) = 1 \tag{9}$$

Say π_1 and π_2 are the proofs of Eqs. (8) and (9), respectively.
  6. Compute the NIZK Groth-Sahai proofs for ρ_2, ρ_5 satisfying,

$$T_2 = e(\rho_2, \rho_5) \tag{10}$$

$$e(T_1, u_t) = e(g, \rho_5) \tag{11}$$

These are two linear pp equations over the variables ρ_2 and ρ_5, and making them to prove in NIZK. To get NIZK for the Eq. (11), we first make it to the form of the Eq. (7) by introducing an auxillary variable ρ_6. That is split into two relations, $e(T_1, \rho_6) = e(g, \rho_5)$ and $\rho_6 = u_t$ (it is of form (6)). Thus commit the element ρ_6 and prove,

$$e(T_1, \rho_6) = e(g, \rho_5) \tag{12}$$

$$e(g, \rho_6) = e(g, u_t) \tag{13}$$

The proof consists of one group element each for the Eqs. (10), (12) and (13), say π_3, π_4 and π_5, respectively. In user anonymity proof, for verifying the Eq. (10) we use the fact that $T_2 = (g, u_t^{\delta s_{\text{id}}})$, refer [17].
  7. Output an ABS: $\sigma = (\{\sigma_i\}_{i=1}^6, \{\pi_i\}_{i=1}^5, T_1, T_2) \in \mathbb{G}^{12} \times \mathbb{G}_T$
Signature length is not dependent on the number of attributes $|\zeta|$, $|\sigma| = 12 * |\mathbb{G}| + |\mathbb{G}_T|$.

---

[1] MA runs $\texttt{BuildTree}$ algorithm and stores the public values for Υ in a public repository. Thus, if the public values already present at the public repository then signer need not reach MA.

– Verify($pp, M, \Upsilon, \sigma, t$): The signature's validity is verified similar to the Eq. (4),

$$e(Z, \sigma_1)e(\sigma_2, \sigma_1) = A_{T_\Upsilon}e(h, \pi_1) \tag{14}$$
$$e(g, \sigma_3)e(\mathcal{F}(M), \sigma_4)e(u^{-1}, \sigma_2) = e(h, \pi_2) \tag{15}$$
$$T_2 = e(\sigma_2, \sigma_5)e(h, \pi_3) \tag{16}$$
$$e(T_1, \sigma_6) = e(g, \sigma_5)e(h, \pi_4) \tag{17}$$
$$e(g, \sigma_6) = e(g, u_t)e(h, \pi_5) \tag{18}$$

Then performs the revocation check: for all $B_{\mathrm{id},t} = u_t^{s_{\mathrm{id}}} \in RL_t$,

$$T_2 \neq e(T_1, B_{\mathrm{id},t}) \tag{19}$$

Returns 1 if the above equations are verified, else return 0.

Equation (14) proves that the signer is a valid user who holds valid set of attributes which satisfies Υ, Eq. (15) links the message M and Eq. (19) ensure that the user is unrevoked.

– Trace(pp, tk, σ): Parse the signature σ and get σ_2. Calculate $(\sigma_2)^{tk} = (\sigma_2)^q = (g^{s_{\mathrm{id}}}h^{t_2})^q = (g^{s_{\mathrm{id}}})^q (\because h^q = 1$ and h is a Groth $-$ Sahai common reference string) and tests:

$$(\sigma_2)^{tk} \overset{?}{=} (g^{s_{\mathrm{id}'}})^{tk}$$

All the $(g^{s_{\mathrm{id}'}})^q$ are available in a list with the tracer, by pre-computation of it. Finally, returns the id' of $s_{\mathrm{id}'}$ which get matched from the list, else returns $\perp$. Note that, all the $s_{\mathrm{id}'}$ are communicated by the issuing authority to the tracer whenever user joins.

– Revoke($\vec{grt}, \vec{RL}, t, \{\mathrm{id}_k\}_{k=1}^{\ell}$): To revoke ℓ users at time interval t, MA adds $\{grt[\mathrm{id}_k][t] = u_t^{\mathrm{id}_k}\}_{i=k}^{\ell}$ from $\vec{grt}$ to the time t revocation list RL_t, as $\{B_{\mathrm{id}_k,t} = u_t^{\mathrm{id}_k}\}_{i=k}^{\ell}$ in RL_t and publishes.

6   Security Analysis

Theorem 1. *The proposed $T\mathcal{VLR} - \mathcal{ABS}$ is correct.*

Proof. It follows from the Groth-Sahai proof system correctness, as per Eq. (4).

Theorem 2 (Anonymity). *The proposed $T\mathcal{VLR} - \mathcal{ABS}$ preserve User Anonymity under SD assumption and DTDH assumption. More precisely,*

$$\mathbf{Adv}_{T\mathcal{VLR}-\mathcal{ABS},\mathcal{A}}^{CPA-anon}(k) \leq \mathbb{T}.N.(2.\mathbf{Adv}_{\mathbb{G}}^{SD}(k) + \mathbf{Adv}_{\mathbb{G}}^{DTDH}(k))$$

Proof. The witness-indistinguishable proofs ($\{\sigma_i\}_{i=1}^{6}, \{\pi_i\}_{i=1}^{5}$) from Groth-Sahai proof system ensures the user anonymity under SD assumption. Where as, for the last components T_1, T_2, it follows the similar approach as in [17] that under DTDH assumption the Eqs. (10), (12) and (13) holds in NIZK proof.

Theorem 3 (Traceability). *Under the chosen message existential unforgeability of the two-level signature scheme, the proposed scheme preserves traceability.*

Proof. As we use the extension form of a two-level hierarchical signature scheme, thus the proof is similar to that given in [5].

Theorem 4 (Attribute unforgeability). *The proposed scheme preserve attribute unforgeability under DL and KEA1 assumptions.*

Proof. The instance of the DL prob, say $(v, v') \in \mathbb{G}_q^2$ is the input to the simulator $\mathcal{B}$.

> **Setup:** $\mathcal{B}$ simulates the $\mathcal{TVLR} - \mathcal{ABS}$ parameters after setting $h = vh'$ and $g = v'g'$, where $h', g' \in_R \mathbb{G}_p$.
>
> $$pp = \left(g, h, u, Z, \mathcal{F}, \{u_t\}_{i=1}^{\mathbb{T}}, \{h_{att_i}\}_{att_i \in U\,Att}\right), ik = (g^\alpha, z, S, \overrightarrow{grt}) \text{ and } tk = q \in \mathbb{Z}$$

> **Queries:** As $\mathcal{B}$ knows all the keys except the relation between v, v', i.e. ξ, so it can answer all the queries as in the **attribute unforgeability** game.

> **Output:** Finally, a signature σ^* on forged attributes on M^* is outputted by $\mathcal{A}$ and Υ^*, where the public values are $\mathcal{T}_{\Upsilon^*} = (\{s_{d_j}\}, A_{T_{\Upsilon^*}}, T_{\Upsilon^*}^{ext})$, and user's private key k_{ID^*} such that $\Upsilon(\Lambda_{\text{ID}^*}) \neq 1$. As per the **attribute unforgeability** game it is a valid signature. Then, from (14) $\sigma_1^* = (g_{\text{ID}^*}^{s_{T_{\Upsilon^*}}} h^{t_1})$. This can be parsed as $\sigma_1^* = (v'g')^{\frac{s_{T_{\Upsilon^*}}}{z+s_{\text{ID}^*}}} h^{t_1} = (v')^{\frac{s_{T_{\Upsilon^*}}}{z+s_{\text{ID}^*}}} X$ for, $X = (h^{t_1})(g')^{\frac{s_{T_{\Upsilon^*}}}{s_{\text{ID}^*}+z}}$
>
> $$\text{Then, } v'^{s_{T_{\Upsilon^*}}} = (\sigma_1^*/X)^{z+s_{\text{ID}^*}} \tag{20}$$
>
> can be extracted by $\mathcal{B}$ using ik. Since $s_{T_{\Upsilon^*}}$ is unknown to $\mathcal{A}$, this get resemblence to the KEA1 assumption, that $\mathcal{A}$ is given an input $(v, v^{s_{T_{\Upsilon^*}}})$ (which is incorporated in $(h, h_{T_{\Upsilon^*}})$ and $\mathcal{A}$ finally returns $(v', (v')^{s_{T_{\Upsilon^*}}})$ (which is extracted as above in Eq. (20)).

Then according to KEA1 assumption, there exists an extractor $\bar{\mathcal{A}}$ which on same input as given to $\mathcal{A}$ will output $\xi : v' = v^\xi$.

6.1 Comparison

In Table 2 we compare our proposed scheme. Our proposed scheme signature contains total 13 group elements. Following notations used, ζ - set of attributes used in signature, m - total number of attributes, $m = |U\,Att|$, χ - user's attribute set length, $\chi \leq m$, N - no. of users, r - no. of revoked user at any time interval, VLR - verifier local revocation, $\vec{e}$ - one exponent operation, $\vec{p}$ - a pairing operation and na - not applicable.

Table 2. Comparison with other schemes

	[9]	[16]	[21]	[12]	Our scheme
User's private key length	$O(\chi)$	$O(\chi)$	$O(\mid \log_2 N.m.(\chi + \mid\Upsilon\mid))$	$3 + \chi * m$	$O(\chi)$
Signature length	$O(\mid\zeta\mid)$	$2*O(\mid\zeta\mid)$	$O(\log_2 N)$	$O(m)\mid G\mid$	$7\mid G\mid+\mid G_T\mid$ $=O(1)$
Signing cost	$O(\mid\zeta\mid)\bar{e}$	$O(\mid\zeta\mid^2)\bar{e}$	$O(\log_2 N + \mid\zeta\mid)\bar{e}$	$\frac{(\mid\zeta\mid*m+7)\bar{e}}{+1\bar{p}}$	$O(\mid\zeta\mid)\bar{e}$
Verification cost	$O(\mid\zeta\mid)\bar{p}$	$O(\mid\zeta\mid^2)\bar{p}$	$O(\log_2 N)\bar{p}$	$(\mid\zeta\mid + 4)\bar{p}$	$(r + 7)\bar{p}$
Key update cost in revocation	na	$O(N - r)\bar{e}$	$O(r \log(N/r)))\bar{e}$	na	0
Revocation	No	Yes	Yes	No	Yes (VLR)
Suspension of users	No	No	No	No	Yes
Traceability	Yes	No	Yes	Yes	Yes
Predicate	Threshold	Monotone	Threshold	Monotone	Monotone

7   Conclusion

We have proposed a traceable and revocable ABS scheme with VLR feature having constant-size signature and proven that it is secure in the standard model. Our scheme is comparatively better than the existing ABS schemes as depicted in comparison table. The size of the signature with proven security in the standard model makes it suitable for practical real-time applications. Further, to make the scheme realistic, attribute revocation feature need to be developed.

References

1. Ali, S.T., Amberker, B.B.: Dynamic attribute based group signature with attribute anonymity and tracing in the standard model. In: Gierlichs, B., Guilley, S., Mukhopadhyay, D. (eds.) SPACE 2013. LNCS, vol. 8204, pp. 147–171. Springer, Heidelberg (2013). https://doi.org/10.1007/978-3-642-41224-0_11
2. Bellare, M., Palacio, A.: The knowledge-of-exponent assumptions and 3-round zero-knowledge protocols. In: Franklin, M. (ed.) CRYPTO 2004. LNCS, vol. 3152, pp. 273–289. Springer, Heidelberg (2004). https://doi.org/10.1007/978-3-540-28628-8_17
3. Boneh, D., Goh, E.-J., Nissim, K.: Evaluating 2-DNF formulas on ciphertexts. In: Kilian, J. (ed.) TCC 2005. LNCS, vol. 3378, pp. 325–341. Springer, Heidelberg (2005). https://doi.org/10.1007/978-3-540-30576-7_18
4. Boneh, D., Rubin, K., Silverberg, A.: Finding composite order ordinary elliptic curves using the cocks-pinch method. J. Number Theor. **131**(5), 832–841 (2011)
5. Boyen, X., Waters, B.: Full-Domain subgroup hiding and constant-size group signatures. In: Okamoto, T., Wang, X. (eds.) PKC 2007. LNCS, vol. 4450, pp. 1–15. Springer, Heidelberg (2007). https://doi.org/10.1007/978-3-540-71677-8_1
6. Datta, P., Okamoto, T., Takashima, K.: Efficient attribute-based signatures for unbounded arithmetic branching programs. In: Lin, D., Sako, K. (eds.) PKC 2019. LNCS, vol. 11442, pp. 127–158. Springer, Cham (2019). https://doi.org/10.1007/978-3-030-17253-4_5
7. El Kaafarani, A., Ghadafi, E.: Attribute-Based signatures with user-controlled linkability without random oracles. In: O'Neill, M. (ed.) IMACC 2017. LNCS, vol. 10655, pp. 161–184. Springer, Cham (2017). https://doi.org/10.1007/978-3-319-71045-7_9

8. Emura, K., Miyaji, A., Omote, K.: A dynamic attribute-based group signature scheme and its application in an anonymous survey for the collection of attribute statistics. JIP **17**(1), 216–231 (2009)

9. Escala, A., Herranz, J., Morillo, P.: Revocable attribute-based signatures with adaptive security in the standard model. In: Nitaj, A., Pointcheval, D. (eds.) AFRICACRYPT 2011. LNCS, vol. 6737, pp. 224–241. Springer, Heidelberg (2011). https://doi.org/10.1007/978-3-642-21969-6_14

10. Goyal, V., Pandey, O., Sahai, A., Waters, B.: Attribute-based encryption for fine-grained access control of encrypted data. In: Juels, A., Wright, R.N., di Vimercati, S.D.C. (eds.) ACM Conference on Computer and Communications Security, pp. 89–98. ACM (2006)

11. Groth, J., Sahai, A.: Efficient non-interactive proof systems for bilinear groups. In: Smart, N. (ed.) EUROCRYPT 2008. LNCS, vol. 4965, pp. 415–432. Springer, Heidelberg (2008). https://doi.org/10.1007/978-3-540-78967-3_24

12. Gu, K., Wang, K., Yang, L.: Traceable attribute-based signature. J. Inf. Secur. Appl. **49**, 102400 (2019). https://doi.org/10.1016/j.jisa.2019.102400, http://www.sciencedirect.com/science/article/pii/S2214212616303106

13. Hada, S., Tanaka, T.: On the existence of 3-round zero-knowledge protocols. In: Krawczyk, H. (ed.) CRYPTO 1998. LNCS, vol. 1462, pp. 408–423. Springer, Heidelberg (1998). https://doi.org/10.1007/BFb0055744

14. Herranz, J., Laguillaumie, F., Libert, B., Ràfols, C.: Short attribute-based signatures for threshold predicates. In: Dunkelman, O. (ed.) CT-RSA 2012. LNCS, vol. 7178, pp. 51–67. Springer, Heidelberg (2012). https://doi.org/10.1007/978-3-642-27954-6_4

15. Laguillaumie, F., Paillier, P., Vergnaud, D.: Universally convertible directed signatures. In: Roy, B. (ed.) ASIACRYPT 2005. LNCS, vol. 3788, pp. 682–701. Springer, Heidelberg (2005). https://doi.org/10.1007/11593447_37

16. Lian, Y., Xu, L., Huang, X.: Attribute-based signatures with efficient revocation. In: 2013 5th International Conference on Intelligent Networking and Collaborative Systems, pp. 573–577. IEEE (2013)

17. Libert, B., Vergnaud, D.: Group signatures with verifier-local revocation and backward unlinkability in the standard model. In: Garay, J.A., Miyaji, A., Otsuka, A. (eds.) CANS 2009. LNCS, vol. 5888, pp. 498–517. Springer, Heidelberg (2009). https://doi.org/10.1007/978-3-642-10433-6_34

18. Maji, H.K., Prabhakaran, M., Rosulek, M.: Attribute-Based signatures. In: Kiayias, A. (ed.) CT-RSA 2011. LNCS, vol. 6558, pp. 376–392. Springer, Heidelberg (2011). https://doi.org/10.1007/978-3-642-19074-2_24

19. Okamoto, T., Takashima, K.: Efficient attribute-based signatures for non-monotone predicates in the standard model. In: Catalano, D., Fazio, N., Gennaro, R., Nicolosi, A. (eds.) PKC 2011. LNCS, vol. 6571, pp. 35–52. Springer, Heidelberg (2011). https://doi.org/10.1007/978-3-642-19379-8_3

20. Sakai, Y., Katsumata, S., Attrapadung, N., Hanaoka, G.: Attribute-Based signatures for unbounded languages from standard assumptions. In: Peyrin, T., Galbraith, S. (eds.) ASIACRYPT 2018. LNCS, vol. 11273, pp. 493–522. Springer, Cham (2018). https://doi.org/10.1007/978-3-030-03329-3_17

21. Wei, J., Huang, X., Liu, W., Hu, X.: Practical attribute-based signature: traceability and revocability. The Comput. J. **59**(11), 1714–1734 (2016)

Correction to: Side-Channel Analysis of CRYSTALS-Kyber and A Novel Low-Cost Countermeasure

Meziane Hamoudi, Amina Bel Korchi, Sylvain Guilley,
Sofiane Takarabt, Khaled Karray, and Youssef Souissi

Correction to:
Chapter "Side-Channel Analysis of CRYSTALS-Kyber
and A Novel Low-Cost Countermeasure"
in: P. Stănică et al. (Eds.): *Security and Privacy*, CCIS 1497,
https://doi.org/10.1007/978-3-030-90553-8_3

In the originally published chapter 3 the first and last name order of one of the authors was incorrect. The author's name has been corrected as "Bel Korchi, Amina".

The updated version of this chapter can be found at
https://doi.org/10.1007/978-3-030-90553-8_3

Author Index

Printed in the United States
by Baker & Taylor Publisher Services